MW01032538

"The unexpected death of a spouse presents life-altering questions about what to keep and what to let go. Through stories, photographs, and family recipes, Huehn's memoir repairs a life nearing collapse from the weight of grief. Memories resist sentimentality to reveal the strain and humor of building a life with a partner. Whether navigating life in Germany as a young wife and mother, entering the emergency room where her beloved lies, or lifting the surfaces of her old farmhouse to understand two decades of her husband's quirky renovations, Huehn brings her training as a nurse to each new understanding of grief and healing. Like her journey to fix the old farmhouse and occupy it fully, this memoir is a one-of-a kind, empowering response to loss and a life in progress."
—Diane LeBlanc, Director of Writing, St. Olaf College

"This is a compelling and candid love story about a cross cultural romance. It's also an immigrant story, which carries the remnants of war and loss, and the difficult work of bridging very different temperaments. Finally, it is a beautifully written eulogy to Klaus, whose abrupt death left his wife and their children bereft. A seasoned nurse, and educator, she felt competent at work but 'unmoored with sorrow' and unsure at home. Her endearing, yet eccentric husband, who had no experience building a house, enthusiastically tore the entire roof off theirs, and it remained that way for months. When he died, his improvised, makeshift house projects left her with a run-down old farmhouse, a crippled septic system, and equally crippling self-doubt. Yet she responds to 'the assignment fate' had given to her, with courage and pluck. This is a wonderful, memorable read."
—Julie Neraas is a spiritual director, ordained minister, and former professor at Hamline University.

"*A Widow's Guide to Becoming a Handyman* will warm your heart while also, gently, breaking it. Susan Huehn takes us on a tumultuous and chaotic journey of love and grief that is both tender and transformative. Telling the story of her marriage and her sudden, unwanted widowhood, she reminds us that the work of love is always, necessarily, also the work of repair. Her candor, vulnerability and wisdom make this a grief memoir that is as much about self-discovery as it is about healing from traumatic loss."
—Karen Hering, *Trusting Change: Finding Our Way through Personal and Global Change* and *Writing to Wake the Soul*

"Susan Huehn's story of love and loss set in Germany and a German-American Minnesota town, is honest, intimate, and emotionally powerful. Alternating chapters take the reader back to youthful love and yearning and forward to devastating grief, while reflecting on the evolution of a transatlantic relationship. The crumbling farmhouse home becomes a metaphor for the challenges of the marriage, the dreams, the setbacks, the frustrations, and ultimately forgiveness—of herself and of her partner. A great read!"
—Susan Bartlett Foote, Professor Emerita, University of Minnesota, author of *Crusade for Forgotten Souls: Reforming Minnesota's Mental Institutions 1946-1954*. Winner of the 2019 Minnesota Book Award.

"Susan Heuhn's book is a big-hearted and artfully-crafted memoir of passionate love, sudden loss, and messy grief set in a farm house restoration project. Readers whose anguish hasn't followed the stages of grief in blueprint order will appreciate Susan's DYI-ing of her emotions and renovations after the premature death of her husband, Klaus. I love memoirs that interrogate and challenge accepted norms: this book gives us all space to rethink the grieving process."
—Nicole Helget, author, *The End of the Wild*

A Widow's Guide To Becoming A Handyman

Susan Huehn

ice cube press, llc
north liberty, ia, usa

A Widow's Guide To Becoming A Handyman

Copyright © 2023 Susan Huehn

ISBN 9781948509435

Library of Congress Control Number: 2023932873

Ice Cube Press, LLC (Est. 1991)
1180 Hauer Drive North Liberty, Iowa 52317
www.icecubepress.com steve@icecubepress.com

The paper used in this publication meets the minimum requirements of the American National Standard for Information Sciences—Permanence of Paper for Printed Library Materials, ANSI Z39.48-1992.

Made with recycled paper.

Manufactured in Canada

For Peter, Sonja, and Alex

CHAPTER 1

The loud ringing from the house phone broke the silence. Sandhill cranes had already left for the winter, and no tractor rumbled down the road to disrupt the unfettered quiet of country living. The remaining birds were silenced by the unusually stark cold this early in the season. The conservative farmers living around us were especially reverent on Sunday mornings for rest and church. Sonja, Peter, and Alex slept upstairs. The phone's ringing startled me. A cup, half full of cold coffee and congealed cream, sat on the table in front of me. Klaus had made the coffee that morning so that I didn't have to move from my worn leather chair or rearrange the items on my lap: a computer, a granny-square afghan, books on research design, and Gabe, my trusted Jack Russell Terrier, who was snoring peacefully, qualitative research design failing to keep him awake.

Klaus knew just how I liked my coffee. Dark and strong with just enough cream to remove the bitter edge so the coffee tasted smooth. The cupboard was stuffed with mugs that carried logos with nurses and hearts and loons to mark vacations at lakeside cabins. My favorite cup had a certain shape: a wide top, and round to provide enough surface area to warm both of my hands without fingers overlapping. The table between us hosted the morning's conversation. So many different tables over the years, but the conversation threads were always the same. What should we make for dinner? How was dinner last night? What could we have added to make it better? What was on the schedule for the day? Over the years, concerns about our children moved to the top of our priority list, and there was always a catalog of my questions addressing the current idiosyncrasies and needs of our old farmhouse, in endless disrepair:

> What about the water in the kitchen, Klaus? Can we do anything to make sure the pipes don't freeze?
> Is the electric heater on in the wellhouse to keep the pump from freezing?
> Can the electric heater cause a fire?
> Have you finished the insulated box around the well so our electric bill isn't so high?
> Why can't I lock the bathroom door without lifting it a little bit?
> And could you fill that mouse hole behind the washing machine with steel wool and glass shards so they don't keep getting in?

Klaus responded with a quick "Ja, ja, Susanne," followed by a change of subject to something, anything, else. This morning he turned the conversation to last night's pizza, the smell of oregano and garlic still hanging in the air.

"Do you think they liked the tuna fish one?" I asked this morning. "Maybe we should have put on less garlic?"

Before going to bed, I nuzzled into his neck, my nose and chin fitting perfectly. The warmth was welcome against the arctic air that was seeping through the cracks of our house and underneath the covers of the bed. Into his familiar smell, I whispered, "I love you so much." After over two decades I had the angle of my head just right so that I averted too much scratch from his beard on my cheeks. "Dat's so nice" he whispered back, his mouth directly by my ear.

At the table, my coffee in hand, he asked, "Schudd I stay at home mit you today, Susanne?"

"No. Go ahead." I encouraged him out the door. "Cooking for everyone at church is your thing. Please go and do what you love." At that moment, discernment between grounded theory, narrative research, case study, and phenomenology seemed imperative to my wellbeing and the future I had planned for me.

Sitting on the bottom step, he groaned as he leaned over and tied his new, fur-lined ankle boots. "My feet feel farther away every day," he said and chuckled under his breath.

A small kiss on the cheek. "I'll see when you get home." He grabbed his fur-lined coat and was out the door. Forever.

No more Saturday night pizzas. Who could have known? Looking back, would I have wanted to know? Would I have wanted to participate in the countdown that led to the end of his life?

This would be our last conversation. No more conversations over coffee. Would we have said anything differently had we known? Would our conversation have centered on something other than the thickness of the crust or the use of feta instead of chèvre? Would I have wanted to say goodbye? I certainly would have asked some questions about how the house worked.

How is it again that you keep the wellhouse door from being swept open by the wind? At which temperature do you set the thermostat on the portable heater so the well pump doesn't freeze?

The bright sun had warmed the living room, but the leather chair remained cold against my skin. Was it just an hour ago over coffee that he had asked me if he should skip going to church? "Should we do something together today? I want to be a good husband." I wonder about the questions that would haunt me, still, had he stayed home.

Had I known these were the last words that would pass between us, I would have considered them more carefully, maybe looked into his blue dancing eyes as I was saying them. Smiled. Touched his rough, but always warm, hands, calloused from hard work. I should have said, "I love you."

It was the end of Thanksgiving weekend. Thanksgiving was always full of melancholy since my dad died on Thanksgiving Day four years earlier. Since then, we had celebrated the holiday with just the five of us, Klaus and I doing what we loved and did best together: Planning the meal weeks ahead of time, then shopping for the freshest and finest ingredients, and finally spending the days before cooking. The menu this year included triple ginger cranberries. "We haFV to haFV cranberries, Susanne." New to Klaus since we moved from Germany, they were his favorite and not to be missed.

I continued to consider the merits of various qualitative research designs and wondered what we'd do that afternoon. Sunday afternoon would perhaps consist of a chai latte on tatami mats at our favorite tea shop, then crossing the street to a Russian grocery store that sold dense rye bread and put small pieces of tissue paper between thin slices of Havarti. "Dis is how it should be done, Susanne," he would say as the woman laid the large square block of Havarti on the professional slicer. Appreciation for professional slicing was one thing from the Old Country that Klaus wouldn't give up.

We still had a landline. I had to get up and walk to another room to answer the phone. I carefully placed my papers and books on the sofa so as not to disrupt the haphazard organization that made sense only to me. I tried to reach the phone before it woke the rest of the house.

Was it just one hour ago that Klaus had kissed my cheek and asked if he should stay home with me today? A simple kiss, done so often. Each time I assumed it would be the same as the last one.

"Hello?" My thoughts were still on the notes on the couch. I did not know that the split-second pause after my greeting would end this life and force me into a new, unwanted one. Gabe, who looked just like Eddie on *Frasier*, shook himself awake, the jingle of his tags familiar and reassuring. Grief was not new to Gabe. He had recently accompanied me through the deaths of both of my parents. He knew when my parents were close to death, and he knew when I needed him most, pushing his small wire-haired body against mine to share my pain. He stood by my side, pushing his body against my leg to make his presence known as if he intuited the impact of that phone call.

The short phone cord tethered me. A familiar voice from the church said, "Something has happened." My hands turned cold and clammy. The curls of the phone cord warped my fingers bloodless.

The only sound in that split second of eternity was the steady dripdripdripdripdripdripdripdripdrip from the kitchen faucet. It was bitterly cold outside. By keeping the water running at a steady drip in our special needs house, we could ward off washing dishes upstairs in the bathtub. Klaus had the rate of drips down to a science, a science he often lectured me about, using a teacher's voice, even though he had never been a teacher. "You have to let da vater drip so the drips run close together, almost in a steady stream but not qvite. And don't run the vater too fast. Vee can't vaste vater." Just before walking out the door, he stopped at the kitchen faucet to correct the speed of my drips, dripdrip dripdripdrip drip dripdrip drip

"Please come now," the voice startled me back to the current moment. The receiver in my hand grew larger as I held it, stared at it.

"We think it may be his heart," the same voice said. The phone cord now seemed to be transmitting a fog-inducing smoke that enshrouded my head and made things hard to hear and equally hard to understand. It seemed as if the person delivering the message had suddenly traveled thousands of miles between sentences.

It was Stone Soup Sunday, one of Klaus's favorite Sundays of the church year. All of the children of the church brought their favorite vegetables: rutabaga, carrots, potatoes. This year, to honor the German leading the soup project, someone had brought spätzle, a small dumpling-style noodle common in German soups.

Cooking for the church community was Klaus's contribution. While the adults were in church, Klaus cleaned and chopped the vegetables with the children. He loved to cook with them, teaching them how to use knives carefully without cutting themselves. "Roll your fingers just a little bit" he would say holding a carrot in his left hand while cutting with his right. Sometimes they had a hard time understanding him through his thick German accent, so, he would show them. "This way your fingertips aren't as easy to cut." He also always insisted that the knives be as sharp as possible: "they are less dangerous that way." Together they washed and prepared the vegetables for the broth simmering on the stove. The spätzle went in at the very end.

My nurse brain quickly switched on, talking over my rising feelings. I had learned early on that what I showed on the outside mattered more than what I felt on the inside. With my immigrant parents, what mattered was hard work and the accomplishment of goals. Feelings got in the way. As if I was separated in two, I could hear my nurse's voice through the fog-inducing smoke say, "I will meet you at the hospital" and rather than the phone receiver growing larger, I realized I was shrinking.

I moved upstairs to change out of the Lanz of Salzburg flannel pajamas that had protected me from the worn leather that was always too hot or too cold. The flannel now seemed porous, and I shivered uncontrollably. I wrapped my arms around myself to stop the shivering. It was always colder and draftier upstairs. My teeth chattered, the kind of cold that went straight to one's marrow. Or was it fear I was shivering from?

"Don't people have symptoms before they have a heart attack?" I asked myself as I pulled on yesterday's clothes still conveniently on the floor. Elastic-waist pants require no effort or thought; a t-shirt pulled over my head; a black cardigan, the color fortuitous, with only two large buttons that were easy for my trembling fingers to fasten. Klaus was a little overweight, but not by much. And he certainly didn't have the personality type most frequently associated with heart attacks. Tolerant and patient, he served as the tethered end of the kite string when I spun anxiously out of control, calmly talking me back to earth. He was the voice that reassured my ever-doubting self and encouraged me to go back to graduate school. "You can do it, Susanne. You haff to."

So, I did: first my Master's degree in Nursing Education and now eleven credits into a PhD program. I wanted to obtain the credentials I needed to teach nursing, my beloved profession.

Klaus hadn't been sick. Well, there had been indigestion during the night. Damn that pizza, I had thought as I reached to give him one of the chewable cherry Tums I always had on my bedside table. It took only one for him to fall back asleep. Not bad on the indigestion scale. Sometimes I had to chew three or four for indigestion to abate. Was the indigestion a clue? If so, it was the only one. My nurse brain ticked through a checklist of symptoms. Chest pain? No. Arm pain? No. True to his German heritage, a little stubborn perhaps. But not sick. Not symptomatic of a heart problem and certainly was not symptomatic of a heart problem bad enough to cause him to die.

My nurse brain monopolized my growing fear as I got dressed. Above all else, be calm on the outside, I whispered to myself. My training was to tend to the feelings of others. "Schlucken," my mother would say to me as my feelings bubbled up. Swallow. Just swallow your feelings. Joy. Rage. Amazement. Sadness. Fear. The goal was independent of the source and always the same. Swallow. It was extremely helpful training in my role as a nurse when my foremost goal was always that patients feel safe in my care.

My brain reassured my wife-self. "No one dies of a heart attack anymore."

Swallowing my fear, I remained composed for my children, now awake from the phone call. "Something has happened with your dad. I'm headed to church." Sonja, a first-year college student, teared up. Alex, introverted and sensitive, was 16 and a sophomore in high school. He and Klaus were kindred souls, united in their love of teasing me. They would often sit together in a chair wide enough to hold them both and blow the tapioca pearls from the bubble tea Alex loved through the wide straw, laughing when they hit me squarely between the eyes.

"They think it may be his heart."

Peter, a junior in college, was up and getting ready to cut down the family Christmas tree. "Should I still go?" This was something he and Klaus had always done together, but this year's schedule did not allow for that. Klaus was committed to cooking soup and Peter had a six-hour drive back to college that afternoon. It was an event we had previously done as a family. Up and down the rows we went, in search of the perfect Christmas tree. A colorful hat would be placed on an ornament contender. Nein. Nicht gut genug. No. Not good enough. Too tall, too thin, too short, a bare spot. The hat was moved from tree to tree. Klaus's search drove us crazy. For the last few years Sonja, Alex, and I had retired, and it was left to Peter and Klaus. "Yes, I think you should still go. Everything will be ok."

Alex was silent. Sonja asked, "Should I come along?"

"No, I'm going to go by myself," I said, in my best, most reassuring, nurse voice.

Gabe, sensing something was wrong, wove in and out of our legs nervously.

"I will call you as soon as I know something. Try not to worry."

What I didn't say was "I need to go alone; I'm not sure I trust myself to take you with me." Putting on my warmest coat and gloves, I walked out the door.

SPÄTZLE

After failing at making perfectly round dumplings, I became the official "Spätzle-maker" in the hotel kitchen I worked at. Every day I cracked 30 eggs into a huge bowl and made enough spätzle to feed hungry hikers and tourists in the remote alpine village where I was spending the summer. My arms haven't been that strong since.

Begin with twice the number of eggs as mouths you wish to feed.

Crack eggs into a large mixing bowl. Add ½ an eggshell of water for each egg.

Add salt and nutmeg to taste. I recommend using a whole nutmeg and freshly grating it for better flavor.

Begin adding flour by the spoonful. Using a wooden spoon beat the dough as you continue to add flour, scooping and pulling it from the sides of the bowl. Continue to add flour until the dough is moderately sticky. Once "bubbles" appear during beating you are done – this usually takes 10-15 minutes. This is a helpful task to share among Spätzle eaters.

Bring a large pot of salted water to a boil and then reduce it to a simmer. I have a glass of cold water handy to add in case the water gets too hot and the spätzle threatens to boil over. Using a Spätzlemaker of your choice scrape the dough into the simmering water and cook until the noodles float to the top, this only takes 2-3 minutes. Remove the spätzle from the water with a slotted spoon into a bowl of cold water, then into a colander.

Toss them with butter and serve warm!

Chapter 2

I struggled to know where I fit in, east or west of the Atlantic. My parents, both German natives, joined other immigrants in settling in the small central Minnesota town I called home in the early 1950s. New Ulm, named after a town of the same name in Bavaria, is located in a triangle of land at the confluence of the Minnesota and Cottonwood rivers. Residents of one of the most ethnically German communities outside of Germany are watched over by an impressive bronze "Hermann the German" set on a hillside overlooking the river valley. Manifestations of the town's motto, "See Germany in America," are everywhere, from the Wilkommen sign at the town's entrance to grocery store ads identifying sale prices on "Bananen" and "Äpfel." Tourists can shop for hand-carved wooden ornaments on year-round Christmas trees, dumpling mixes, beer steins, and imported chocolate of all shapes and sizes while being serenaded by traditional German polka music piped throughout downtown. Three times a day tourists congregate at the 45-foot-tall Glockenspiel to hear programmed German music and watch as three-foot-high animated figurines appear and move to music that depicts the history and development of New Ulm.

Our family life was governed by their nostalgia and attempts to recreate a traditional German way of life in south-central Minnesota. Daily my hair was separated into three equal sections, each tightly braided and bound with a matching rubber band. One braid for the right, one for the left, and one wound tightly on top and named the "nest" after our parakeet Hansi found a home there. German was spoken in our house.

Packages with highly valued commodities arrived from Germany for Easter and Christmas from Oma and Tante. They were wrapped in brown paper and tightly bound with twine. Dresses, chocolates, lotions, and perfumes unavailable in central Minnesota were safely snuggled in the box to withstand jostling from the trans-Atlantic voyage. Knit Strumpfhosen worn under dresses and pants were the most highly valued as they were deemed to keep me warmer than any American-made tights. My favorite was the Prinzenrolle, sandwich cookies filled with chocolate cream. There were always two rolls, one for my brother and one for me, to prevent arguments.

Donut earnings funded a summer trip to Germany the same summer I was to get my driver's license. I stayed with Tante Luise, my mother's sister, and her husband, Onkel Hans, 30 plus years her senior. Luise was of the generation that lost marriage-aged men in the war. I barely remembered them from my last trip to Germany to visit my Oma, my mother's mother, as a four-year-old in braids and red short lederhosen with hearts trimmed in white as pockets.

They lived in Kreis Böblingen a small village south of Stuttgart. There was no fancy travel, just participation in everyday life. Mornings I would rise and go to the bakery to get my beloved freshly baked Laugenbrezeln, the twisted middle crunchy and perfect for dipping in soft butter, the bottom half thick and chewy and ready to be sliced horizontally and spread with sweet cream butter. They would be eaten in the Eckbank in the kitchen over lively World War II stories that often ended well into the morning with my aunt in tears. Dishes were quickly washed and put away, and a grocery list was made for the day. I headed off with a healthy dose of anxiety and an Einkaufskorb. My aunt's billfold and the shopping list were securely tucked in the bottom of the basket. Could I bag the groceries quickly enough today? Would I understand how much something costs? My German was good but not up to the village's strong Swabian dialect and I would fumble as I misunderstood.

Afternoons I walked through the Kurgarten with Onkel Hans, stopping to rest on a bench and collect town gossip. Evenings we leaned out of the window together, human satellite dishes that collected news from the village. Onkel Hans would yell at familiar faces and together we watched the town's events on the Hauptstrasse directly below us.

At the peak of my debilitating insecurity as a teenager, I was confronted with a pleasant discovery that summer in Germany: I fit in. The way of life felt strangely familiar even though I had only been to Germany twice as a young child. I felt a sense of belonging and of being understood. No one made fun of me for being bilingual. Everywhere I saw validation of what my parents identified as a better way of life on the east side of the Atlantic. If anything, I returned home at the end of the summer with more questions than answers and a burning desire to return to that feeling of belonging.

Rotary offered me that opportunity when I was accepted as an exchange student, all expenses paid, for a full year following high school. A year in Ulm would allow me to spend more time figuring out which side of the Atlantic I belonged on.

"I won't sign," my dad said angrily. The blue permission slip flew back across the oval kitchen table on Jefferson Street. A personal dream I dared to reveal evaporated. The dream didn't fit my parents' values of hard work, attendance to tasks, frugality, and attainment of goals.

The plan was for me to go to college and study nursing, a career that offered lifetime job security. My mother had always wanted to become a nurse, but the war interrupted her education in the eighth grade, and her dream had to become mine; there was no other option.

Travel and postponing my plan to attend college directly after high school were unnecessary extravagances. Frugality was a virtue of the highest regard, which my parents acquired from living in post-World War II Germany and later from living as immigrants. A use was found for everything. I was taught to squeeze the very last dollop of toothpaste out of the tube. And no food went to waste. Ever. What some might see as necessities were seen, by my parents, as indulgent luxuries. "Why do you need those?" my father asked as we were driving up Fourth Street past the light-green rambler where I often played with Beverly. "Your glasses are perfectly fine. You do not need contact lenses." Dresses had added-on crocheted hems to extend their life as I grew.

My Dad was also afraid I would not return following my year as a student at the Gymnasium. "You will find someone to marry and stay in Germany forever." Nostalgia had boundaries. Despite the desperate longing for their homeland that seeped out of their pores and into my upbringing, their greatest fear was that I would meet a German man, fall in love, move to Germany and they would be left behind in America.

I knew this was not a battle I could win. My dream of spending a year in Germany was shattered, my snow globe shaken and my feelings, unsupported and unprocessed, remained locked inside. I became what I *should* be and survived by being quiet, not demanding or seeking attention, and staying out of sight.

When I graduated from college, I returned to my childhood home. In the mornings, I frosted and sprinkled donuts at my grocery store job. When not working, I cared for the 14-year-old family dog, a long-haired dachshund, and studied for the national licensing exam that would give me the initials RN after my name.

This dog was not the first long-haired dachshund in the family.

"We want a dog" my brother and I begged as we offered up combined earnings from our paper route and babysitting jobs.

"The only dog that is ever coming into this house is a long-haired dachshund," my father responded. This dachshund would replace the original full-sized red long-haired dachshund my father had grown up with in Slovakia.

Second condition. The dog had to be named "Mausi."

Customers familiar to me from my donut career, which spanned high school and college, greeted me over the bakery counter. "Are you home for the summer?" they would ask. "Do you have a nursing job yet?" Others who knew my family more closely asked about my parents. "Have you heard from them? Are they having a good time?"

Emotions and regrets had kept them from returning to Germany for a visit until now when my parents were making their first return trip to Germany in nearly two decades.

"Heritagefest" was an annual opportunity for my parents to be fully immersed in their longing for "the old country." This year, I was attending Heritagefest without them. It was a blazing hot evening as I sat in the bleachers eagerly awaiting the performance of a choir from Stuttgart. I hoped to connect with a choir member or two to practice my German and reminisce about things I loved in and around Stuttgart. Sitting on the bleachers and sipping my ice-cold beer in the sultry shade, the choir began singing the tunes so familiar to me. In between songs, I lifted my beer to Ein Prosit, Ein Prosit der Gemütlichkeit.

"Fritz, turn down the music," my mother, Frieda, would yell down the stairs on Saturday afternoons. My father was under the dark green Volkswagen Fastback fixing the problem du jour. She hated the music that was alphabetically arranged in a small vinyl suitcase made especially for cassette tapes. In actuality, her disdain was a cover for the painfully vivid imagery the tunes evoked of her beloved Germany. It was too much for her. She desperately missed her family and the small village of her youth. My mother dealt with her longing and remorse by suppressing it. Swallowing. It came out occasionally and sideways.

The lyrics were like a cheese grater on her skin and frayed nerve endings. But Fritz was oblivious to her requests and the scratchy lyrics from the too–loud cassette player, and my father's accompanying voice continued with no change in decibel level. My father also longed for Germany, which he expressed in singing along to the German folk tunes to which he knew every word. The door slammed shut between them, each left to their coping mechanisms.

Beer stealing some of my inhibition, I loudly sang along with the choir. I spotted him in the back row, swaying in time to the music. The youth choir members stood on the stage in direct sunlight and blazing heat. His mature beard raised the median age of the choir and broadened the definition of "youth." They were singing "Kornblumen Blau," a German ode to the special blue of the cornflower. I knew that shade of blue so well: a muted blue with hints of lavender offset by the sharp orange of poppies that grew alongside the cornflowers in the ditches around Stuttgart.

He was wearing sunglasses and a goofy straw hat, which I followed through the crowd following the concert.

A careful "Hallo" and compliments for the choir performance led to a beer in the beer tent where a brass band blasted polkas and waltzes. Underneath the straw hat were eyes as blue as the cornflowers he had been singing about and reflected depth, generosity, and kindness.

"Vaaatt? Ein Yin und Yang?" he yelled over the oompah music. The dime-sized Chinese pendant that was a permanent fixture around my neck caught his eye. We felt an immediate connection over our shared philosophy of interconnectedness that the pendant symbolized.

We sat close enough so that I could smell the sweet scent of sweat coming off his body. "Möchtest du tanzen?" he asked when a familiar waltz began. My chin snuggling into his collarbone I fit perfectly into his arms. He was an experienced ballroom dancer; I had no experience beyond the bear hug variety of American high school dances. We awkwardly danced to "Kennst du die Perle, die Perle Tirols." He swung his sunglasses, on a red rope, around to his back so that he could hold me tightly as we danced. Realizing my inexperience, he guided my steps with a firm hand on the blue floral Laura Ashley look-alike dress I had sewn for myself. His blue eyes smiled at my missteps. The air was hot and heavy, and it seemed there was no one else on the makeshift dance floor set up on the dirt of the fairgrounds. Those eyes caused a voracious pining in my core. My breath shortened, and heat rose along my face and down my neck. I fell in love with him during that dance. I had known him for less than thirty minutes.

Klaus was visiting the United States for the first time and spoke almost no English. His host family, who lived a few houses down from my parents' home, did not speak German. I became the interpreter for the three days of the festival. Together we went to festival events and tourist excursions in and around my hometown.

I went to all of the performances of the choir and looked for the goofy straw hat and piercing blue eyes in the back row. He wasn't easy to pick out in the choir; others loomed over him. His eyes were the most remarkable thing about him, not only for their beauty but also for their expressiveness. It was as if they looked through me and sensed how separate and alone I had felt growing up. They were eyes that conveyed a ripple of intimacy and made me feel understood. It was as if his thoughts floated on the surface and wanted to be read.

I anguished about the love I felt and the questions I had. The deep doubt I had in myself and the world around me prevented me from trusting this could happen. I had never had a serious boyfriend and felt unlovable. I questioned my every move, my every thought. Could he love me too? Were the feelings reciprocal? I certainly did not believe that I would ever find someone to love me and someone to love in return.

How could a relationship in which an ocean separated us ever work? Klaus had just ended a relationship with a woman from Hamburg, on the other side of Germany. That relationship ended, in Klaus's eyes, because of the great distance that separated them.

Did he reach up and stroke the nape of my neck that Sunday afternoon from the back of my dad's dark green Volkswagen Fastback on our way home from a picnic at Fort Ridgley? I couldn't be sure. It could have easily been beads of sweat rolling down my neck from the summer heat. If he had reached over, was it an accident or was it intentional? It was my only clue that he was having the same feelings as me. My questions remained unanswered for a year and a half.

We said goodbye that Sunday evening after that picnic. Holding my hand, he kissed me on the cheek and promised to write and send a cassette tape of music sung by his choir. Only Mausi, the dachshund, was witness to this promise, and he was deaf.

I waited and waited and waited for him to write. I passed the licensing exam and started my first job as a psychiatric nurse at the New Ulm hospital. The long nights I worked alone gave me ample time to think about Klaus and to wonder what he was doing. I asked myself if he was dating someone else and wondered if the promised letter from him was lost in the mail.

He never wrote.

CHAPTER 3

Despite two pairs of mittens, my hands shivered so badly as I got into my Nissan Versa that I had to stabilize one hand with the other to get the key into the ignition. "Dammit," I cried to myself as I missed the keyhole again and again. After several tries, I finally managed to hit the keyhole, and my car stuttered reluctantly to life.

My Dad's voice was loud in my head as I backed the quarter mile down the driveway onto the gravel road, careful to avoid the ditch. "The gravel road is so hard on your car, Susi." My urgency was controlled enough to consider the damage the gravel was doing to the undercarriage of my car. "It is like sandblasting the bottom of your car" my dad, ever an auto mechanic would say. "As soon as you hear the gravel hitting the bottom of your car, you have to slow down." He kept a nail-polish-sized bottle of paint in his glove compartment to touch up dings from the gravel after each visit.

Thankfully I was driving the ten miles to town, rather than the ambulance driving the ten miles to my house, I thought. I had called 911 once in the twenty years we had lived in our house, which sat on the borders of three counties in southeastern Minnesota.

"My husband cut his fingers off, I need an ambulance."

"Ma'am, you have the wrong number. You need to call Rice County. This is Scott County." Senseless. I lived in Dakota County. The hinterland location made accountability for things like hooking up our phone and emergencies murky. "Please call Rice County."

I tried to find my voice. My voice tried to find a response. Nothing came out of my gaping mouth so I just hung up the phone.

I tried again. 9-1-1. I pushed each digit intentionally as if that were going to make a difference. After nine rings another person answered. "I live in Dakota County and have an emergency. My husband cut his fingers off."

This operator didn't make an issue with the number I dialed or the county I lived in. Twenty minutes later the ambulance and snowplow clearing its way arrived.

Thank God Klaus is close to the hospital and those twenty minutes weren't wasted, I thought as I strained out the pinhole of the windshield I had cleared of ice. The heater still blasted cold air and refused to thaw my windshield or feet.

Eight miles to go.

I made phone calls to nurse friends and told myself everything would turn out all right. They reassured me as well.

"It will be okay. Small hospitals are set up for this. Klaus will be stabilized at church and transported to the hospital, a few short miles away," and "There are things like helicopters, bypass surgeries, stents, angioplasties, angiograms, and modern medicine. He will probably be flown by helicopter to a larger hospital in Minneapolis. At most he will need bypass surgery." My friends and my nurse brain reassured me. I swallowed harder.

The flight path of the helicopter was directly over our house. I frequently heard the helicopter and envisioned the frightened families it had left behind. As a nurse, it was my mission to be at their side, reassuring them their loved one would be well cared for and helping them to figure out their next steps.

Six miles to go.

I imagined the next few hours and days as the crunching gravel was replaced by the steady hum of tires on pavement. I sped my car up. Probably, Klaus would be flown by helicopter to a metropolitan hospital with a cardiologist where his heart would be fixed. Soon the blood would be flowing freely through all the arteries and veins again. That was what happened now when someone had a heart attack. Stents were placed. Or would he need bypass surgery? That would mean a longer hospital stay. But whatever treatment was needed, it would be followed by cardiac rehab and a long, healthy life.

Thoughts of how to get my stubborn German husband to comply with cardiac rehab went through my head as I passed the city limit sign announcing that "Cows, Colleges, and Contentment" waited ahead.

When his severed fingers were reattached, he hadn't complied with physical or occupational therapy. Why would this time be different? Why would he apply conventional rules of medicine when the last time he used a coat hanger and Windex to deal with the itching inside his cast?

Four miles.

My cell phone rang, and I reached through the fog enshrouding me to grab the phone and flip it open. The familiar voice from before said, "We haven't left the church yet. Please come to the church." My nurse brain knew that Klaus would have to be stable to transport him to the hospital. Fear rose no matter how hard I swallowed, and a black tendril of panic opened inside my chest.

I shivered in my still too-cold car as I turned right towards the church instead of left towards the hospital.

Almost there.

At the church, flashing red lights, a police car, a rescue truck, and an ambulance greeted me. Inside I was frantic; outside I remained calm. The voice from the phone waited outside the doorway.

The smell of savory vegetable broth filled my nose as I walked into the church and past the kitchen where the soup was simmering. They were attempting to resuscitate Klaus in front of the familiar heavy wooden table that always took at least two people to move, that each Sunday held the cookies and cakes, cheese and crackers, nuts and fruit over which church fellowship occurred following services. I had many conversations over that table. Today, covered with a festive white linen tablecloth, it was to hold the vegetable soup. The terrine sat on the table, empty and waiting, along with the accompanying sliced bread.

The church basement looked like a hospital triage room. I had been in such a room many times beside someone else's family member, holding a frightened hand, explaining what was happening, or actively working as part of a team to resuscitate a patient. The sights, sounds, and smells pulled me in and begged me to engage, to grab a stethoscope or a clipboard and pen, listen for orders, and look for distraught family members. But this time I was the family member. I was the wife fretting at the side of her loved one. There was no clipboard to grab onto.

His wife is here, I heard someone say through my fog. Someone was designated to speak to me, a personal attendant. Together we stood at Klaus's head.

Wrappers from syringes and boxes from used medications were strewn about and the noise was an assault on my ears. "All clear" was shouted loudly enough for everyone to hear and stand away from

Klaus. The announcement was followed quickly by the treacherous sound from the defibrillating paddles shooting electricity through Klaus's heart. His body jerked wildly in response to the shock. My eyes followed the eyes of those kneeling around him to the portable EKG screen which would tell us if the shock had been successful in restarting his heart.

Three people were kneeling around Klaus. Or was it four? I could see his new shoes, splayed to the right and the left. Was it just last week I convinced him to buy them? The fur lining peeked over the top. "You need warm shoes for the winter, Klaus" I had said. Always frugal, it took a bit of convincing to get him to retire the purple plastic shoes that squeaked when he walked. The second pair of shoes we bought were still safely tucked in the box.

We all watched and waited, eyes fixed on the small screen of the EKG monitor. My nurse brain knew I should be hearing an intermittent beeping sound corresponding to oscillation on the screen, which in turn reflected a happily beating heart. Klaus's heart leaped with the electric jolt, reflected on the screen as a sharp jump. Would the line continue in the familiar QRST pattern I had learned as a nurse? I watched as the electrocardiogram briefly complied with the expected normal sinus rhythm.

The image quickly reverted to the ominous flat line accompanied by the persistent monochrome sound synonymous with a heart that refused to beat.

"How long have you been resuscitating him?" My mouth moved like the mouth of a nutcracker doll despite my acrobatic thoughts.

"26 minutes."

This was not the correct multiple-choice answer. My shoulders tensed, and I felt my insides clench in fear. 26 minutes was not the answer that corresponded with a trip in a helicopter to a metropolitan hospital followed by a long and healthy life. It was not even the answer that corresponded to an extended surgery and lengthy cardiac rehabilitation.

I counted seven syringes of epinephrine on his left side. They were almost touching his left shoe. The shoe with the furry lining was meant to keep him warm, now fully incapable of fulfilling that mission. The syringes were empty, and the packaging was scattered, both clues to the urgency of the situation. Epinephrine is a primary drug to restart the heart during cardiac arrest. Seven is not a good number. I had never been in a cardiac arrest situation in which more than two doses of epinephrine had been given that ended in the correct multiple-choice answer, a desired helicopter ride, and cardiac rehab.

"Does he have any health problems?" my personal attendant asked.

"None."

"Cardiac history?"

"None."

"At what point do you consider stopping resuscitation?" I asked my personal attendant.

No answer. Silence. Sometimes no answer is an answer.

Thankfully Klaus and I had had this conversation many times at the kitchen table where we had all our important conversations. My self-reliant and stubborn German husband would not want resuscitation unnecessarily continued.

My nurse brain was nowhere to be found to provide an answer to my question about when to stop resuscitation. I later learned the answer to my question was after the patient was transported to the hospital and an ultrasound was done by the emergency room physician to determine if there was cardiac activity. Cardiac activity equated to a helicopter ride. No cardiac activity; pronouncement of time of death.

"We are getting ready to transport him to the hospital," my personal attendant said. I watched as the other team members performed the carefully orchestrated teamwork of continuing CPR without pause while loading a patient onto a gurney.

One. Two. Three. Continuing CPR. Seat belt on.

They wheeled him past me out the door and into the ambulance. I glimpsed his expressionless pale face, usually with rosy cheeks and a sassy comment. No smile. No smirk. No sassy comment. No flying spittle with a German accent.

The soup was still simmering on the stove as he wheeled past.

"Do you want to ride in the ambulance?"

"No thank you, I'll take my car." I still hoped to need my car to follow Klaus, who would be riding in a helicopter, from the local hospital to the metropolitan hospital where his life would be saved.

I returned to my Nissan Versa and drove, silently, the same Nissan Versa that Klaus had ridiculously thought the five of us could go for a cross-country vacation that summer. I bought the Nissan because the first car Klaus and I had kissed in was a Nissan. It now carried me to the hospital to await my fate. Klaus went with bells and sirens and red lights and a police escort. The familiar voice from the church rode with me to the hospital, knees up against his chest in my car too small to accommodate his height. My personal attendant went with Klaus in the ambulance.

I was strangely calm during the short car ride to the hospital. No one had told me yet how dire the situation was and if they had I would not have believed them.

Fear began to rise as I saw the Emergency Room sign, its red flashing lights signaling urgency and warning. Always taught to do the right thing, I carefully parked my car in the parking lot designated for the emergency room, rather than the fire lane, which would have provided immediate access to the entrance and to Klaus.

I had my insurance card ready for the gatekeeper of the emergency department and compliantly completed the required admission paperwork.

"Please have a seat in the waiting room," the gatekeeper behind the desk said in a tone that was somewhere between dismissive and condescending. This was an appropriate response for someone presenting for a throat culture, not the family member of someone arriving by ambulance in full-blown cardiac arrest. From an early age, I was taught to observe basic social codes. Be polite. Ask nicely. Wait my turn. But don't established codes evaporate during an emergency? Isn't this why ambulances can run red lights and drive on the wrong side of the road?

My compliance reached its limit, and my composure escaped me.

"I need to be in there." Fear that I wouldn't be at my husband's side in his last moments began to leak out.

"You can't be in there," the gatekeeper countered.

The exchange went on until a nurse came to my rescue.

"I need to be in there." My insistence had now changed its focus from the gatekeeper to the nurse. "I know," the nurse nodded. Growing panic sent me into wild and terrified imaginings.

My nurse brain kicked in again. I knew that when family members are at the side of their loved ones during resuscitation efforts emotional burdens and grief response is decreased. My non-nurse mind was wild. I needed to be at my husband's side. I wanted him to know I was there. I was certain he would know. He would sense my presence. He was still close by.

"Come with me," the nurse said.

I do not know the name of the nurse escorting me through the locked door separating the waiting room from the emergency department. I doubt that she remembers me, but I will always remember her rescuing me from the waiting room and letting me witness that every possible effort was made to get my husband that helicopter ride.

The cold air hit me as I crossed the threshold from the waiting area into the emergency department. As a nurse always moving, I welcomed the coolness of hospitals. The cold air not only prevented bacterial growth and infection, but it also prevented the hospital staff from sweating and revealing to patients and families how hard they were working to save lives. I pulled my sweater closer, unable to combat the shivering. The silence of the hallway was broken by the beeps and short commands given by someone in charge of a life-and-death situation. My nurse self recognized the response back as a safety check to make sure that orders had been heard correctly. I swallowed hard and walked stiff-legged toward the largest room in the emergency department. Clop, clop, clop, my black clogs loud against the nurse's silent tennis shoes. The largest room was often the most desirable for doctors and nurses because it had all the equipment we needed and room for the crowd of hospital workers taking care of the most acute patients. But it was the least desirable room for anyone else because it meant the situation was dire. The sickest patients went to the biggest rooms. Charge nurse 101.

The door was open, and I could see Klaus surrounded by a team bent over him. Doctor, nurse, pharmacist, respiratory therapist. Check. Check. Check. And check. Smell from the cautery burned my nose and made my eyes water. The combined smell made a familiar warm tang in the back of my throat, and I bit back my tears as I entered the triage room. The howling in my head was not loud enough to cover the din of the hospital emergency room. I crossed the threshold, the synchronous beeping from machines comforting to me when I was wearing scrubs now sounding foreboding and ominous. Someone was yelling orders. Don't they know not to yell? It scares the other patients and their family members. More Charge Nurse 101. My eyes went directly to Klaus, shirt ripped open. He looked so small in that very large treatment room. His nose and face were bloody. Did he break his nose? Did the table on which the soup was to be served break his fall? When did the hair on his chest turn grey? He was no longer wearing his new fur-lined shoes; his bare feet splayed to each side.

My outside remained composed. I wanted to run but was frozen in place, eyes fixed on the trauma unfolding before me. My insides raged, muscles burning. My gut wanted to heave its contents.

The nurse stood by my side as the emergency department physician performed an ultrasound. My new personal attendant. "Call the helicopter," the physician said. The physician believed he saw a flutter on the grainy ultrasound screen. "Call the helicopter," translated into "there is a chance of survival" in my nurse brain.

A moment of respite from my fear. A split second of relief. Hope.

I recognized the physician. Our children had attended the same elementary school many years ago. "Klaus built you a solar-powered doghouse, Dr. Lum," I blurted.

No response.

The doghouse was a silent-auction item constructed by Klaus with Peter's third-grade class.

"Dotty is always cold," Peter shared one evening during dinner. Dotty was the class dog, and Peter adored her. She was a thin stray who had found her way into Peter's heart. Dotty was a sensitive and gentle mutt, caring for the room full of third graders as much as they cared for her. This conversation came on the heels of the discussion about the upcoming silent auction and what our family would donate.

Those four short words, "Dotty is always cold," were the only prompting that Klaus needed. Soon our kitchen table was filled with diagrams and sketches for a solar-powered doghouse. Only the solar panel needed to be purchased. Always frugal, the rest of the construction materials came from scraps Klaus found in our garage. There was leftover paint in the basement. Weeks were spent in full construction mode with the third graders. It was dark blue with a moon and stars on one side and a corresponding sun on the other.

Seconds later came "Cancel the helicopter," the doctor's response to my recognition. My nurse brain translated "Cancel the helicopter" into "there is no chance of survival."

Had my outburst distracted him? He walked over to me.

"This means you have to stop, doesn't it?"

He met my eyes and gave a silent nod, confirming that my life as I had known it was over.

"He was probably dead before he hit the ground," the doctor with the dog house said. "He probably didn't feel anything." Was that meant to be comforting?

I could feel myself growing hot, not from movement but from the steady pulse of fear in my stomach as the reality of his words sank in.

Through my fog, I could feel the room slipping out of focus. I gripped the back of the chair in front of me as the floor fell away layer by layer. Don't cry. Don't cry. Don't cry. I didn't cry, but a silent internal howl made breathing nearly impossible.

This is what happens to someone else. This is not what happens to me, not to my children. Parents die before their children, but not like this.

Modern medicine failed Klaus as I stood helplessly by. The doctor made the pronouncement. "Time of death: 11:58 am."

Klaus is dead. Dead. Dead. A powerful wave of nausea swept through me. I looked frantically around the room for a garbage can. Just as I started to dry heave a nurse put a ridiculously small pink emesis basin in my hand. It was as if my body was rejecting the fact that Klaus was gone forever. So much rejection could not possibly fit into a basin this size.

The nurse at my side was the only person who remained in the room with Klaus and me. Everyone else had filed out. "Take a deep breath," she said. "And try and hold it for a few seconds." Ironically, I used those very same lines often with my laboring patients dealing with life events at the other end of the continuum.

I tried to stop gagging.

"Now another breath. In through your nose and out through your mouth."

My nurse brain shut off, unable to be resuscitated. I was now a wife without a husband. There was nothing else to attend to.

In my previous experiences with death, both as a nurse and as a family member, the line between life and death had been more blurred. Life gradually ebbed from the body, birth in reverse. Never had I experienced such a firm line being drawn between life and death. Stark bookends. One moment your heart was beating while you were cooking soup, and the next moment it refused to beat again.

Apparently, people could die in the space between heartbeats.

I felt like my consciousness had split in two, no longer my nurse brain and my wife brain. Now, the part that felt things had detached itself from the rest of me. It was on the ceiling, watching.

"I will leave you some time to say goodbye," the nurse said and stood to leave.

And with that, I was alone with Klaus for the last time. I tried to get my eyes to work but their seeing power was reversed. They now looked inward to a white cavity swirling with memories of our years together.

Chapter 4

nearly a year had gone by, during which I thought of Klaus daily. What was he doing? Did he think of me? Surely, he had a girl-friend. Did he remember me at all?

The long nights alone as a nurse on the psychiatric unit gave me ample time to pine for him. Even on dates, he was the bar I measured everyone against, and no one came close to creating the giddy feeling I had with him during those few days.

His birthday was coming up. "Lieber Klaus," I wrote in my head. "Alles Gute zum Geburtstag." Happy Birthday. What else should I write? "I think about you incessantly" would be true. "I think I am in love with you." That's just plain crazy.

I took the step of buying airmail paper, especially thin and light to make use of every gram of weight allowed for air mail postage. Special care was needed when writing on the onion-skin paper so that the ink would not leak through to the other side. Tears also soaked the paper and made it impossible to write on. The paper came with special envelopes flanked with red and blue check marks so that it stood out against all the other envelopes in the mailbag to ensure its speedy travel by air versus ocean liner.

I started again, beginning with Lieber Klaus rather than the more casual Hallo, Klaus. But was Dear Klaus too forward? I wrote the news of the last year, getting my first job working nights with chemically dependent adults. How working alone as a brand-new nurse was difficult. That Mausi had to be put to sleep on Halloween. My parents had a great time on their trip to Germany. I had also moved to St. Paul and had a new job working days on a combined psychiatric and addictions unit. I was glad to be on the day shift. At the end of the letter, before self-doubt and rational thought could stop me, I quickly scribbled the words in my grammatically incorrect and misspelled German: "I have never met anyone who has made such an impression on me in such a short amount of time." Deine, Susanne. Envelope licked shut. Airmail stamp on. Into the mailbox. Off the letter went before I could reconsider.

His response was as immediate as communication allowed. Airmail, 5-7 days there, 5-7 days back, two weeks total. A thick squishy envelope, the kind lined with bubble wrap, arrived in my mailbox. The larger book slipped out first. "Back Vergnügen wie Noch Nie." A book on German bread-baking, complete with recipes for my beloved "Bauernbrot" and "vollkorn Brötchen." A sign that he remembered our conversation from the previous summer about how much I missed German rye bread and multi-grain rolls in the United States. Was that evidence that he still thought of me?

My birthday card slid out next. He remembered that my birthday came shortly after his. "I am sending you a copy of my favorite book," he said among the sparse lines written on the birthday card. "And a book so that you can bake German bread in the United States." Out slid *Siddhartha*, by Hermann Hesse, is the story of the spiritual journey of self-discovery. The protagonist's name, "Siddhartha," is comprised of two Sanskrit words, "siddha," meaning "achieved" and "artha," meaning "he who has attained his goals." I knew the story well. A dog-eared copy lay next to my bed. I wrote back. "My mother and I are planning to be in Stuttgart around Christmastime. Could we see each other? I would like to see you." It was a mother-daughter trip we had been planning for many years, but that motivation was now railroaded by the possibility of seeing Klaus and perhaps getting an answer to my questions. Silence. Again, no response. Self-doubt plagued me. I'd been to the Land of Self-Doubt so many times I should have set up a hot dog stand there. I had been taught to become what I should be rather than what I wanted: quiet, and without needs. And I knew to expect the worst from others. Of course, he wouldn't have time to see me. What was I thinking? There were more here-and-there dates during that year. All without spark, and none measuring up to how I felt with Klaus. After several months I wrote again, this time with specific dates. "We will be arriving the day after Christmas and staying with my aunt until January 9," I wrote. A telephone number where I could be reached would have been helpful, I learned in the 20/20 vision offered by hindsight. Again nothing. More silence. No response. Let it go, I thought. You are making things up. You are telling yourself stories. Give up hope. He doesn't want to see you. You were right all along. Underneath it all rumbled my ever-present self-doubt. No one could love me anyway. Mom and I left for Germany on Christmas Day; my father dropped us off at the airport. We were both full of anticipation, initially directed toward spending time together in Germany. But, unbeknownst to my mother, my excitement was directed at the possibility of Klaus meeting me on a large white stallion and carrying me off into the sunset. I envisioned myself reconnecting with those blue eyes and the smell of Polo in the crook of his neck. I had not given up hope, never mind that I hadn't heard from him since my birthday card in July. While in Stuttgart my mother and I stayed with Luise, my Europa Mutti. Neither knew of Klaus. "I would like to connect with someone I met at the festival last summer," I told them. "I hope I can reach him." Use of the home telephone in Germany was expensive. I was afraid to ask my aunt to use hers, partially because of cost but also afraid that my persistent attempts to contact Klaus would expose the depth of my feelings for him. So, mostly, I snuck out to the telephone booth across the street at every opportunity, tossing my coins in and hoping for an answer. No answer. No answer. No answer. Had I been able to leave a message, it would have gotten more and more desperate with each passing day. Our departure looming ever closer, I was becoming hopeless. Nearly ready to give up, I slipped out to the phone booth after breakfast on the last Sunday morning of our trip. We were returning home that Friday. "Hallo." My heart jumped, and my palms sweat at the recognition of his deep voice on the other end of the phone. "I am just on my way out the door," he said. "I am on my way to my parent's house for Sonntagsessen." Sundays in Germany are sacred. Shops are closed, and unwritten rules abound. Sunday is a day of Ruhe. Lawnmowers do not run, and public hustle and bustle cease to exist, if only for a day. Not so for the women, though. They spent the day in the kitchen, first preparing Sonntagsessen and then Kaffee und Kuchen, all served on the finest dishes resting on pristinely ironed and creased table linens carefully selected to match the china. "My mother is making Rouladen and Kartoffelknödel." I imagined the thin slices of top round slathered with mustard and then rolled tightly around a pickle and bacon slices, served in a puddle of dark gravy with airy potato dumplings on the side. Sweet and sour red cabbage rounded out the meal. "She hates it when I am late." I envisioned the handmade dumplings, light and airy around a buttered and toasted crouton. When out of the water bath, they yielded to a spoon. Fifteen minutes later, the dumplings unacceptably turned from airy to chewy and needed a knife to cut through them. Airy dumplings were the makings of a Hausfrau's self-worth.

"A moment later and I would have missed you. I have been waiting for your call. Did you get my telegram?"

He had sent a telegram?

Bin nicht zuhause. STOP

I won't be home. The then speediest form of communication across the Atlantic, reserved for the direst of circumstances, and he had sent one to me?

Bin bei den Eltern. STOP

The word STOP was used between sentences so that any ambiguous phrases would not be misinterpreted. I will be at my parent's house. Even after punctuation was introduced, people continued to use the word STOP between sentences.

Mich bitte dort anrufen. STOP

Charged by the word, writers kept the message short. Expensive, a telegram was always associated with urgency. Please call me at my parents' number. 07151/63336.

He had sent the telegram the same day we left for the airport, and it was presumably waiting for me back at home.

"When can we see each other?"

Before Klaus went off to Sonntagsessen we hastily made plans to meet on Tuesday, Epiphany, which meant he wouldn't be driving the courier route between pharmacies that was his business. Was it ironic that we would be seeing each other again on the holiday that represented the manifestation of a divine being? He gave me explicit instructions to meet him at the subway stop close to where he lived, which I didn't need as I was familiar with all of the stops between Stuttgart-Zentrum and Gärtringen, my aunt's village south of the city. I stepped out of the phone booth and into the cold to cross the street back to my aunt's cozy kitchen. It was good I had a moment in the cold air to cool my excitement over hearing Klaus's bass voice and the anticipation of seeing him in two short days after 18 months of pining. I was flushed with excitement. My mother and my Europa Mutti, sitting in the same spot in the kitchen with now lukewarm coffee in their cups, were comparing childhood memories, their mutual no-nonsense demeanor meeting somewhere over the middle of the kitchen table. They were still under the impression that I was reading in the living room. "You have such rosy cheeks" my mother exclaimed. "Were you outside?"

"I will be spending Tuesday with someone I met last summer at the music festival," I told my mother and aunt, my palms sweaty at the thought. I hoped my flushed cheeks did not reveal the level of my excitement. "I was finally able to reach him." Adding his name would have made it more personal and perhaps disclosed some of my anticipation. "He is just an acquaintance," I reassured my mother.

"Are you sure?"

"Yes," I lied to protect my mother from the possibility that I was in love with a German man and would move to Germany. Decades of regret at leaving Germany had been a leaden weight on her heart, and she was filled with guilt at leaving her parents. She would see my moving to Germany as her punishment for leaving her parents, now long dead.

I had waited for a year and a half. Now 48 hours seemed endless.

BEEF ROULADEN
Peter calls this "German Sushi"

Ingredients:

Thin slices of top round, two per mouth you plan to feed. Ask the butcher to slice thin slices of top round large enough to stuff and roll up, ideally about 4x6 inches and ¼" thick. Two Rouladen per person allows for hearty appetites and leftovers if you are lucky.

Finely chopped onions
Mustard – any kind that is not too spicy is OK. Choose one you like:
        grainy, Dijon, or yellow.
Dill pickle spears
Bacon slices
Salt and pepper

For the gravy:
1 large onion, finely chopped
2 cloves of finely minced garlic
Butter and vegetable oil
1-2 Tablespoons of tomato paste
1 cup of red wine
Beef broth
2-3 Bay leaves
Salt and pepper

Lay all of the slices of beef out on a flat surface and generously salt and pepper them. Spread each slice with mustard. Next, come the chopped onions, sprinkle them generously on each slice. Top the onions with one or two slices of bacon, laid vertically on each beef slice. Last, place a pickle spear horizontally on each slice of beef, ideally, the ends of the pickle spear will peak out of the beef after it has been rolled up.

Roll up each beef slice and securely fasten each roll with toothpicks, a meat trussing needle, or twine (I have used dental floss in a pinch!).

Fry the Rouladen in a combination of hot oil and butter. Frying in a mixture of oil and butter is the best of both worlds – butter provides the flavor and oil increases the smoke point so you can get a nice sear on the meat. Once the "sushi rolls" are nicely browned, remove them from the pan. In the same pan, adding a little more butter or oil if needed, (without removing any of the browned bits!) saute the onions until soft and translucent, about 5 minutes. Add the garlic and cook just until fragrant, less than a minute. You don't want it to burn or it will taste bitter! Pour in a cup of red wine and simmer for a few minutes, stirring to loosen the brown bits on the bottom of the pan. Add beef broth to cover, a tablespoon of tomato paste, a bay leaf or two, and salt and pepper to taste. Nestle the Rouladen back in the pot.

You can do this a day or two ahead of time and stop here, putting the whole thing into the refrigerator!

Finish the Rouladen on the stovetop or in the oven.

Stovetop: Cook on low for 60-90 minutes, until fork tender.
Oven: Transfer to an oven-safe pot into a preheated 325 F and cook for 60-90 minutes, until fork tender. I have also put them into a slow cooker, a great stress reducer for a holiday meal!

Once the Rouladen are fork tender remove them and pour the remaining cooking liquid through a strainer. Return this liquid gold to the pot and thicken it with either flour or cornstarch, whichever you prefer. Serve in a large puddle of gravy with your choice of gravy-absorbing carbohydrate.

KARTOFFELKLÖSSE

German Potato Dumplings
Makes about 12 dumplings

I worked at a restaurant in Germany for one summer. For my fastidious German boss my dumplings were never perfectly round enough, hence I was not allowed to make them at the restaurant after a few attempts. Since Frau Kleber, no one has complained about the shape of my dumplings and they always disappear whenever I make them. Should you be fortunate to have leftovers, they taste great the next day sliced and fried in butter. Once the slices are golden brown top with a couple of scrambled eggs and fry until the eggs are set.

3 pounds russet potatoes
Salt and freshly ground nutmeg to taste
1/8 cup corn or potato starch
½ - ¾ cup all-purpose flour
1 large egg

Rustic day-old white bread, anything that will stand up to a crunchy, firm crouton.

Trim crusts off the bread. Cut bread into ½ inch cubes and fry in butter until golden brown. Drain on a paper towel and put to the side.

Wash potatoes and cook, unpeeled, in a large pot of boiling water until tender, about 30-45 minutes. Drain and cool slightly. Peel.

Mash potatoes into a large bowl while still warm, taking care to make sure there are no large lumps of potato. Allow to cool completely.

Mix in salt and nutmeg, add egg, ½ cup flour, and the corn- or potato starch. Using your hands, knead until a smooth dough forms, adding flour a tablespoonful at a time until the dough no longer sticks to your hands.

Place a small test-sized ball of dough into a pot of nearly boiling, salted water. Dumplings must be simmered, not boiled! If the ball sticks together you have added enough flour. If the ball disintegrates, knead in more flour. Measure about ¼ cup of dough and form balls around a crouton or two in the middle of the ball. Roll the ball in wet hands until smooth ball forms.

Working in small batches cook the remaining dumplings without crowding them – they should not touch each other in the pot. Simmer for 15 minutes after they have risen to the top. Remove with a slotted spoon.

For over-the-top decadence, garnish with plain bread crumbs toasted in butter. Just gravy works too.

Braised Red Cabbage

Feel free to make this a day or two ahead of time, the flavor only improves.

1 medium head of red cabbage, about 2-3 pounds
2 tablespoons bacon fat, goose fat, or butter
1 large yellow onion, finely diced
1 large apple, cored and finely diced
1 cup water or dry red wine or a combination of the two
¼ cup apple cider vinegar
2-3 whole cloves
1 bay leaf
Salt and pepper to taste

Saute the onions in your fat of choice until translucent, about 5-6 minutes. Add the thinly sliced cabbage and stir. Cook until the cabbage wilts. Add the rest of the ingredients and mix until combined. Cover, reduce the heat to low, and simmer until the cabbage is softened, about two hours.

CHAPTER 5

I was suddenly left alone with Klaus in the emergency department treatment room, the stainless steel reflecting cold and sterile. No more urgent voices calling out orders. No more beeping and alarming. I had been told to "say goodbye."

How do you say goodbye after two decades of constant companionship? There had been no time for preparation, no forethought, no planning.

The nurse left me alone. "Wait! Help!" I screamed in my head. "I don't know how to do this from this side of the nurse's station." My kite was spiraling out of control. I needed someone to grab the trailing string and hold on tight. I needed someone to tell me how to do this. Countless times I had left bereaved parents with the same instructions. "I will leave you to have some time with your baby to say goodbye," I said in my most compassionate nurse voice. "Put the call light on when you are ready for me to come back." Did they too want me to return with an instruction manual providing details on how to say goodbye to their stillborn baby? Those parents had each other. I was alone without someone to tether me to the ground. Maybe the nurse was ringing the chaplain on call. If I were the nurse, that is what I would be doing right now. The chaplain could certainly tell me how to do this. At least I wouldn't be alone.

I smelled coffee from the nurse's station. Coffee. The best friend of nurses. One of us always had beans from home in our bag when substandard hospital coffee was just not going to be enough. "I'll go make the coffee," one of us would say after a tragedy while another foraged in the refrigerator around lost lunches with questionable smells for half and half with a reasonable expiration date. We sipped the strong brew that was made just the right color with the perfect amount of cream and readied ourselves for the next emergency. The next tragedy.

I approached his body, dressed in his leather vest, button-down flannel shirt, and dark green corduroy pants. He had certainly become a more adventurous dresser in our two decades together. When we met, he owned two white shirts and two pairs of grey pants. The braided leather belt I had gotten him for Christmas last year was unbuckled. That and his torn shirt provided access to his chest, which lay bare. His chest hair had just recently started turning grey. I inspected his hands and knees through my tears. Were there any scrapes? Had he tried to brace his fall? Had he felt anything before he fell? Any pain?

His nose was bloody and swollen; was it the manifestation of a hard and fast fall with nothing breaking the moment between life and death?

I remembered that hearing is the last sense to go. "I love you, Klaus," I said through sobs as I bent to kiss him one last time, certain that he could hear me. The scratch from his salt-and-pepper beard on my cheek was bristly and rough, as it always was. He kept his beard well trimmed because I hated it when the hairs went up my nose. But this time the cold radiating from his face underneath the beard startled me. How could he already be so cold? I had always used his hands and feet to warm my own perpetually cold extremities. Less than an hour earlier, those hands had been chopping vegetables with the children of the church, warm and full of life and eager anticipation. Those feet had moved to the serving table to determine where to place the soup terrine.

The life that had made him warm was gone. The soul that knew just how to reassure me in moments of self-doubt was no longer there.

Blood from his face mixed with my tears and left a watery smear on my cheek. Unsure of what to do next, I walked out of that room to the nurse's station.

"I'm waiting for my children. I'm not sure what to do next."

"When are they coming?" a voice from the desk asked me. Everyone suddenly looked the same. "They are on their way." Coffee mingled with antiseptic, phones ringing, a cacophony of loud and muffled voices, all so familiar to me yet strangely different from the other side of the nurse's station.

"Will they want to see their father? Will they want to say goodbye?"

"I have no idea," was what my brain said on the inside. On the outside, my mouth said, "I'm not sure."

The nurse escorted me to a much smaller emergency department room. My clogs clomped through the hallway, evidence that I was tethered to the ground, yet the rest of me seemed to be detached from my body and floating. A beeping IV pump and the smell of fresh coffee in the background would have, under normal circumstances, roused an immediate reaction. No, I didn't need to go turn off the alarm, but I would love a cup of coffee. With cream, please. Now they were otherworldly and seemed to reach me through cotton-filled ear canals. There were hushed voices at the nurse's station. No laughing. I knew these conversations well. "Oh, how sad. I wonder how long they were married." And then, because the sadness was sometimes just too much, "What are you doing this weekend?" I had been on the nurse's side for the better part of two decades, engaging in conversations anticipating weekend plans or what their spouse had recently done to annoy them.

I had clearly moved down the scale of acuity as measured by the size of hospital rooms. Smaller rooms were for the less acutely ill; larger rooms were for the more acutely ill; the largest rooms were for the trauma patients needing the most equipment and hospital personnel. As a charge nurse, I made those discernments quickly and effortlessly. Now I was regarding the full impact of those decisions as a family member. I was brought to an empty patient room, tiny, with no equipment and no stainless steel. This room became my waiting room to tell my children their father had died. I listed grievances with God in my head. They are at the cusp of adulthood. They have so many difficult decisions to make. And Klaus's parents didn't deserve to lose a son. Dammit. Fluorescent lights gave me a headache.

One plastic chair. A portable stand that held equipment to monitor a patient's blood pressure, pulse, and oxygen levels: a patient's vital signs; signs that are vital to life. Or are they? Or are signs vital to life how many vegetables we chopped with children? How much soup we had cooked for those we love? I had wheeled a similar stand around hundreds of times, maybe thousands. The noise level of the wheels existed in direct proportion to the urgency of the situation. The bed in the room had only a sheet covering it. The acuity of those assigned to this room was so low it did not even warrant a bedspread.

A nurse put Klaus's wallet and wedding ring into my hand. No, my mind screamed. I need to take all of him home, not just his wallet and wedding ring.

"Could I please have a glass of water?"

A too-small glass of water in a Styrofoam cup with a bendy straw, which in my mind was reserved only for hospitals, was placed at my side. How would this cup ever hold enough water to replace the amount of water my body had already lost through the tears I had shed in the last hour? There was no ice in the glass.

Did the nurse think that the extra cold would be too startling for my current state? Would it shock me into reality? Or maybe the resuscitation had exhausted her as well and the extra steps to the ice machine were just too much. She had removed only part of the wrapper from the straw, putting the exposed part of the straw into the water. The nurse had left the remaining wrapper for me to remove myself so that I would know she had not touched the drinking end of the straw. I had delivered thousands of glasses of water that looked just like this one to distraught patients and family members. But now, as a distraught family member, germs did not matter, and I wondered why the hospital used Styrofoam and straws. Didn't they know these were bad for the environment?

The water came with cheap tissues, the kind that are rough and aggravate your nose with too much rubbing. Hospitals should at least get the kind of tissues that have lotion for family members, I thought. Trivialities flooded my mind to keep out the thoughts of how I would tell my children their father had died.

With a whoosh of her arm, the nurse closed the stained plaid curtain, the rattle of the rings against the rod startling. What story of tragedy and pain was behind that stain on the curtain? The whoosh, curtain, and rattle created a border, a wall between my raw grief and the outside world.

The dog-house doctor came in to see me. Usually, I am full of questions. Usually, I want to know everything. Usually, the more information I have, the more in control I feel. But this time I just said, "With all due respect, Doctor, I am not interested in hearing what happened." I just wanted my children to come. I no longer wanted to be alone.

I could hear people whispering at the nurse's station. Were they wondering how many children I was waiting for? Were they asking who wanted to go to lunch? I was frightfully alone. There is surprisingly little to do in a hospital after a loved one has died. I waited for my children for what seemed like hours. I anticipated with agony telling them their father had died. Their emotions frightened me.

As I waited, I rehearsed various lines in my head. All lines ended with the same message: "Your dad has died."

Different words? Should I add I am sorry?

"I'm sorry. Your Dad has died."

More words? Fewer words?

Different approach? Maybe I should make the delivery longer to soften the blow.

"Once your dad got to the hospital, they tried many things. They called the helicopter but, in the end, they couldn't save him."

But this was no acting exercise. This was the real deal. I choked on the words in my mouth.

Peter would be solid when I told him. He would be the one to carry on family traditions.

Sonja would cry, but only briefly. Her focus then would shift quickly from her own grief to reading my feelings, followed by a determination of what I needed, which she would then promptly carry out.

For Alex, the sadness and grief would be turned inward in his attempt to hide his pain and protect me.

I heard them come through the main entrance of the emergency room. Whoosh. The automatic door opened. Whoosh again and it closed. They were as silent as their boots were loud. Clomp. Stop. Getting directions. Clomp, clomp, clomp. Stop. They were shown to where I was waiting. In the hospital room for low-acuity patients. CLOMP. STOP. I took a breath. Then another. Trying to stop my spinning thoughts before they came into the room. The plaid curtain was moved back a little as they came in. They scanned my face for clues of what was going on.

No amount of rehearsing had prepared me for this. I wanted more than anything to stretch this moment. To expand the time before they know. To shield them from what has happened for as long as I can. I took a deep breath to calm my spinning thoughts.

The sound of my voice scared me. "I am so sorry, but your father has died." Their faces unraveled. Sonja shed enormous tears, like heavy pearls. Peter, ever the pragmatist, paced anxiously and wondered about returning to school and taking his finals. Alex was quiet, his face a perfect, younger image of his father. I watched his eyes sink deeper and deeper into his face, which was becoming whiter by the moment. I went to each of them and took them in my arms.

"Would you like to see your dad?" My nurse brain knew I should allow them to see Klaus and say their last goodbyes. But not all things are worth knowing. Sonja and Peter chose not to see his body and live with their last memory of Klaus making pizza.

Alex and I walked to Klaus. Death had silenced the incessant beeping and yelling of orders in the large triage room. Tears blurred my vision, running down my face and neck and between my clothes and skin, soaking the front of my shirt. The tears seemed to come from every pore of my body.

He is dead.

He is dead.

He is dead.

Would it become more real the more I repeated the mantra to myself?

The three words contained no sense. I could not bend my mind to their meaning. It was impossible that my husband, healthy and exuberant and cutting vegetables just over an hour ago, should be dead.

Alex bent over his dad and then looked over at me, his eyes deep dark pools of sorrow. "Enough?" I asked. He nodded, and together we fled a room so full of feelings they threatened to capsize me.

"What do I do now?" I asked at the nurse's station. Previous life experience had not prepared me for what to do next. As a nurse, I knew the next steps for my patients and their families. But at this moment, I was a family member first and had no idea what to do next.

"The coroner will call you with the report" and "get some rest" were my first instructions on how to handle the land of the newly widowed

I now inhabited. Get some rest? Rest eluded me for months. It was the first platitude of many. Someone saying something to make me feel better. But I came to envision these platitudes as though I were swaddled in a layer of bubble wrap as self-protection. Sometimes the platitude required two layers.

"Is there anything else I have to do?"

"There is nothing else for you to do here," were the spoken words. "Please go home," was left unspoken. I was excused from the hospital.

My family of five—now a family of four—filed through the automatic door. Open. Whoosh. There was a short hallway between the emergency department and the outside. Was it designed to soften the blow between the threshold of events in the emergency department and the changes the outside world held for us? To extend the moment between my before-Klaus-died-life -and-after-Klaus-died life?

Freezing ice hit our faces, the individual sharp edges cutting the skin on my cheeks as if to drive in my changed reality. My husband is dead. He is gone. Klaus is gone.

The door closed with an equal whoosh as if I was being vacuum-sealed out of one world and thrust into another.

Chapter 6

finally, Tuesday morning arrived. I made my best clothing choice from the limited options in my suitcase. A little lipstick and a touch of mascara. The rest of my face was already flushed with excitement and in no need of extra color. My knees were shaky as I waited for the subway. Alle einsteigen. All aboard. All aboard for the rest of my life? Vorsicht bei der Abfahrt. What did I need to be careful of? What is waiting for me on the other end of this trip? Herrenberg. We made a large loop and the Stiftskirche with its familiar onion-shaped dome came into view on the hillside. I wanted the train to go both fast and slow at the same time. Böblingen. We passed by lots of Mercedes in all colors, shapes, and sizes waiting to be shipped to auto dealers across the world. For me, the town was not associated with luxury cars, but with swimming and shopping and leisurely afternoons that include Kaffee und Kuchen on the top floor of Hertie. Familiar woods streaked by the window. In a moment the lights would switch on automatically and we would enter the tunnel. The tunnel came to an end a moment later. My heart jumped as the tracks sloped to my favorite part of the journey. First, I would see the Fernsehturm, a 217-meter telecommunications tower overlooking Stuttgart. In the next moment, we left the woods, and the tracks opened into an expansive view of the city. Stuttgart lies at the base of a fertile valley known as the Stuttgarter Kessel. The Neckar River threads through the city. I traced the muddy river and followed it to the Old Castle and the Staatsoper and the familiar downtown passage. In summer, steamy heat would sit in the cauldron and the view would be hazy. On such days, city dwellers escape to the surrounding vineyards and woodlands for frische Luft and relief from the heat. This January morning it was bright and chilly, and the view was clear.

Universität. Here I watched the students hurrying to their next Vorlesung, their worn leather satchels filled with books crisscrossing their backs. My heart beat faster. Mine was the next stop. Would he be there?

"Schwabstrasse," the automated metallic voice announced as the S-Bahn slowed. The small plaid curtain clamped to the side of the narrow horizontal window allowed for a perfect balance between looking out and not being seen. I peeked from behind the curtain. Was he there? The butterflies in my stomach were so active, I was certain those next to me could hear them banging to the left and right of my insides.

The train slowed, the loud wail from the screeching brakes temporarily drowning out the voices of self-doubt in my head. Maybe I should just keep going? Only two more stops and I would be at the center of the city with coffee shops, street musicians, and storefront windows to fill my day. My worldview that things didn't work out and I was unlovable would remain intact.

My wobbly knees somehow kept me upright as I made it to the double doors and waited for the small light to turn green before pulling the handle. Whoosh. The doors opened quickly and easily. The rest happened automatically. The feet attached to my wobbly knees stepped over the large gap of open tracks between me and what I did not yet know to be the rest of my life. I stood on the platform shivering—from anxiety or cold—and scanned the milling crowd.

The holiday crowd was thin enough so that individual faces were not hidden in the mass of many. What if he had shaved his beard? Maybe he had grown his hair longer than the close crew cut he had a year and a half ago. What if I didn't recognize him? It was winter. He would be dressed differently than in the hot summer. Would he look different with a thick winter coat, a hat, and gloves? What if I got the wrong stop? He said Schwabstrasse. I was sure of it.

No Klaus. My self-doubt was screaming loud believable thoughts. Of course he is going to stand you up. I nervously paced among those whose direction had a purpose. Five minutes felt like hours.

Movement off to my side caught my attention. Someone was running. It was Klaus, flying down the concrete steps two at a time, having judged the long escalator ride from the street level not being fast enough for the urgency of the moment. He hugged me, a hug that lasted a split second longer than the hug you give a friend.

Increasing anticipation. You are here. It is you. It is really you. I wanted to pinch myself to make sure this was happening. Polo by Ralph Lauren filled my nose and erased my doubts. All of the phone calls, letters, and yearning converged into the small spot I was standing on and into this moment. This is the kind of love delivered on moonbeams and in thunderbolts. Some moments shift the trajectory of one's life. This was one of those moments.

Every molecule in my body was awake, alert, and excited.

"Let's go have tea," he said as he took my hand, its warmth lessening some of my self-doubts. We made the long escalator ride up to street level, the heat from his body radiating through his wool-lined leather coat from my hand into the rest of my body slowly thawing the nervous tension at my core. His Nissan van was parked crookedly in the fire lane at the top of the escalator. At the time, his blatant disregard for rules and prescribed order was a novelty.

Settling in with our tea in a quiet corner away from the others I felt wholly and completely alive. He pushed a small wrapped box across the table. "Frohe Weihnachten. Eine Kleinigkeit für Dich." A small Christmas gift for me. "Danke." I reached across the Chinese teapot for the small box. The thought of bringing him a Christmas gift had crossed my mind, but I knew him too little to have any idea what an appropriate gift might be. I slowly unwrapped the jewelry-sized box where I found a modern version of the yin and yang pendant I had worn around my neck in the beer tent a year and a half ago.

This half-dollar-sized pendant was completely silver, not the traditional black and white. The two pieces of the yin and yang were slightly offset, reflecting the dark and light components integral to the symbol. A jade and black onyx were in each section. "I designed it for you." No smile was necessary, his eyes said everything that needed to be said. He had not forgotten.

Tears spilled from my eyes and words escaped me as he hung the chain around my neck.

"I haven't stopped thinking about you," he said. "I have loved you since our dance in the beer tent." There really was a touch at the nape of my neck last summer from the back of the Volkswagen.

Finally. It didn't make any sense, but we had fallen in love last summer during that awkward polka. Our love really had begun in an instant.

Finally, some solid evidence for my doubting mind.

We went for a walk in the woods. Here the passionate kisses I had until this point only imagined became reality over a trespassing barrier in the woods. In our rush to have privacy, Klaus parked in a mud puddle, his Nissan van failing to go forward or back when we were ready to leave. Years of experience pushing cars out of snowbanks during Minnesota winters proved useful and impressive to Klaus, as I pushed his Nissan van backward out of the mud.

For the remainder of the afternoon, Roman archaeological treasures were witness to passionate kissing to make up for the longing of the last year and a half. He deposited me back at my aunt's house just before dinner. Walking into her apartment I quickly went to the bathroom to splash cold water on my face to cool my passion and hide the flush on my face.

"It was great to see him again," I reported to my aunt and mother. My aunt grabbed the chain around my neck holding the Yin and Yang and pulled it out from under the sweater where I had intentionally placed it to hide it from them. Boundaries were not my aunt's strong suit. "What's this?" she asked.

"Just a gift from a friend."

It was Tuesday. My mother and I were returning home that Friday. I spent the remaining few days accompanying Klaus on his courier route during the day. My aunt's house happened to be on his tour, and he picked me up along the way in the morning and returned me in time for dinner. In the evenings, I reassured my mother that he was only an acquaintance. The simplicity of accompanying him at work was made magic by our passionate love that had only been part of our dreams for a year and a half. We talked and kissed and kissed and talked. We carried boxes together into the pharmacies and walked out holding hands. We stopped at the Schokozentrale for chocolate and I learned that Klaus was a lover of all things chocolate and his delivery van rarely made it past the Schokozentrale. Dark chocolate covering thick, chewy marzipan was his favorite. We wanted to climb inside each other and get to know everything there was to know. We were also terrified because we did not know where this love would go or how it would end, and with each passing minute, we realized how just how short our time together was.

Barriers and oceans seemed to fall away as we stood in each other's arms kissing goodbye on the curb in front of my aunt's apartment that Friday afternoon. The yin and yang pendant swayed between us, its symbolism of parts that cannot exist without each other taunting our fate.

CHAPTER 7

The vacuum of the hospital door firmly sealed me into the Land of the Newly Widowed. Icy sleet and biting wind hit my raw face. We hurried across the emergency department parking lot to find my Nissan Versa encased in a sheet of ice. All I wanted was to get back to the safety of my warm home. Maybe then I would wake up from this cruel joke.

The sound of the ice scraper grating and squeaking across the ice crystals on the frozen windshield was intolerable to my frayed nerve endings. The car's engine didn't want to start; it simply refused to respond to the arctic circumstances, as if sympathizing with my not wanting to cross over into my new life without Klaus.

On the third try, an obnoxious squealing sound came from under the hood, and the engine reluctantly sputtered to life.

"We have to get Dad's car," Sonja reminded me. "It's still at the church."

To do that, I needed Klaus's keys.

Klaus had driven his friend's Honda Accord to the local Farmer's Market the day before because his white Dodge caravan was on the skids and he was too cheap to fix it. The steering wheel needed to be turned a certain way for the car to travel in the desired direction. It was downright scary, but I had long given up trying to get him to fix it. My laments only made him dig his heels in even further. There were certain things I just couldn't engage with him about. Instead, I refused to ride with him.

In Germany, the car would never have passed their routine rigid inspections. Repair and a follow-up inspection would have been mandatory for the car to maintain its registration. Klaus hated mandates and protocols. The slightest suggestion of a prescribed order to things caused him to bristle and rebel. Instead, he channeled the nomadic cowboys on the Westerns he watched, choosing to follow his internal abstract law and social order.

Together with his friend Luigi, who I called my other husband, Klaus plotted, stirred, peeled, and chopped fruit all week long to prepare for Saturday's market. They were a team who provided entertainment for market goers, bantering with each other and their regular customers in thick German and Filipino accents.

But Luigi was traveling, so Klaus had done the market the previous day alone. They sold jam that reflected the prime fruit of the season. Varieties such as "Strawberry Champagne" and "Rhubarb Orange" were hot commodities to market goers. Klaus and I loved to linger over coffee in the morning accompanied by English muffins buttered just so and topped with a dollop of jam. If the English muffin was still warm from the toaster, the jam would also warm and spread to the edge of the English muffin and mingle with the butter. Pluot and Jack Daniels was our favorite.

There were two remaining cases of strawberry jam. Klaus had completely sold out of the mustard, which everyone loved. The variety didn't matter: brown with ale, yellow with tarragon. Homemade mustard was created to solve the problem of substandard American mustard. The mustard problem came after the much bigger problem of substandard American sausages had been solved.

It is no secret that Germans like their sausages, and Klaus was no exception. He loved sausages and longed to find the ones he remembered so fondly from his homeland. The German love affair with sausages is for good reason: the variety and availability when you step onto German soil are astounding. Wurst, like beer, defines Germany's cities and regions. A wurst map of Germany would be a mosaic of ungraspable complexity, ranging from classic fried bratwurst to tangy Currywurst, dependent on the region and whim of the local Metzger.

Klaus spoke with wurst-laden pride of the sausages from his native Thuringia. "It is da wurst of Martin Luther and Goethe," he boasted. Thüringer Rostbratwurst is a long, thin white bratwurst, with the distinct flavors of caraway, marjoram, and garlic, which are produced for centuries and served in pairs with mashed potatoes, roasted onions, and gravy. Alternatively, the pair of sausages are served with a bun comically small for the task. Unable to find a palatable substitute on the American sausage market, Klaus resorted to collaborating with a butcher to have sausages made to his specification. Relying on memory and an old recipe, Klaus traveled back and forth to the butcher shop to fry up small bits of sausage as the recipe was tweaked and re-tweaked to satisfy his scrutinizing wurst palate.

He ordered dozens at a time to keep in the freezer.

"VAT are you doing?" he screeched in clipped guttural German as I placed the precious sausages in simmering water to be heated. "Dey must be grilled, deesze sausages. NO VAATER." The only thing exceeding his distress at putting sausages in water was serving them with ketchup. Seeing ketchup going on his precious sausages resulted in a large guttural screech with a German accent and flying spittle. My children did it just to set him off.

"I don't think they gave me his car keys," I said to Sonja. A search of my coat pockets and purse revealed only his wallet and wedding ring.

Peter and Alex had already left to return home. Sonja watched me for clues about our next step.

Were the keys still in the front pocket of Klaus's favorite corduroy pants?

Whoosh. Open. Through my fog, back over the threshold, and into the emergency department I went, briefly leaving the Land of the Newly Widowed.

"I need my husband's car keys," I said to the nurse who had sent me home with the discharge instructions to get some rest. I wondered if she was already on to the next patient, the next tragedy or joy that defined her days as a nurse. Had she already forgotten us?

I pictured Klaus on that cold stainless-steel table. Would the wide wale dark green corduroys that he wore all winter still be keeping him a little warm? Did that even matter? I pictured the nurse reaching into his right pocket to get his keys. Or maybe she reached into the left pocket first because she didn't know that he always carried his keys in his right pocket. I should have told her that.

She returned quickly with his keys and silently pressed them into my hand. How could the keys feel so cold? Their weight was so familiar and now so strange. The nurse's eyes were sympathetic.

I hoped my eyes had the same reflection as I helped to deliver babies: joyful when the outcome was good, kind and understanding when it wasn't. I pictured those same eyes moving on to the next patient, the next family that needed her comfort and understanding.

Whoosh. Out again. Back into the Land of the Newly Widowed, this time for good. I dropped Sonja off at the church. She took the keys, stuffed herself around farmer's market paraphernalia, and drove the Accord home.

Having retrieved the car, there was nothing left for me to do but to also return home. One foot perched on the gravel driveway, the other foot still in the car, I felt the undertow of the distant life I had led as a married woman less than two hours ago. I heard the dripdrip dripdrip-drip drip dripdrip drip from the kitchen sink as I walked through the back door. The drips were exactly as Klaus had adjusted them before he left the house a lifetime ago. Peter unloaded the Christmas tree from the back of his pick-up truck and cut the end to fit into the Christmas tree stand as if Christmas was still coming. Alex disappeared into his room. Sonja walked the pasture with Abby, her horse.

Gabe pushed himself against my shin as I walked in the door. "I am here, I am hungry" he was saying with his entire body as if to give purpose to my being. "Oh Gabe" I squeaked out as I bent to pet his wiry hair. I entered the home of my previous life where Klaus's half-empty coffee cup with congealed cream floating on top still sat on the coffee table in the living room. Dammit. "Can't he ever put his coffee cup into the dishwasher? would have been my former self's reaction. The home in which Klaus's dirty underwear and socks from yesterday still lay on the bedroom floor. I hate that that would have been my former self's reaction. The towel from his morning shower was still damp, hanging on the side of the bed. "That will mold and stink," would have been the reaction. The book he had been reading, "Paganism," lay open on his page. Our argument over this book just a few weeks before seemed like years ago. It was the book he selected to read in the waiting room at the hospital a few weeks ago while waiting for me to have a minor procedure. "What are people going to think? Can't you take another book?" In my previous life, I worried about what other people thought. Some things had so annoyed me last week. Yesterday. This morning. My former self was so concerned with the orderliness of the bedroom floor, the integrity of a book's spine, and what other people thought. All of these had seemed imperative to a good life. There were times I considered these things so important to my wellbeing that I actually could start a fight over them.

People began to arrive. I felt airless. Phone calls were made. More people. Was there enough air in my house for all of these people? More phone calls. It seemed as if the house phone never stopped ringing. Was it the cell phone? Or the house phone? Loud ringing in stereo demanded my attention. Some people I wanted to talk to. Others I didn't. Another person stepped in to be my personal attendant. "Would you like to take this phone call?" they asked. "How about this one?" When I couldn't speak anymore, the personal attendant took over. "Let me finish this call for you." I didn't have to think or respond. Everyone should have a personal attendant at times like this.

The worst call was to Klaus's parents. It was evening in Germany. They were watching Tagesschau, the daily news program. Bonnggg. The familiar sound that signaled everyone to be quiet as the news Germans took so seriously was about to begin. Heute die Nachriĉten......Today's News, from the day your son died. I punched in the numbers starting with the international area code - 011, then the Germany code - 49, followed by the area code, 7151. Finally, I dialed their phone number, 63336, whispering to myself, just as I heard Klaus whisper to himself hundreds of times as he dialed his parent's phone "eins-zwei-drei" to make sure he dialed not two, not four, but three threes in succession.

My father-in-law. "Hühn" he answered his deep voice nearly identical to Klaus's voice. "Hallo" I said tentatively. "Ach Susanne!" It was his usual bright response still mingled with a bit of a surprise to get a phone call from overseas. He was always glad to hear my voice. The time the bright surprise lasted only a split second.

"Ich habe eine schlechte Nachricht." I have bad news.

The shock was too big to absorb the details. Klaus's parents had already had their quota of losses. For Klaus's mother, it was three brothers, and her father in the war. For his father, a brother, a sister, and both parents by age 17. The tragedy and shock were too big for many words. They would call back the next day. And the next. Each day asking for more bits of information, as if receiving the information over several days and in small bits rationed the pain.

"You aren't going to be able to do this alone, you know," someone said to me that day. "You are going to have to ask for help." Asking for help was not in my repertoire of skills. I had grown up in the company of those for whom self-reliance was of the utmost importance, and asking for help was seen as a character flaw.

The food began to arrive in casseroles, bags, aluminum pans, and disposable containers. Warm and cold, large and small, sweet and savory.

Boston brown bread, thick and dense, slightly sweet and ever so comforting arrived. Cookies for my children. A simple mix of pasta, hamburger, and canned green beans was particularly appealing. It didn't require much chewing. Its blandness presented no further assault on my senses.

Most valuable were the sandwich fixings.

"How odd," I thought as sliced ham and cheese and white sandwich bread came out of the bag, after the tissues and paper towels. I had delivered soups and casseroles, but never sandwich fixings. I quickly learned sandwich fixings were valuable commodities, especially the soft white kind of sandwich bread that didn't require a great deal of effort to chew and allowed me to conserve my finite amounts of energy. Sandwiches have a normalcy and a control over them that other provided food doesn't. You can make a sandwich when you want it and the way you like it and not have to have it when someone else brings it or the way someone else makes it, unlike baked pasta, which all had to be reheated at 350 regardless of the ingredients.

I vowed to ask for help. "I am going to do whatever is necessary to work through the five stages of grief as quickly as possible," I said to whoever would listen, mainly to convince myself that I would soon return to my former self and my former life. Those infamous five stages.

Denial. Anger. Bargaining. Depression. Acceptance. "That was the correct order, wasn't it?" I checked with my nurse brain. I had learned about them as a nurse, never questioning their accuracy. I had talked about them with patients, never once considering how they would play out if I was the actor on the main stage. It did not yet seem ridiculous to me that I could order my emotions into tidy and linear boxes with a distinct beginning and end.

Sonja came in from outside and put Klaus's keys into my hand. She had driven the Accord home. His keychain was held together by the bronze tag with "Susanne" on it. Susan in German. What Klaus called me. I loved how musical my name sounded in German. Would someone ever call me "Susanne" again? The bronze tags had been given to us as a wedding gift. Mine said "Klaus."

What an odd wedding gift, I thought at the time. Now I clung to it as if my life depended on it. It had some dents and scratches nearly twenty-five years later, but it still bound the keys together.

Chapter 8

Was it just two days ago we had been kissing goodbye on the street corner over 4,000 miles away, the rumbling of the diesel engine of his Nissan cargo van drowning out my sobs? The heaviness of the yin and yang pendant that rested against my heart was the tangible reminder it had happened and I wasn't just imagining it.

It was Sunday and the wall phone rang at exactly 4 pm. I lifted the received and heard the short high-pitched "beep," that signaled a rare and expensive international call. "Hallo? Klaus?" No more words squeaked out, they were blocked by crying.

"Ja Schatz, ich bins. Seit ihr wieder gut nach hause gekommen?"

"Yes, we arrived home safely." Frieda was back home with Fritz; I was back in my apartment.

Monday morning my search for work opportunities in Germany began in earnest. The Department of Defense employs thousands of civilians in critical positions worldwide; nursing was a critical position. I called the central office in New York City and requested information on how to work as a civilian nurse for the military in Germany. A thick envelope arrived after a few weeks with pages of instructions, a checklist of all the paperwork required to become a federal employee, an application, and a list of all the army bases in Germany. "Please check all of the places you would consider being placed. Your chances of getting employment will increase the more selections you make." Should I check them all and increase my chances of being on the same side of the ocean but risk being on the other end of Germany? Or should I check only Stuttgart?

The 34-mile commute from my apartment to the psychiatric unit where I worked took me past the international airport. Twice daily jumbo jets close to landing roared over my car. I could almost make out faces in the small oval windows as I wondered if they were coming from or going to Stuttgart where I so desperately wanted to be.

I meticulously followed the instructions and enclosed all of the requested verifications of my citizenship so there would be no question about my eligibility for federal employment and no delay in my offer because of a mistake I made. Last, I slipped in the preference sheet, indicating I would only accept employment in Stuttgart. I magically believed the new, crisp envelope would make my application stand out among the other envelopes. I took the pudgy envelope to the post office and prayed as the mail clerk tossed it onto the outgoing mail pile.

The waiting began. While we waited, we wrote letters on onionskin paper to save every penny in postage, pennies that went toward the phone bills we racked up.

After a few weeks, my patience waned and I randomly called offices associated with APO addresses.

"Have you received my application?"

We are not in charge of those applications, Ma'am.

"I am eager to accept employment and ready to move to Germany."

We get hundreds of applicants, Ma'am. I have no way of knowing where your application is.

"Do you anticipate openings anytime soon?"

We have no idea when openings will occur, Ma'am.

I felt as if my application was sitting in a big, black hole and I wondered if such jobs even existed.

In our Sunday phone calls, we exchanged information about what his mother had made for lunch that day and my most recent disappointments with the Civilian Personnel Office, but then the conversation stalled. Long-distance love needs touchpoints, especially a love built on four afternoons spent together in the front of a Nissan van dropping boxes of medications off at pharmacies. "Is this sustainable?" I started to ask myself. We were heartsick with love, but for our love to be sustainable we needed touchpoints.

"Would you like to go on a sailing trip to Corsica with my sailing club?" It was mid-March. He was inviting me to be part of a crew of twelve that would share the responsibilities of sailing and living on a boat for ten days.

"I have never been on a sailboat."

"You don't need to know how to sail. I will teach you."

"Ok. I will come." Our Sunday phone calls had renewed energy as we made plans for our trip. Outwardly I made plans to meet Klaus in Italy and join the sailing club. Inwardly was another story.

The doubt began instantly. I didn't even need to sleep on it. Oh my God, what have I done? What have I agreed to? I don't know any of these other people. I have never been on a sailboat. I don't even know Klaus except through a handful of days spent together and weekly phone calls.

And then the big one: What will my parents think? How will I tell my parents I am going on a sailing vacation with Klaus?

The doubt broke me and just days before I canceled. "Klaus? I can't come, I have to move."

It was only kind of a lie. The lease in the townhome I was renting with my roommates was up and I was ready to live alone. I just didn't have to move during the time we were supposed to be sailing the Mediterranean.

"I will come and help you move."

Oh God, doesn't he know that I just can't deal with having him around? I can't decide if I can love him or not?

"Please don't come."

The Sunday phone calls resumed after I moved and he sailed the Mediterranean.

We wanted to be together but there was the problem of a visa and immigration. I couldn't just move to Germany and move in with him, just as he couldn't just move to Minnesota and live with me.

It was fall and I had been trying for the past nine months to get hired by the Civilian Personnel Office. Desperation led me to meet with an Army recruiter, my longing for Klaus obscured the fact that being in the Army came with quotas for push-ups, sit-ups, timed two-mile runs, and a weight limit which the recruiter kindly told me I exceeded.

"Could you please orient a new nurse tomorrow?" the nurse manager asked before leaving for the day. "She has spent some time in Germany, I think you would be a good fit."

Victoria had just left a position as a civilian nurse in Garmisch-Partenkirchen, where she had worked for four years after being hired on the spot when traveling through the area as a tourist.

"The system is screwed up," Victoria told me. "You have to just move there and call them until you get hired." Immigration laws gave me three months to do that.

"What do you think?" I asked Klaus the next Sunday telling him about Victoria. Klaus, much more trusting of the world and good outcomes than me, was eager for me to come right away. My amygdala, the part of the brain that is associated with producing feelings of fear, was certainly much larger and more active than Klaus's and dread and fear rang like tinnitus in my ears.

I don't even know the guy.

I haven't seen where he lives.

I don't know if he likes his coffee black or with milk and sugar.

Does he keep secrets?

Does he leave dirty socks and underwear on the floor?

I haven't met his parents.

I don't know if he squeezes the toothpaste tube from the middle or the end.

Does he clean up after himself?

Does he rinse the sink after he spits in it when he is brushing his teeth?

Is he a cautious driver?

Does he regularly change the oil on his car?

Will he make me soup when I am sick?

Until now our relationship was based on an awkward polka dance, Sunday afternoon phone calls, letters on flimsy onionskin paper, a kissing exhibition at the *Landes Museum Stuttgart,* and four afternoons in the front seat of a Nissan van. I couldn't just go over there and move in with him.

"I will come and visit," Klaus announced the next Sunday. It was nearly the holidays. Plans were set for Klaus to arrive the Sunday after Christmas. I told my parents reluctantly. My mother's narrative had stopped when we left Germany nearly a year ago. My father didn't even know of Klaus.

"This Klaus," my dad asked from underneath my Pontiac T1000 while changing the oil, "this isn't somebody serious, is it?"

"Oh no," I said. I was an expert keeper of secrets and swallower of my innermost wants and desires. "He is just someone I met at Heritagefest two summers ago."

I rented a sleeper sofa for the living room to maintain the false pretense that he was just an acquaintance.

Klaus arrived to 30 below temperatures, but the passion we had contained over twelve months of phone calls kept us from feeling any of the arctic Minnesota air. We couldn't still ourselves; there was fire and unraveling when we touched. We spent our days exploring each other and loving, getting out of bed only occasionally to cook something to fuel more lovemaking. We put our passion and love into a container when we went to New Ulm for Klaus to meet my parents and pretended to be acquaintances.

After two weeks, we were committed more than ever to being together. "Please just come," I will take care of you." It was the evening before Klaus was returning to Germany and I was again beside myself at our impending separation. "You don't have to worry about having a job."

I reenergized my attempts to find work overseas. Victoria continued to encourage me to "just move over there and call them until you get hired." "This is just not going to work," I told myself over and over again until I believed it. Self-doubt, lack of trust in good outcomes, and fear of telling my parents the truth led to full-blown self-sabotage.

But I could not give up on love and finding love. I made plans to travel to Germany in early spring to visit the Civilian Personnel Office to make a personal plea for a job. Just before leaving my fears and self-doubt got the best of me. Two days before I left, I saw no way through my craziness and fears and broke up with Klaus. "Es geht einfach nicht weiter" I told him over the phone. I just don't see any way forward I said trying to believe the words as they came out of my mouth.

The airline ticket paid for, I called my Europe Mutti and asked if I could come and spend a few days with her. I told my parents I had gotten a great deal on a flight and was going to Germany for a long weekend.

When traveling to Germany I always had the same pattern. I flew to Frankfurt and traveled to Stuttgart by train. Depending on how the transatlantic flight went, it was never certain which train I would catch and what time I would arrive in Stuttgart. After I landed, had gone through customs, and purchased my train ticket I would call my aunt letting her know when to pick me up at the train station in Stuttgart. Klaus and I had made the same plans before I broke up with him. Unwilling to give up on our love, yet uncertain if I was still coming to Germany as planned, he spent the morning at the train station watching passengers arriving on all trains from Frankfurt. There are 16 platforms with arriving trains in Stuttgart. He strategically placed himself at the top of platforms where all passengers funnel to enter the central *Bahnhof*. This way he could scan all passengers arriving by train. Shortly before he was to give up, he spotted me on the platform greeting my aunt and cousin who had come to pick me up. Not ready to reveal himself, he hid behind a pillar and made plans to surprise me on Sunday.

Following Sonntagsessen, my aunt, cousin, and I were going out for a Spaziergang. A Spaziergang, best translated as a stroll or leisurely walk, is a beloved German pastime. It can occur at any time of day during any day of the week, but is obligatory on Sunday afternoons with family, the object being to walk at a slightly slower pace than usual in an attempt to absorb the surroundings. We were driving a short distance to nearby woods and just pulling away from the curb. Unbeknownst to me, Klaus was coming from Sonntagsessen with his parents, to pay me a surprise visit. He panicked as he saw us pulling away from the curb, fearing he would miss us. I saw him coming alongside my cousin's Jetta. Just like in the movies, he careened in front of us, stopping us short. Rather than going for a walk with my family, I went for a walk with Klaus.

How could I turn my back on this persistence and love? How could I deny his faith in our love? He made me believe that love was possible.

"I promise I will be here by your birthday." It was March and his birthday was June. That gave me three months. I returned home and made plans to do just that.

I returned home after my long weekend in Germany and told my parents I had been offered a job at a civilian hospital in Germany, and, once I arrived in the country I would report to the main Civilian Personnel office in Heidelberg and they would tell me in which hospital I would work. In reality, I sold all of my belongings, quit my job, bought a one-way ticket to Germany, and made plans to move in with Klaus.

I left three days before his birthday with two suitcases and $900 in American Express Traveler's Checks in case things didn't work out.

CHAPTER 9

I stepped over the threshold of Klaus's dirty socks and slipped under the dark green and purple paisley flannel duvet that still smelled of him, the bed that in the span of one day became an alien and unfamiliar landscape of loneliness. Waking alone in bed just one morning ago was as unthinkable as waking up with a set of wings on my back. Gabe, who usually slept curled at my feet, spent the night on the floor. It was all just too much for his peanut-sized brain. After a long and sleepless night, amazingly the sun rose again. Es geht immer weiter. Klaus's voice was in my head. Whenever my fears and insecurities fed my beliefs that the world would no longer go on, Klaus would laugh and reassure me that life will continue, the world will change, and we must be open to whatever passes before us, because, well, what other choice did we have?

Getting up was unthinkable. Klaus's trademark sweet smell of Irish Spring laced with sweat froze me to his side of the bed.

"Hi Sheila," I said from under my cocoon of blankets to my best friend who had materialized through my fog. Sheila was that friend who knew everything about me. We started the same day as Labor and Delivery nurses and yearly celebrated our anniversary. There were no pretenses between us, and she was not scared of my emotional complexity. Knowing there was nothing she could say to penetrate my fog, she simply crawled into bed with me.

The reality of Sheila lying in bed next to me instead of Klaus catapulted me back over the threshold of Klaus's dirty socks. "Go take a shower, and I will make coffee." Simple instructions with a small reward were exactly what I needed. You do this and I will do that. These were the same type of instructions I had used with my young children when fear prevented forward movement.

Dutifully I followed her instructions, the hot water shockingly soothing. As I relaxed into the water, a whole new round of sobs released. I gasped into the running water as I shed a layer of skin, sadness, loss, and fear.

Sheila handed me a cup of coffee with just the right amount of cream when I stepped out of the shower. No words needed to pass between us. We had worked together so long and so often that people often got us confused. If anyone was to be with me this morning, it was her. Sheila was my work wife. She brought me lunch. I brought her lunch. We shared coffee and Special K bars and frustrations about our husbands not getting home projects completed. We worried about our children together. Together we navigated the emotional dents of nursing. The work was so much easier with Sheila at my side. This morning she was acting solo, keeping us all from teetering over the edge: washing towels, unpacking bags of groceries that held dinner, and even managing to make my children laugh. Making their children laugh should be at the top of a list on an instruction sheet for the most important ways to help new widows.

"I am going to make meatballs and mashed potatoes for dinner," she announced as cans of soup, potatoes, and ground beef came out of the grocery bags.

Klaus loved Sheila's cooking, especially her chicken enchiladas. For years, Klaus raved about the tidy chicken enchilada she served smothered in green chile sauce when he was helping with a basement project at her house. And Sheila loved the throwing of the tools, running feet, and guttural German squeals of joy when she announced "lunch" by yelling down the basement stairs. "Susanne! It vasz a neat enchilada all rolled up." My enchiladas, on the other hand, were cut in squares regardless of where the tortilla stopped and started. How could someone with tools strewn across our entire property find value in a neatly rolled enchilada? "Was this even a conversation worth having?" I wondered at the time, and every time after when he brought up neat enchiladas.

"I call these funeral meatballs," Sheila said. "I make them anytime someone dies." Large soft meatballs and creamy mashed potatoes were just the right comfort meal. But first, we had to go to the funeral home.

Was it only yesterday that the funeral director had told me to be at the funeral home at 1 to plan my husband's funeral? Was that the same day that he was chopping vegetables for soup? It seemed as if so much time had passed between cutting vegetables, the funeral director, and now. The events could not possibly be connected. Could they? Sheila confirmed it was time and that indeed the events were connected. It was time to go to the funeral home except I still had my bathrobe on.

"Umm. Do you think you should put some clothes on?" Sheila asked carefully. She recognized that any request might make me spontaneously combust.

I looked at her blankly as if I didn't understand, my hands wrapped around my coffee cup to keep them warm. It was the wrong cup with the wrong size. My hands awkwardly lapped over each other. There was not enough surface area to warm my fingers and palms. Intimacy between friends has its boundaries. She did not know which cup was my favorite and why. Wordlessly she took my hand, set the wrong coffee cup down, and led me up the stairs to find something to wear other than my fuzzy grey bathrobe and slippers.

After zipping my coat as if I were a kindergartener, Sheila poured me into her Toyota Corolla, leaning over me to fasten my seat belt. She put the cup of coffee back in my hand. It was still the wrong cup, I could tell by the feel of its shape in my hand. I tried to get my eyes to work but somehow their seeing power was reversed again. I can't do this. Planning the funeral of my mother and father was one thing, but Klaus? I alternated between heaving sobs and nothing. Can you become dehydrated enough from crying to prevent more crying? Sheila's speed while driving into town was not influenced by my father's voice so we were in the parking lot of the funeral home in no time. I'm not sure I would have walked in if she hadn't been at my side. I might still be sitting in the funeral home parking lot in that red Toyota, an attraction for the town. Come and see the widow who can't get out of the car to plan her husband's funeral. Bring her some peanut M&Ms or a Fillet-O-Fish. We don't know when the attraction will end.

The particularly heavy door to the funeral home was flanked with audacious brass handles as if to signal the significance of the doors I was about to open. The reception area felt full of ghosts and long-lost sounds of crying, laughing, and whispering. Andy, the funeral director to whom I had spoken on the phone—was it just yesterday?—was waiting on the other side of that large door. He had the presence reserved only for those who work with the newly bereaved, kind and soft-spoken, with eyes that can convey expression when there are no words to adequately fill the gap. He made no quick movements so as not to startle those who are fragile and traumatized. "Are you Susan?" I nodded. How could he miss the swollen eyes and splotchy face? Only squeaks came out of my tightly constricted chest and throat. Translation of squeaks must be a foreign language learned in mortician school. "I am so sorry for your loss." More sobbing proved my theory of dehydration preventing more crying wrong. The strong smell of coffee made me gag between sobs. The entourage of two, Sheila and Andy, guided me to the type of furniture reserved only for funeral homes, soft and squishy so that you could easily shrink into a corner, away from the terrible circumstances that had brought you to this place. The beige furniture was accented with a few throw pillows in another shade of beige. How many shades of beige can there be? Table lamps muted the light and a scent only identifiable as artificial irritated my nostrils. Sheer beige curtains covered the windows, floor to ceiling. Were they to match the beige furniture? Or were they, like the muted tones and muted light, meant to mute the view of my new painful reality? Or were the muted tones meant to protect the eyes of the newly bereaved made raw from saltwater tears?

"The minister has not yet arrived," Andy confirmed. "She should be here soon."

Everything had fallen out of place. It was Monday, wasn't it? Who would roll the garbage can up the driveway? Was it a recycling day? It was Klaus's job to keep track of that. Who would cook dinner? Not Klaus. Dinner was in the bags of groceries that arrived that morning. How I hated those daily morning phone calls from Klaus. "Susanne. Vat shudd I make for dinner?" God, can't you figure it out for yourself for once? What I wouldn't give to hear my phone ring now with Klaus's voice asking if it should be spaghetti or fish tacos.

It seemed as if time had stood still, and I was suspended in space. When would the tidy grief I had learned about in nursing school begin? I needed the kind of grief that started with one stage, proceeded along a linear path, and cleanly ended with following the last stage.

The minister arrived. Funeral planning could now commence.

The drill of planning funerals was not new to me; my parents had died not that long ago. Minister. Check. Choosing the readings and selecting the songs. Check. "My Life Flows on in Endless Song" reminds me so much of Klaus, the minister suggested. "Perfect," I squeaked out through my pinhole-sized throat as a new round of sobs emerged, remembering the singing thread that had connected us and continued throughout Klaus's life.

In 24 short hours, my future had become wholly uncharted and full of uncertainty. Sheila passed me dry Kleenexes from the box and deposited my soaked ones into the trash can next to her. What would happen to the life Klaus and I had planned together?

Writing the obituary. Dedicated husband and father. Passionate maker of mustard and jam. Sailor. Check. Planning the lunch. Lutheran funeral lunches from my life thus far were easy to plan. They included deli ham on soft white buns and potato salad that had a particular yellow color from just the right amount of Frank's mustard. Bars baked by the Ladies Aid Society. Who would make bars for the lunch? We weren't Lutheran. Klaus hated American white bread that stuck to the roof of your mouth as Softie buns were sure to do. I couldn't serve those.

"Would you like to serve the soup at the funeral?" the minister asked, startling me back to current time and place. Was I hearing correctly? Did she just ask me to serve the soup my husband cooked for his own funeral?

"What?" I asked haltingly, my voice sounded alarmingly loud.

Those who had stayed behind at the church after Klaus's trip to the emergency room had cleaned the carpet, picked up the syringe wrappers and medication boxes, and ladled the soup into round plastic containers that now lined the inside door of the church freezer.

Yes, I had heard correctly. There was a new round of sobs from being overwhelmed and exhausted by what life was asking me to do.

ARE YOU NUTS?

I didn't say it. But in my mind, I screamed it. Screaming silently to myself had become a new coping mechanism overnight. How was I going to do all this alone? When would the roof of the house fall in? Who was going to help me launch our children? I was being asked to do things that I didn't feel remotely capable of doing alone. And now

I was being asked to do the unthinkable: serve the soup cooked by my husband at his own funeral.

A deep inhalation got stuck somewhere mid-chest and resulted in breathing that was fast and shallow. The lack of oxygen resulted in a tingling feeling in my lips, fingers, and toes. With each breath I became more anxious, causing me to breathe even more quickly and more shallowly which only made the sensation of suffocating worse.

My nurse brain spoke to my wife brain. "Take a deep breath, down to your toes, and hold it for one-two-three." I had done this with thousands of anxious labor patients.

"Now let it go. One-two-three."

Who cooks for their own funeral? "There is no way I can even look at that soup," I thought, "much less have it served at the funeral."

Klaus cooked many dinners in the church basement kitchen. They were Rainbow Meals to raise money to pass the Marriage Amendment. He ordered people around in his brusque German voice in a space too small for more than a couple of people. With Klaus, more than one cook was too many in the kitchen. The brave souls who volunteered to help him were at the beck and call of his impatience to carry out the elaborate plan he had created after weeks of poring and planning in his favorite cookbook, Essen Wie Gott in Deutschland. Eating Like a God in Germany. Tears and exasperation with spittle were as much a part of the meal preparation as the recipes. Most recently, he had made sausages and carefully curled them in springform pans too numerous to count, and wurst cake that earned a standing ovation was served with mixed salads.

That world of Klaus planning, cooking, and serving meals for a cause was so far away. This new world was surreal. My nurse brain reminded me that grieving is a normal and necessary part of the human experience. How many times have I reminded patients of that as they held their dead baby? Grief is as normal as exhaling after inhaling. But inspiration and expiration were no longer a given in my world. The pause between the two had been harshly interrupted. Klaus had inhaled expectedly, yet the inhale was not followed by an exhale. Nothing felt normal. And if this was a necessary part of human experience I wasn't interested. I tried to name what I trusted, to provide a stronghold and firm ground. All that I had trusted was gone. I knew that life equated with change and movement. But this? Life had given my future a pink slip.

"Klaus, are you vexing me from the heavens?" My mind was wild. Klaus hated waste more than anything else, and he wouldn't want the soup to be wasted. I was certain of that. With even more certainty, I knew that he would forever haunt me if I wasted the soup.

Klaus's father's salary as a teacher at a vocational school in former East Germany provided for a comfortable life. Yet comfortable margins only extended to what was available in East Germany at the time. Basic needs were readily provided for, but circumstances, necessities, and living situations could change at a moment's notice, and the family didn't know if life, as they knew it, would exist from one day to the next. Luxuries from their capitalist cousin, West Germany, were widely unavailable. Klaus told stories of being sent by his mother to the market when word on the street was that they would have bananas. Klaus, a small boy having just started school, would stand in line for hours, only to have the last banana sold to the person ahead of him. Oranges, coffee, and Swiss chocolate were enjoyed only during the holidays when they were sent as gifts from their affluent West German friends and relatives.

The scarcity the family lived with left long and deep impressions on Klaus, motivating him, to the horror of our three children, to dig spaghetti out of the trash and eat it for dinner.

Within the span of a few minutes, I went from thinking I would be unable to even see the soup, much less eat it, to planning the funeral around it. Klaus would be euphoric that he catered his own funeral.

Sheila poured me back into her Toyota Corolla and again fastened the seat belt around my still trembling body, and home we went.

Chapter 10

the connection had an eight-hour layover in New York City, providing me one last opportunity to reconsider my decision.

"This is the final boarding call for KLM flight number 64 to Amsterdam." The snaky line of passengers was reduced to just a few stragglers running to the gate with urgency and carry-ons flying behind them.

What would my life be like if I turned around? If I didn't board the plane? Could I get my job back in St. Paul?

The artificial booming metallic voice might as well have said, "Susan, it's time to make a decision. Are you going to board or not?"

What if I never explored this relationship with Klaus? Would I become the Old Maid that I desperately avoided being dealt during many raucous card games around my grandmother's Formica table? I had never had a boyfriend before and desperately wanted to be loved. I knew I did not want to live with unanswered questions that began with "if only." I knew I did not want to live with eternal regret. This time I was not going to succumb to whom I was supposed to be and what I was supposed to do. This time what I wanted mattered, and I was going to follow my dreams.

Weak-kneed I passed through the gate my paper boarding pass crumpled in my sweaty fist.

The distinct smell of jet fuel filled my nose as I walked through the tube of in-between places to connect the dots between the current place and the new place, the old life to the new life. The new life with potential? With love? The space is filled with hope, possibility, and fear. I heard the engines running, almost but not quite loud enough to drown out the voices in my head: "Are you sure you want to do this?" My feet moved forward, ignoring the voice. I bumbled into the plane and through the aisle to find my window seat. My eyes looked for seat 32F while I avoided the irritated looks of the passengers anxious for the flight to get underway.

"Excuse me, I need to get to the window seat." A huff from my aisle seat companion let me know that he was annoyed with my tardiness. I hoped my new teal backpack, the exact measurements allowed for a carry-on, didn't slam him in the face as I crawled over his knees to get to the window. In my mind, I screamed back at the huff, "I was not late. I have been sitting at the gate for eight hours contemplating the future trajectory of my life. And the meaning of life. Do you know what a monumental decision I just made?"

Moments later, the doors locked, and we pivoted to the east, flying into the sunset over the Hudson River, the Statue of Liberty getting smaller and smaller while she raised her hand in farewell. Instead of talking some sense into me, the person beside me left me alone, my pores radiating the sense that I would prefer to be with my thoughts, fears, and dreams while I ate crackers and drank 7-Up to settle my queasy stomach.

Radiant sunshine woke me after a restless night of intermittent sleep as we descended through a sunrise over Amsterdam. I decided to spend a few days here before moving on to Stuttgart, another opportunity to reconsider my decision and fly home to the safety and security of the known. I sent the two tan canvas suitcases, heavy with my best-guess-of-what-one-needs-when-one-moves-to-Europe-and-moves-in-with-a-man-one-barely-knows, ahead to wait with Klaus in Stuttgart as some kind of insurance plan to myself that I would follow through with my plan. It was as if I was saying, "I must arrive in pieces, I cannot just jump in with both feet and do it all at once." I wandered through the cobblestone streets of Amsterdam in the early morning hours and slept off the jet lag at my downtown hotel adjacent to the city park.

Shiny trinkets and colorful wooden clogs for flowers and feet lined the canals as I walked later that day looking for dinner. What can I bring Klaus from Amsterdam? A t-shirt? I could only estimate his size. Drop? I didn't know if he liked candy. Stroop waffles? I didn't know if he liked cookies.

The Masters stared back at me through painted eyes the next morning at the museum. Rembrandt and Vermeer seemed to be chiding me into buying the one-way train ticket to Stuttgart. Van Gogh picked up where they left off. They were silent witnesses to my indecision and insecurity. I could only take one small step at a time, and the next step was buying that ticket. I called Klaus just before boarding the train. "Alles Gute sum Geburtstag." I was keeping my promise of arriving by his birthday. "I am arriving this afternoon at 1:47." My promise was kept with just under twelve hours to spare. I worried about the fact that I didn't have a job and what to tell my parents as the scenery changed from green pastures, canals, and windmills to the industrial cities of northern Germany. Yet part of me was also excited, the excitement building as the train passed the Cologne Cathedral and the University in Heidelberg. Oh, to rest my chin on your shoulder, Klaus, and snuggle into your itchy neck whenever I wanted. No longer would I have to imagine the smell of Polo filling my nose or the warmth of your hands. You would be a real player in real-time.

The train station is the ideal scenario for greetings and farewells. The powerful beast of the locomotive thrusts itself into the station, clanking and squealing as the train slows. The last moments of waiting begin. Eyes focus on the platform keen to possess a loved one. The train slows, slows, slows, teasing everyone on both sides of the divide, making them savor the tension between absence and presence. It is agonizing how long it can take a train to come to a full stop. People jump up, collect pets and children, and organize shopping bags, flowers, backpacks, and suitcases so nothing is left behind. They hustle to the doors anticipating being in the arms of their loved ones. The train inches to a stop. If this were an old regional train people would be hanging out of the windows calling to the waiting, but, on this modern Intercity, anticipation is tightly sealed inside the bullet-shaped cabin. With a sigh and a last jarring squeal, the locomotive finally came to a dead stop. It is still, and yet the doors cannot open. Why is there such a long wait on trains—ten seconds, twenty, almost a minutes sometimes—between the locomotive stopping and the green light that tells you that you can push the button that allows the doors to open? All along the track buttons are pushed and with agonizing slowness, the doors open and people begin to spill out of the carriages. Some passengers must wait while others fuss with clumsy bags on steep steps. It is as if the whole of railway technology has been designed to maximize the emotional drama of return from afar.

I allowed those around me to scramble and gather their belongings before I exited down the metal stairs that folded out of the train.

Only a few short months ago Klaus had been hiding behind the pillars in the Bahnhof wondering if I would arrive. This time, I wanted to do an about-face, duck, and hide behind the pillars, both from hope and from my potential future. Was I doing the right thing? Why was it so hard for me to consider the possibility of being loved? I was back in my Candy Pink closet, that braided little girl full of shame, fragility, and fear hiding from life and afraid of being seen, living a life in reaction to the existence of others.

There was no hiding as I stepped off the rung of the locomotive and into the familiar smell of grilled wurst mingled with cigarette smoke and diesel. Few were on the platform in the sweltering heat of midday, and I easily spotted him waiting in a crisply ironed tan and white striped button-down shirt with equally crisp khaki pants, the crease dangerously sharp. The same gold-rimmed sunglasses from three summers ago were suspended around his neck as he looked up the corridor. Our eyes met. There was no running toward each other but a slow intentional walk holding each other's gaze until we were close enough to embrace.

He gave me a kiss on the cheek and one Sweet William. The maroon blooms at the end of a long stem tightly bonded together, protecting the fragile unseen center of the flower. No violins played or trumpets sounded. The spell was broken by Klaus's unfamiliar brusqueness. "This is all the flowers you are going to get." We retrieved the suitcases that had arrived well before me and left the Bahnhof hand in hand and stepped into the hot summer sunshine to his Nissan van illegally parked in the loading zone. "Does he ever park legally?" I wondered.

"I'm sorry, I didn't bring you a birthday gift," I said as we stepped off the hot pavement into the cool stone apartment building. Not yet accustomed to climbing the 88 steps and four flights, I reached the apartment landing panting and well behind Klaus. He was waiting inside the dim, windowless entryway with his hands behind his back.

They emerged holding 21 red roses as I crossed the threshold into the apartment. "You are the best birthday present I have ever gotten," he said tearfully. "Three and seven are lucky numbers, so three times seven roses so our lives will be filled with luck," he said, taking me into his arms.

He led me into the bedroom. We tumbled onto the new crisply ironed yellow duvets and tatami mats, a large blooming orchid providing a heady scent to fuel our passionate reunion.

I woke first and explored the rest of the apartment, a wide rectangle with a bedroom in the middle. Street sounds lured me to the left and I found the living room. It was furnished with a wire coffee table and three wire garden chairs that, without cushions, would leave a checkerboard imprint on bare skin. The fourth chair looked more at home on the balcony off the living room that was just large enough for the chair and nothing else. From the balcony, the bell of the Strassen Bahn could be heard as it moved swiftly along the tracks and stopped in a steady rhythm every seven minutes. People disappeared into the small neighborhood stores to do their daily shopping. They emerged a few moments later with their Einkaufskorb overflowing with a loaf of bread or brötchen from the bakery, packages of sausages tightly wrapped in white butcher paper from the Metzger, or bundles of fresh vegetables and bright flowers from the farm stand. I looked forward to shopping with my own colorful basket and wondered if Klaus already had one for me to use.

Off the living room was a dining room that smelled of lemon oil. The table was covered with an ironed lace cloth and set with matching china and fancy napkins intentionally folded into the delicately flowered coffee cups. Evidence his mother had been there earlier in the day preparing for my arrival. There was a festively wrapped present in birthday paper and a yellow cake layered with raspberries and whipped cream. Remembering I hadn't eaten since leaving Amsterdam early that morning, I was unable to resist and grabbed a raspberry peeking out from the middle of the cake. It was tart, and the whipped cream stuck to it tasted of vanilla and rum as I slowly licked it off my finger.

In search of a snack, I wandered back through the entryway and past the bedroom where I heard Klaus loudly snoring. The kitchen was on the opposite end of the rectangle. I rummaged through the cupboards and found the furnishings of a bachelor who worked long hours and spent little time at home. The kitchen was stocked with bare necessities: a coffee maker, one frying pan, a small pot, and a few utensils. The refrigerator was bare except for a few bottles of beer, some mustard, and a pickle jar with more brine than pickles. The late afternoon sun poured in through a large window in a second small balcony that hung off the kitchen like a second hip to the first balcony on the opposite end of the apartment.

Klaus had told me in our phone conversations that his mother cleaned for him, but I didn't fully register the impact of this until I saw the evidence everywhere in the apartment: the ironed table linens, the filter, and the coffee in the coffeemaker only requiring someone to flip the switch, the waxed linoleum on the kitchen floor and the bathroom smelling piney fresh with towels hanging next to the sink that carried a sharp crease just like the crease going down the front of Klaus's khaki pants.

I opened the door to the glassed-in balcony off the kitchen, hoping for a quieter space to drink coffee in the mornings and read. On the other side of the door was an abrupt end to evidence of Klaus's mother's presence. This balcony had no room for a chair. It was stuffed floor to ceiling, with tools and what appeared to be junk spilling out from an assortment of cabinets and drawers. The disarray spilled out and over. Bags holding who knows what littered the floor and made a walk to the window for a view of the back of the house treacherous. Evidence of a messy bachelor life had been removed from the rest of the apartment and stuffed into twelve square feet.

Klaus was suddenly holding me from behind and nuzzling my ear lobe.

"I was hoping for a quiet place in the sun to read and drink my coffee in the morning."

The smell of Polo and his nuzzling pulled me away from the chaos on the balcony and my vision of reading in a comfy chair by the window. I turned around in his arms and leaned into the crook of his neck, deeply inhaling the smell of Polo. The smell of Klaus.

"I will clean up. I promise," he whispered into my ear. "Come back to bed with me."

We followed the heady scent of the orchid back to the tatami mats and consummated my decision to move to Germany for the remainder of the night.

I woke early the next morning to the yet unfamiliar sounds of my new home. The digital clock next to Klaus's side of the futon blasted 5:37AM in large red numbers.

I knew he left early, but I didn't know he left this early. It was the beginning of long days spent alone while Klaus worked 12 to 14 hours at three jobs. I made myself coffee and waited until I could call 5th General Hospital about a job. At 8AM, I dialed the number for the chief nurse's office, this time without the international prefix.

"Colonel Keaton here."

"This is Susan Weissmann. I've relocated to Stuttgart and am ready to work. I can start anytime."

CHAPTER 11

Decades earlier my parents had had their own transatlantic love story. My father's ancestors were part of a group of German settlers that began to immigrate to the fertile mountain valleys of central Slovakia in large numbers in 1250 in response to an invitation from the Hungarian monarch who was trying to resettle the northern reaches of his kingdom. As an incentive to bring trade and establish businesses in the area, the king offered these Germans the right to own property and an elevated status in local society

My ancestors settled in Pezinok, a village of about 10,000, at the foothills of the Carpathian Mountains. Oma Rose and Opa Edward, neither German citizens nor Nazis, were prosperous merchants, owning vineyards, a blacksmith shop, and a gas station. Oma managed the vineyards and Opa the blacksmith shop and gas station. As a businessman, Opa was known not only for his talent at bending red hot iron to ornate designs but also for good conversation and a kind word. Oma was known for an abundant kitchen and always having an extra place at the table. Full of shrewd wit, she was always concerned with the bottom line. "How much money did you make today, Eddy?" she asked daily at Feierabend.

In the mornings, Oma would ride her bicycle out to the vineyards to oversee the 12 to 15 workers and get them started on the day's tasks of pruning, picking, or weeding. She was a diligent vintner and proud that the quality of her grapes prevented the need to add additional sugar to sweeten the wine.

Mid-mornings, Oma returned to her kitchen to cook for the vineyard workers. I loved hearing her reminisce about the robust lunches of Nudelsuppe, Rostbraten mit Zwiebleln, Salat, and Semmelknödel. These stories were shared on long Saturday afternoons from her rust-brown Lazy-Boy with knitting needles poking out from the left and right sides of the chair and her snack of a turkey carcass and sharp paring knife for scraping every last bit of meat off the bone. The knitting needles were as much for cleaning her ears as they were for knitting countless afghans. I would walk the two blocks to her house every Saturday from my Arts and Crafts class with Mrs. Cook, carefully carrying whatever stunning creation I had made that day awaiting her praise. The smell of paprika and freshly baked Semmeln would greet me from the short gravel driveway where I checked the mail. On weather-permitting days, I found her in the large garden weeding, mowing the lawn, or cutting irises. Other days I went in through the garage door and found her standing at the stove, stirring the tough cuts of chuck roast that had been cut into bite-sized pieces and braised all morning with an equal amount of onion and three to four heaping tablespoons of Schilling's sweet Paprika. Homemade Semmeln would sop up the dark-red sauce made thick from disintegrated onions. Regardless of the weather and setting, a large clean apron with pockets was a constant. In the afternoons we sat together, me on the brown couch with her rat terrier Fifi at my side, and she in her Lazy-Boy knitting. She told me story after story of growing up, speaking Hungarian in school, German at home, and Slovak in the streets. Mostly the stories were of dancing in glorious ball gowns or shenanigans growing up with five brothers.. Occasionally a story of war and loss crept in, for which a lace-trimmed hankie was at the ready in her apron pocket.

When the entire family came, she would make Apfelstrudel or Zwetschgenknödel. For Apfelstrudel, Oma would put two extra leaves in her Formica kitchen table. The plain white Strudel cloth came next. The small ball of dough that had been resting underneath a kitchen towel on her cutting board was placed in the middle of the cloth and, with her expert hands, stretched across the table. As small children, we watched in amazement as the dough stretched and stretched, our backs to the wall, not daring to speak or touch the dough ourselves. If things went well, we could see the age spots on the tops of her hands through the dough. If things didn't go well, which was rare, it was always the flour's fault. The dough would tear into large holes, the size of the holes in direct proportion to the length and volume of Hungarian profanities that came from Oma's mouth. We eagerly awaited our turn to help spread the thinly sliced apples tossed with cinnamon and sugar evenly across the dough. Oma finished with spoonfuls of melted butter, cream, and cottage cheese mixed with eggs splashed at regular and calculated intervals across the dough. There was always a rearranging of apple slices to Oma's satisfaction before she would pick up the long end of the strudel cloth and roll the apple-filled dough into a bumpy log, expertly stopping just so the strudel wouldn't flop onto the floor. Once snaked onto a baking sheet, the strudel got a healthy basting of butter and was baked to golden-brown flaky perfection.

In the short weeks of August and September, when Italian prune plums were available, she would make Zwetschgenknödel. No other plum was an acceptable substitute. The plums were washed and placed on a clean kitchen towel to dry. Once dry, a slit just large enough to extract the pit was made. A sugar cube was pushed in to replace the pit, two if the plums weren't to the satisfaction of Oma's sweet tooth. Potatoes put through a ricer and mixed with enough flour to make a stiff dough were wrapped around the plums. The large dumplings would be placed in simmering, not boiling, water, and then rolled in bread crumbs, cinnamon, and powdered sugar. A healthy dousing of melted butter satisfied our genetic predisposition to high cholesterol.

The meals were always preceded by a soup of beef stock, made from long-simmered bones the day before, thick with handmade noodles, and topped with a sprinkling of chives from the garden. A bottle of Maggi seasoning sat on the table so that everyone could season to taste. Mausi would sit quietly under Oma's chair and wait for the large nuggets of beef she secretly fed him under the table despite my father's admonitions. She also recalled fondly the Mausi from their home in Pezinok and remembered him vicariously through our Mausi replacement.

Early in World War II, the original Mausi was left behind with Opa by a German soldier moving with his troop through their small village to the eastern front. The soldier stopping for a chat at Opa's gas station and lunch from Oma's kitchen was heartbroken he could not take the dog with him. The red long hair dachshund had been the Officer's companion, sharing his meals of Wurst finished with coffee. My grandfather assured him the dog was being left to a good home and that her sophisticated palate for wurst and coffee instead of kibble would be maintained. Thus, the family legacy of soft-heartedness for long hair dachshunds was born.

Mausi became my father's dog. My father, then in his early teens, had cobbled together a bicycle from parts he found in my grandfather's blacksmith shop. Mausi was trained to sit on the bicycle seat. The full-size dachshund would put his front paws on my father's shoulders and together they would go for bicycle rides at the foothills of the Little Carpathian Mountains.

The fall before the end of World War II, my father began classes with dreams of becoming an engineer. Daily the Bummelzug took him the 20 kilometers to Bratislava, Slovakia's largest city and an important center for trade along the Danube. Among the brightest and best, my father had gained selective admission to the Gymnasium, the level of high school that prepares students for higher academic learning. In a few short months, the world was in the final throes of World War II and the Germans in the area feared for their lives. The family fled their home in January 1945, on my father's 15th birthday.

This group of Germans is part of a story few history books have ever told. It is the story of millions of German-speaking civilians living in eastern Europe and driven out of their homes at the end of World War II. Most families were deposited amid the ruins of the Third Reich and left to fend for themselves as best they could. Some families, including my father's family, were detained and held in captivity at concentration camps. During the day, my Opa and father worked for a farmer which helped the family get more of the scarce food. My grandmother worked for the camp supervisor. Oma, educated by life experience rather than lessons in a classroom, possessed knowledge far beyond the years of schooling that had been cut short due to the First World War. She had sewn family jewelry, gold coins, and watches into the lining of clothes and coats, valuables that she then used as bribes to get the family out of the work camp and Czechoslovakia. She bribed the head of the camp to arrange for a truck to pick up the family of six, my grandparents, my father and his two siblings, and Omamama, my father's Oma. A date was arranged. It was dark as the truck and Russian driver came. The bribe ensured that the gate guards would look the other way as the family of six climbed into the back of the truck with their one shared suitcase.

"Where are you going?" the truck driver asked my grandfather in Russian.

"Where are you going?" My grandfather countered.

"Vienna," was the reply.

"Then we are going to Vienna as well." The homeless family first hid in the ruins of a house in Vienna so they would not be on the street. After a week, Opa made contact with some distant relatives from whom the family received a room in a cellar where the family could live. The family moved to where my Opa and my father could find work, the two of them supporting the family of six in war-torn Europe.

As work dwindled, the search for more work always took them farther west. And with each subsequent move farther to the west, the realization deepened that they would not be returning to their home in Czechoslovakia.

Because the family was without citizenship, they were unwanted by the Austrians as well as the Slovaks. They ended up in Germany in mid-April, 1946. Large areas in cities were, at that time, uninhabitable because of the bombings, so refugees were distributed among smaller villages. The village where they arrived, Bondorf, near Stuttgart, had 1600 inhabitants and had to accept 800 German refugees from the East. Struggling to feed themselves, the villagers wanted nothing to do with these displaced Germans, and no one wanted my father's family of six. The farmer assigned to take them initially refused. Finally, after sitting in front of the courthouse all day, the police intervened and the farmer was forced to take them in. Together they lived in a single room.

My father, 16, secured a job as an apprentice to an auto-mechanic. He and my mother met at a ballroom dance class shortly after my father's family settled in Bondorf. My mother was working as a seamstress for Bleyle, one of the largest German manufacturers of knitted goods and hosiery in the first half of the 20th century. "She didn't smell like a cow," my father remembers of his first dance with my mother. They danced and struggled to understand each other, as the Schwäbisch and Viennese dialects of German were vastly different. Early mornings, they rode the train together to work, and they fell in love.

By 1950, my father had passed his Journeyman's examination in Auto Mechanics, and he and my mother planned to marry and start a family. Opa had other plans.

"Wir gehen nach Amerika," he announced to the family. My grandfather, after losing his businesses, his home, all of his possessions, and four years of not being wanted anywhere, dreamed of a new beginning. He dreamed of emigrating to America.

"Ich bleibe hier." My father, finally feeling some hope for his future, had no intention of leaving my mother or Germany.

"Die Familie bleibt zusammen." A slap across the face made clear my father would not be staying behind. The family would stay together. They left for America in 1950, my father leaving behind a lock of his hair to remind my mother of her promise to come to America.

After two years of letters, my mother kept her promise and left her village for the first time to emigrate to America, which, in the early 1950s, was akin to a family death for my mother's poor agrarian family. When my mother left for America, her parents felt as if they had buried her.

The loss of the possibility of education was one of the biggest war casualties for both of my parents. Physical access to school and teachers because of bombings, enlistment, and transportation difficulties disrupted my mother's primary school education after the eighth grade and her lifelong dream of becoming a nurse. Once in America, my father, as the eldest son, was expected to work to help support the family after leaving Slovakia. He was never able to resume his education, a regret that followed him to his grave.

The remorse my parents suffered at having left Germany plagued them for the remainder of their lives. They felt anger at lost opportunities, regrets, and guilt at having left my mother's parents behind. These emotions infused every cell of their bodies, every aspect of their lives, and every part of my upbringing. The trauma they endured became my responsibility, and with that, I became bound up in their grief and regret.

Moving to Germany permanently was absolutely out of the question. Their pain would be unbearable. The war never left my parents. Their trauma became my trauma, their fear my fear.

Slavic Peasant Goulash

This is the Goulash Oma Rose made every Saturday. The goulash was always ready by the time I got to Oma's house, so it was something I did not learn how to make at her side. Ironically, Martha Stewart made this goulash on one of her TV shows, saying the same thing Oma used to say: the amount of beef and onions must be equal. This recipe is an adaptation of what I remember from Oma's stories about how the goulash is made and a recipe derived from Martha Stewart.

Ingredients:
Vegetable oil
5 pounds beef chuck, trimmed and cut into 1-inch cubes; alternately
        you can use the prepped stew meat from the store
5 pounds yellow onions
**Oma always said the key was to use the same amount of onions
        as beef!
Sweet Hungarian paprika
2-3 cups beef stock

Directions:
Heat oil in a large Dutch oven. Season meat generously with salt and pepper. Cook meat in batches, not overcrowding the pot, adding butter and oil as needed. Cook each batch of meat until well browned on all sides, about 4 minutes, and transfer to a plate.

Once all the meat is browned, reduce the heat to low and add onions, and cook, stirring occasionally until the onions are translucent about 10-15 minutes. Return the meat to the pot and add the paprika followed by the stock. Stir well to combine.

Cook, covered over low heat until the meat is tender and the sauce is thickened about 2 hours. Serve with crusty bread to sop up the sauce.

SEMMELKNÖDEL

(BREAD DUMPLINGS)

Dumplings in Germany vary with the region. While Klaus's mother made dumplings from potatoes and called them Klösse, Oma Rose made dumplings from stale bread and called them Knödel. Oma would make these thick chewy dumplings on special occasions and serve them alongside her goulash.

1 pound of stale bread, preferably of a sturdy variety. Squishy
     American white bread won't do here.
1 cup milk
1 medium onion, finely chopped
½ bunch parsley, finely chopped
2 tablespoons butter
2 eggs
Salt to taste
You may need additional milk or dry bread crumbs

Chop the stale bread into small cubes, no more than ½ inch in size. Warm the milk (do not boil!) and pour over the bread cubes. Allow the bread cubes to soak up the milk.

Melt the two tablespoons of butter in a pan and saute the onions until translucent, about 5-6 minutes. Add the onions and the parsley to the bread cubes and allow the mixture to rest for at least 15 minutes.

Beat the eggs and add them to the mixture after the resting time. Add salt and pepper to taste. Knead the mixture with clean, wet hands, adding milk if it is too dry and dried bread crumbs if it is too wet.

Form into 8-10 dumplings of equal size – they don't have to be perfectly round to taste great! Press the balls with your hands to make them compact.

Bring a large pot of salted water to a boil, then lower the heat. Dumplings are not to be boiled, only simmered. Placing a dumpling into boiling water will cause it to disintegrate.

In batches add the dumplings to the simmering water – they shouldn't touch - and allow them to simmer for 20 minutes. Remove with a slotted spoon.

OMA ROSE'S ZWETSCHGENKNÖDEL

Makes 12 dumplings

Oma and I made these side by side every year in late August or early September, depending on the availability of the Italian prune plum. As we made the dough and shaped the dumplings, she would regale me with stories of making them by the dozen to feed those that worked for her and Opa Edward in the vineyards of Slovakia.

Ingredients:
12 Italian prune plums, available August through October, smaller
        and firmer than ordinary plums
2-3 medium russet potatoes
1 beaten egg
½ - 1 cup all-purpose flour
Pinch of salt
2 cups plain toasted bread crumbs
1-2 sticks of butter
Sugar cubes
Powdered sugar and ground cinnamon to taste

Boil the whole, unpeeled potatoes until tender when pierced with a fork. Peel while still warm and pass through a potato ricer. A potato ricer is a kitchen gadget that resembles a large garlic press. It will force the cooked potatoes through a sheet of small holes, which are about the diameter of a grain of rice. The same can be accomplished with the diligent use of a potato masher and fork.

Add the egg and a pinch of salt, and mix gently. Begin adding flour, small bits at a time. The amount of flour will depend on the size of the egg and the water content of the potato. You should end up with a firm, malleable dough similar to play dough.

Prepare the plums: slice open with a sharp knife and replace pit with one sugar cube. Do not do this too far in advance or the sugar will begin to melt and the plums will become too juicy.

Begin to form the dumplings. For each dumpling take a piece of dough about the size of a golf ball. Roll it gently into a rough ball. Using both thumbs and begin to flatten the dough into a small disc. Place the plum, slit side down, onto the disc and mold the dough around the plum, firmly pinching it closed. Be sure the plum is completely covered in dough.

Bring a large pot of water to a boil and decrease the heat to a simmer. Gently drop the dumplings into the water, making sure they are not too crowded. Simmer, do not boil, for 15 minutes after they float to the top.

While the dumplings are simmering melt a stick of butter in a saute pan over low heat. Add the breadcrumbs and cook, stirring constantly until the breadcrumbs are golden and fragrant. Be careful not to burn them. Season the breadcrumbs generously with powdered sugar and cinnamon.

Remove the dumplings and roll in the crumb mixture until they are completely covered.

Oma's Apple Strudel

How I wish I could spend a Saturday afternoon with Oma making strudel. This was one recipe she did not write down and the memories between the cousins are inconsistent. Over the years we made several attempts, mostly unsuccessful. Most problematic was the strudel dough itself, each attempt at recreating Oma's strudel resulting in a strudel dough full of holes that would have elicited a string of Hungarian swear words from her.

Our most successful attempt was using the following dough recipe from "Binging with Babish," a you-tube channel that Peter follows.

For strudel:
1 ½ cups bread flour
4 tablespoons vegetable oil
2 egg whites
¼ tsp salt
½ tablespoon lemon juice
¼ cup warm water

For the filling:
5-6 granny-smith apples
Juice of one lemon
1 cup bread crumbs, toasted in butter
½ cup sugar
1 tablespoon cinnamon
1 cup cream mixed with 1 egg, beaten

To make the dough:
Place the bread flour in a medium bowl and make a well in the middle. Into that well pour the vegetable oil, egg whites, salt, and lemon juice. Mix until it barely comes together. Add warm water and mix with your hands until you have a smooth dough. Once the dough is smooth, knead until the dough becomes smooth and supple; about 10 minutes. You want the gluten to develop so your

dough is very elastic. When finished, place in an oiled bowl and let rest for 1 hour.

While the dough is resting peel and finely slice the apples, and add the lemon juice to prevent the apples from browning.

Cover your table with a large, clean tablecloth. Oma had a special "strudel cloth" that was brought out for this occasion. Liberally dust the cloth with flour. Plop the dough onto the floured cloth and begin rolling the dough with a floured rolling pin, sprinkling the dough with flour as you go to prevent sticking. Roll out the dough until it is a large circle, about 18-24 inches. Now pick up the dough and using the backs of your hands, particularly your knuckles, stretch the dough like a pizza crust. Get it as large as you can without tearing it and then set it down. Gently pull at the edges of the dough using the back of your hands until you can read a word on a slip of paper slid under the dough. Or in our case, until you could see Oma's age spots on the backs of her hands.

Mix bread crumbs, cinnamon, and sugar.

Spread the thinly sliced apples evenly across the dough, then the toasted bread crumbs. Using a large tablespoon, "sprinkle" the strudel with the cream and egg.

Grab the long edge of the tablecloth and roll the strudel, being careful to not flip it off the opposite side of the table. Tuck and seal the edges.

Preheat the oven to 350F. Place the strudel on a parchment-lined baking sheet and brush the entire strudel generously with melted butter. Bake until golden brown, about 1 hour. Leave on a wire rack to cool.

After cooled, cut the strudel. Dust with powder sugar and don't forget to serve it with schlag, a generous dollop of sweetened whipped cream.

Chapter 12

struggled to fit Minnesota Nice and Midwest Values into my new-found German residency.

My parents believed I was traveling while I awaited placement by the Civilian Personnel Office in an Army hospital somewhere in Germany. The most direct I could be with my parents was using Klaus's address as my return address on the flimsy air mail envelopes that contained letters I wrote home about everything I was doing except living with Klaus. They responded by ignoring my return address and sending letters to me in the care of my aunt. My Europa Mutti was close by and witness to my real living situation. She did an excellent job of reinforcing and deepening the guilt I was already experiencing over leaving my parents and moving to Germany. "This is surely your mother's punishment for leaving her parents behind." Her home was no longer the trusted haven it had once been for me.

Monday, Wednesday, and Friday mornings I called Colonel Keaton at 5th General Hospital in Bad Canstatt.

"Any word yet on a job for me?"

"Not yet."

"Do you anticipate any openings?"

"I am not sure."

I was desperate for work. I wanted my own money, my own friends. I was desperately lonely.

I spent long days alone walking up and down the "Fussgängerzone" filled with people, shops, food vendors, and street musicians. My daily extravagance was a cappuccino on the Schlossplatz, where I watched street life moving in front of me and wondered if not wearing tennis shoes was enough to not give me away as an American. In the late afternoon, I returned to our apartment and waited for Klaus to come home from work. Often, the late afternoons turned into the late evening.

Our Wohnung, in the heart of Stuttgart West, was in a grand old building from the early 1900s. Stuttgart is in the heart of Swabia, a region of Germany well known for various things. It is the area famous for Mercedes Benz and Porsche, Bosch and Stiehl, and much delicious food such as Käsespätzle and Fleischküchle. It is also known for a strong German dialect, Schwäbisch, that makes understanding the locals always an experience for both non-native German speakers and Germans from other areas of the country. The dialect had been in my ear from an early age, and although my German was nearly flawless, it often took me a split second longer than expected to process and respond, which led people to believe that I was just plain stupid.

Our Wohnung was amazingly spared during the war and was now transformed into a multi-family apartment building. The heavy wooden front door opened to hand-painted murals on both sides of the hallway and the mailboxes that had held my love letters for a year and a half. There were five landings with two Wohnungen per landing, one to the left and one to the right. We lived on the fourth of five floors. Built before elevators, the 88 steps to our apartment door often kept visitors at bay.

A large key opened the door to our apartment. The weight of the key in my hand provided the security I so craved as I locked the door. Even more than the key, I loved the large keyhole associated with it, which was also part of the other doors in our building and allowed delicious smells to escape from the kitchens into the stairwell, revealing what was being cooked for dinner. Out of the keyholes came smells of onions being sautéed in butter or Braten, the Sunday roast.

Most people would agree that Germany is a country where cleanliness is an important value and that Germans are some of the tidiest people on earth. In Germany, there is a "tidy" continuum and Swabians are on the far-right end of that continuum. Even among Germans, Swabians are regarded as ridiculously industrious and punctilious.

Swabia is also known for the dreaded Kehrwoche. Of all the variables on the cultural dashboard, there is none more likely to spark a clash than Kehrwoche, literally translated into "sweep week." This compulsory task of sweeping the street in front of the house is passed from Wohnung to Wohnung each week in the form of a small sign hanging outside the door announcing Kehrwoche.

Alternating weeks, the residents share the responsibility of cleaning the landing, the windows, the banister, and the stairs. The entire building alternated mopping the communal entryway and sweeping the street in front of the building. The Swabians around me, frugal and tidy, knew exactly how Kehrwoche was to be done and the expectations surrounding it. It was bred into their genetic make-up just as the color of their eyes or the resilience of their spirit. I, as a foreigner, lacked this inherent knowledge, and given that there was no instruction manual I never quite seemed to live up to the Swabian bar of completing my responsibilities adequately.

Frau Horlacher, who lived on the landing above us, meticulously counted the dust bunnies in the stairwell or dirt swirls left behind by a mop, collecting each one as evidence of my inadequacy as a Hausfrau. Her disdain for my cleaning competence was communicated regularly with nasty notes left tacked to our door, reading "Kehrwoche vergessen?" Of course, I hadn't forgotten, I was just too scared to leave my apartment for fear she would ridicule me as soon as she heard the door latch.

Other under-the-breath comments about "die Amerikannerin" resulted in quickly and carefully timed departures from the apartment to minimize exposure to my scrutinizing housemates.

I wished for instructions on how to deal with German neighbors. It seemed to me as if annoying, and subsequently fighting with, one's neighbors was a common pastime in Germany. These annoyances and arguments often led to longstanding silences that spanned years and generations, often with those in recent generations having no idea of the root cause of the argument.

Stuttgart is the sixth largest city in Germany, with a population of 2.7 million people. The total area of the city is just over 80 square miles. This boils down to 7,800 people in each square mile. In Brown County, Minnesota, where I grew up, the population density was just 44 people per square mile. Heightened acuity over boundaries and personal space fueled arguments I didn't understand. To say that living in such close proximity to others was an adjustment for me would be a gross understatement.

"Sonntag ist Ruhetag!" Loud angry words mingled with spittle were coming through an open window into the back courtyard just as I turned the hose on my car. What have I done wrong now? I was not making any noise washing the car, but I learned that work and noise on Sundays are strictly verboten, prohibited with a capital P. A little quiet snoring in a hammock is allowed, but house and garden appliances and machinery are off-limits. No Sunday lawn mowing as well as no Sunday afternoon car washing.

Finding a parking spot for the 1970 Mercedes diesel Klaus had purchased for me was nearly a full-time job and another prime source of contention. Larger than most German cars and less worthy because it was not new, shiny, and without dents, the car required daily decisions between getting a parking violation for illegal parking or risking eggs on my windshield because I had parked too closely to someone else, or, God forbid, in their parking spot.

When he had a rare day off, Klaus and I would go to a Badezentrum. Germans love to visit the many health resorts and spas throughout the country to use therapeutic water from natural springs to alleviate an assortment of complaints. Our favorite was the Filderado.

Saunas were always included in the experience and required an understanding of rules and deeply held traditions ingrained in Germans at a cellular level. For a modest Midwesterner, German sauna culture came with a steep learning curve. My experience with indoor pools was limited to the pool in New Ulm, Minnesota.

"Let's do the sauna first," Klaus announced on our first Saturday out.

"Vatt? A schwimming suit?" Klaus laughed as I emerged from the dressing room. First mistake. I learned that a swimming suit in the sauna inhibits circulation and the release of toxins. I returned without my swimming suit; essential body parts covered with a too-small white towel.

I wish I had known, I thought to myself; I would have brought a bigger towel.

Naked men and women were milling about, in and out of various saunas. Afraid but having to ask I squeaked out the next question: Where is the women's sauna? More laughter provided my answer as Klaus disappeared into a sauna. The Saunameister, just closing the door took pity on me and asked if I wanted to come in. Klaus had taken the last spot in the other sauna. I was the last one in, which meant crawling over nude bodies of all shapes, sizes, and genders to the top bench.

Naked bodies were settled on the benches, hogging as much space as possible for themselves. The Saunameister, a fit-looking blond woman, began speaking to us in a meditative voice. I took a deep breath and willed myself to enter a state of blissful calm while worrying about which rule I was going to break next. It didn't take long. Was it my imagination or were accusing glances flying my way? What was I doing wrong now? Squinting through the dark I searched for a clue. Directly opposite me, a naked woman sat in a cross-legged position showing me a view I didn't want to see. Apparently, that was OK, but something I was doing wasn't. The Saunameister's lovely intoning stopped to tell me to get my bare skin off the wood. A key rule of German sauna. No skin on wood. I took the towel from around my body and placed it between me and the wood.

The Saunameister began a dramatic performance of towel wizardry with snaps, twirls, and waves, spreading scented air created by pouring water onto hot coals infused with essential oils, disbursing the searing scented air in all directions around the dimly lit sauna. I was mesmerized by the heady smell. But the hot air was hitting me like an herbal tornado. I hadn't properly cooled down before entering the sauna. Another mistake. Klaus, couldn't you have told me all of this?

Bursting out of the sauna through a cloud of lemongrass, I was in a foggy haze, my face as flushed as a German red cabbage. A sheen of sweat coated my body as my white towel fluttered behind me like a broken wing. Vaguely, I was aware of disapproving faces following me through the gloom. I had disrupted the Aufguss. Feeling like a microwaved schnitzel, I staggered down the hallway in search of a cold shower. I felt like a sauna pariah. How could I have screwed up something as simple as going to the sauna?

After eight long weeks, a job offer was finally made on Friday afternoon.

"Hallo?" I answered the olive-green rotary phone in our entryway.

"This is Colonel Keaton. I would like to offer you a job. Can you start on Monday?"

Wild animals could not have kept me away.

"Yes, absolutely!"

"I am sorry it has taken me so long to get back to you. We have had a hiring freeze in place for two years and I have been working to momentarily lift it so I could hire you."

I learned later the freeze was reinstated after my hire and remained in place for an additional two years. Was the universe telling me this was meant to be?

Klaus and I celebrated my job with a bottle of champagne that Friday evening as Klaus wondered aloud when I would tell my parents that we were living together.

ZWIEBELROSTBRATEN

Four 7-ounce sirloin steaks
Salt and pepper
Flour
Vegetable oil
Unsalted butter
Beef broth to make gravy

Fried onions:
1 onion per person, thinly sliced
Butter
Salt

Salt and pepper the steaks and turn in the flour. Quickly sear the steaks on both sides in oil in a cast iron skillet. They should still be pink on the inside. Remove the steaks from the pan and keep them warm on a preheated plate in a warm oven.

Add the butter to the drippings from the steak in the skillet and make a gravy with the beef broth.

In another skillet fry the sliced onions in butter on medium heat until browned. Serve the steaks topped with onions and a large puddle of gravy.

CHAPTER 13

"I don't know if there is any help for me," was my response to the "good morning" on the other end of the phone from another Sheila in my life. This Sheila I had observed from hard white plastic chairs that belonged on a patio rather than in a dental office. For nearly two decades, I had peered over the top of the most recent issue of *Better Homes and Gardens* as she flapped large pages of an appointment book filled with pencil marks and erasures looking for appointments that would work between soccer, theater, and play practice. I marveled at her unwavering equanimity as patients called in to contest which custodial parent was paying the dental bill. This time, I was to be the recipient of her unwavering composure.

"Hi, Sheila. This is Susan Huehn," I choked out.

"Good morning, Susan. How can I help you?"

"MycrownfellofflhaveterribletoothpainandKlausdied," came out all once before another sob choked out.

It seemed as if the pain my body was holding since Sunday was just too much and it exploded through the root of my lower left molar. The protective cover blew off, leaving the skeleton of my tooth exposed, raw and throbbing.

"What now?" I wondered as I stared at my tooth cap in the palm of my left hand, my toothbrush in my right. Google told me there are three things to do when you lose a crown.

1. Find the crown.

Check. I have it.

2. Clean the crown.

It came out while I was brushing my teeth so it must be clean. Google also said, "a crown comes out when chewing something unusually hard or sticky." That hadn't been the case since chewing had become too much work and most foods made me want to vomit. Thick, soft slices of slightly sweet Boston Brown bread delivered by a neighbor had been my sustenance since Sunday.

3. Call the dentist and have the crown reseated as soon as possible.

Check. It was the day of my husband's funeral, and I was calling the dentist.

"The funeral is in a few hours and I don't know what to do."

"Do you have the tooth?"

"Yes." The tooth was in a sterile urine cup that I usually carried in my bag with an emergency snack of almonds.

"Just come on in and we will take care of it."

"Could you please make sure Dr. Jenos knows that Klaus died before I see him?"

Klaus and the dentist had a special relationship. The dentist marveled at his adamant insistence to refuse pain control except under the direst circumstances. And never gas. "I hate dat" was his consistent and emphatic response, regardless of how deep the drill needed to go.

The dentist always greeted me with a "How's that stubborn German husband of yours?" before he inquired about my wellbeing. This morning, I couldn't bear the thought of his hand on my shoulder inquiring about Klaus.

My Nissan turned north out of the driveway to the dentist instead of south to the church. The urine cup sat on the passenger seat next to me, the orange lid tightly fastened so I wouldn't lose one more thing.

Sheila was waiting for me as I slunk through the door of the office, scooting me past those in the waiting room and into a chair. This time the dentist greeted me with a silent hand on the shoulder and no inquiry about anyone's wellbeing. My state was obvious from my tear-stained face and rumpled flannel pajamas with terriers to match Gabe and winter boots, my cheek raw and throbbing from saltwater tears and the pain directly behind them. Could I go to the funeral in this outfit too?

Sometimes a firm hand on the shoulder held a second longer than intended for a friendly greeting conveys a message that words cannot.

I left the dental office my tooth firmly cemented back into its rightful place; the gap closed. But what would fill the gap that Klaus left?

Sonja, Peter, and Alex were just leaving as I headed into the house to change out of my pajamas and don the same black funeral suit in which I had bid farewell to my parents. My mother eight years ago. My father four years ago. Do people in my life now die in a four-year rhythm?

Expired passports prevented Klaus's parents from coming.

"I can wait with the funeral if you would like to come" I offered.

"Nein, wir kommen nicht."

Failure to be physically present did not halt their propensity to regulate Klaus.

"Cremation? We want him properly buried."

For them, proper burial included embalming, a fancy casket, and a headstone engraved with flowers and a schmalzy declaration of enduring and unending love.

"Das ist nicht OK," they hurled across the Atlantic. "How could you burn him?"

It was Klaus's wish, I hurled back.

We are his parents.

I am his wife.

Thank God I don't have to tend to them, I thought as I pulled a brush through my hair and fastened it with a binder. Black clogs without a slip-proof rubber tread forced me to walk slowly and consider where I was stepping. "Stay upright," I repeated to myself as I shuffled out the door and back to the Versa.

This time, as the gravel crunched under my tires, I practiced the eulogy I was going to give. The eulogy, lying next to me on the passenger seat, was typed in 26 font and double-spaced to allow for easy reading through tears. I made it through once before the gravel stopped crunching and I had to pay attention to traffic.

I drove to a different and larger church, one in which my husband's blood wasn't still on the carpet waiting for the carpet cleaner. I walked through a different back door, but the same smell of savory vegetable broth filled my nose as I passed the kitchen where the soup was simmering on the stove.

I am attending my husband's funeral.

I am attending a luncheon for which my husband cooked.

What. The. Fuck.

The minister gathered my family in an alcove of the church out of sight of funeral attendees. I teetered on the edge of something, an edge of separation where lingering felt creepy. Was Thanksgiving just last week when Klaus and I served butternut squash soup with cilantro cream, brined and roasted turkey, cornbread and cranberry stuffing, and mounds of mashed potatoes to our then family of five?

The alcove was the in-between space of stairwells and airport terminals, places with the purpose of getting you from one place to another.

Behind me existed a life with expectations of growing old with Klaus. A large white space that was my future loomed ahead of me.

The funeral would celebrate Klaus's life and mourn his death. The funeral would ask me to leave behind my expectations for moving forward in life without Klaus and transition from wife to widow.

What will I need in this place I am going? How can I know if I have never been there before?

When the precise hour arrived, my family and I followed the minister in a single line out of our hiding place. The church was completely silent. Sunlight streamed in through unfamiliar stained-glass windows. How is it that all churches smell the same?

As the alcove opened into the front of the sanctuary, I looked out at the faces standing and recognized a mosaic of my life, my children's lives, Klaus's life, and our life together.

Each direction I looked someone was there from a different segment of my life. Childhood. High school. College. First job. Those who knew me before Klaus. Those who knew me in Germany. Those who encouraged me to go to Germany and move in with Klaus. Those who knew Klaus from the farmer's market. Those who knew us together. Every time I blink, a memory from a different section of my life rippled across the undersides of my eyelids as I seated myself in the space reserved for the widow.

The organ began to play the familiar tune that reminded me of the thread of music in our lives.[1] One round resonated in the sanctuary. With the second round, the words began and I sang as loudly as I could through my tears.

My life flows on in endless song
Above earth's lamentation.

Where are you, Klaus? Are you lamenting now? Or are you singing? Maybe you are in a place where no one laments that the outlet cover and the screw holding it in place match?

I hear the real though far-off hymn

That hails a new creation.

Are you far off, Klaus? Or are you near? What is the new creation? I hope, for your sake, it has no right angles. You hated right angles.

No storm can shake my inmost calm
While to that rock I'm clinging.

Klaus, you were the rock I clung to. You understood my self-doubt and nagging fears. When they spun out of control you squeezed my cheeks with one hand and stroked the back of my head with the other and said, "Oh Susanne. It vill be OK. The four of us can do this together. You and me and me and you." You tethered me to the earth. Is there any way I could talk you back to earth now?

How can I keep from singing?[1]

Are you singing now, Klaus? Will I ever sing again?

We celebrated his soul to the other side with a collage of memories and then toasted him with teacups of holy soup in the parish hall. It was mid-afternoon when I returned home, the time we would usually be sharing a cup of coffee and conversation about how our days had been, and the time when you most recently reassured me that yes, I could be a college professor. And yes, I could finish a PhD

Instead, I was greeted by the jingling of Gabe's dog tags as I entered the eerily quiet house. The missing sound was the dripdripdripdripdripdripdripdripdrip from the kitchen faucet. I had forgotten to leave the water running in my rush to leave the house. The pipes were frozen, a haunting premonition of my life to come.

---

[1]From *Singing the Living Tradition*, Hymn #108, "My Life Flows on in Endless Song."

Chapter 14

We were kissing wildly on the hillside where triumphant processions, chariot races, and public executions had entertained Romans centuries ago. The kissing was making up for our fight just a few hours ago on the Piazza Navona, with throngs of Christians who wanted to catch a glimpse of the Pope as our audience.

Roman soldiers usually lined up for battle in a tight formation. After a terrifying burst of arrows and artillery, the Roman soldiers marched steadily toward the enemy. At the last minute, they hurled their javelins and drew their swords, before charging into the enemy.

Klaus and I had lined up like soldiers arguing about which direction we needed to walk to find the Coliseum.

"It is disz vay!" German spittle hurling at me like arrows.

"No, Klaus, the map says it is this way," I yelled back.

Instead of a terrifying burst of artillery, our words hurled at each other like javelins. Rather than drawing a sword, I walked slowly toward him and threw the travel guide at him.

It was coming up close to a year of living in Germany, and I wanted to celebrate with a trip.

In the past year, we went from passionate phone calls full of "if only" to working out where we put our dirty dishes: Klaus on the table, me in the sink. Our relationship was like a pendulum that crashed to the far right and far left of an emotional spectrum. We entertained the spinster, Frau Horlacher, who lived above us with either raucous lovemaking or loud arguments about who last took out the trash. Her pinched face when I encountered her on the stairs counting dust bunnies seemed to remember screams of "ja, ja" or "I took it out the last time."

"Can we go to Rome for Easter, Klaus?"

Until now, our travel had been limited to short distances allowed by our temperamental old Mercedes and the limited time off we had from our jobs. Klaus was still 12-to-14-hour days at three jobs. Working for the Army, I rotated days, evenings, and nights and worked most weekends.

We traveled when we could on one and two-day trips across Baden-Württemberg, guided by a dog-eared copy of *Traumstrassen durch Deutschland*. The less traveled the road the better. We took sudden turns to follow signs for artists and castles and stayed in villages where restaurant choices were guided by Klaus's conviction that the best restaurant was the one closest to the village church. Our travel was spontaneous and without a detailed map or agenda. Driving in the car Klaus would reach over and grab my hand. "I am so glad you are here, Susanne. I luff you." Our phone calls full of longing seemed so far away. We ate out twice a day and spent leisurely mornings in bed with slow sensual lovemaking or intimate conversations about our dreams for the future.

Rome, however, was farther than we trusted our Mercedes, now fondly nicknamed Daniel Dusentrieb, to take us.

Daniel Dusentrieb, or Gyro Gearloose in English, was a cartoon character created as part of the Donald Duck universe. A genius inventor always coming up with new ideas, Daniel's creations caused trouble for his friends who frequently bought into them.

Our Daniel was intermittently reliable and had bumps, dents, and scratches. The car was multiple shades of forest green, reflecting Klaus's ongoing but intermittent effort to restore the car. He viewed himself as a master of car restoration and a genius of mechanical ability, which may have been true had he had the attention span to stick with the project. In reality, he didn't bother to get the same shade of dark green spray paint, so his patching efforts remained pink, white, and far from smoothly sanded.

Daniel was Klaus's way of saying "fuck you" to the German love affair with cars that were pristinely clean, undented, and unscratched. He didn't care about the multiple shades of dark green or the frowns from those who parked close by.

"Klaus, please. Could you work on Daniel this weekend?" My hopes were dashed on Monday morning as I saw yet another shade of dark green sprayed on the car.

I desperately wanted the car to be one color, reliable, and not to be a beacon to random vehicle inspections at the side of the Autobahn. Polizei saw me coming and automatically waved me to the side of the road. These inspections paralyzed me with fear.

"Papiere bitte." I leaned over to the glove compartment to retrieve the vehicle registration as another Polizist circled Daniel, bending and stooping to note the car's flaws. Sometimes I got away with a warning. Sometimes I needed to go to a follow-up inspection or have something repaired. And sometimes I pretended to speak only English. In frustration, they would wave me back onto the Autobahn without shaming me or a necessary follow-up.

Daniel Dusentrieb had a thinking cap shaped like a combination of a roof-top and a nest that only worked if three blackbirds lived inside it. Wearing this thinking cap helped him figure out particularly difficult problems.

We did not get off so easy the time that Klaus rigged up the windshield wipers with string because the motor controlling them was broken. String was tied to each of the wipers which ran into the car through the front windows, open just far enough to allow the string to pass through. The small beads of rain that made it through the crack bounced off the forest green leather seats. We were on our way to Bavaria for a weekend adventure on the Ammersee.

dee-doop, dee-doop, dee-doop.

Flashing blue lights and a siren passed us on the left shortly after we pulled out of our parking spot. An intercom bellowed to match the flashing sign on top of the police car, "Bitte folgen." We obediently followed the Polizei until we found two parking spots on the side of the road. My hands were now quiet in my lap, holding both ends of the string as we waited for the police officer to approach the window.

"Das Auto bleibt am Platz stehen," the Polizist screeched at Klaus in guttural German, his spittle mixing with the streaming rain coming in as Klaus turned the crank to roll the window down. This car will not move another inch. He took our keys and issued a ticket for driving an unsafe vehicle. Our instructions were to call a tow truck and have the car repaired before driving it again.

Instead, we walked to the nearest Gasthaus. Over beers, I fretted and Klaus fumed.

Me: "What are we going to do? We can't just take the car."

Klaus: "They can't tell me what to do."

Klaus prevailed, and once the rain stopped, we returned to Daniel and, with my keys returned to our weekend plans.

Daniel Dusentrieb in the cartoon was often assisted by Little Helper, a small robot with a light bulb for a head who helped keep an inventory of his shelves containing odds and ends labeled "geegaws, gimcracks, gadgets, and gizmos." Short of a light bulb on my head, I was Klaus's little helper on the passenger side, pulling the strings of his invention in time to the beating rain and keeping a mental inventory of all the geegaws and gimcracks of Daniel. Little did I know how apt this description would be of the future Klaus and me: multitudes of ideas not always working out, helper with a nest on their head, and bins and rows of items distinguishable only to Gyro.

After an overnight bus trip with sleep induced by dirty-foot smell, we unpeeled ourselves from the bucket seats in Vatican square on Good Friday afternoon surrounded by huge crowds of visitors. What have we done? Did I think we were going to be the only ones visiting Rome over Easter?

Crowds involuntarily pushed us towards St. Peter's Basilica to attend Good Friday Mass with Pope John Paul II. This was the only arranged part of the bus tour. We were now officially on our own.

Spontaneity, while fine for the countryside of Baden-Württemberg, did not work for me in Rome. On Saturday morning, I got up early and armed myself with my detailed agenda and map that was made just for tourists, the kind with streets in bright colors and large pictures of the sights not to be missed.

The Sistine Chapel, Vatican Museum, Trevi Fountain, Spanish Steps, Forum Romanum, the catacombs, the Pantheon: I was determined to see it all in less than 48 hours.

"I want to go to the Sistine Chapel first," I said to Klaus at the café overlooking the Tiber on Saturday morning as I refolded and redirected my map to the agenda I had in my head. It was on my short list of "things not to miss." The ancient cobblestones were already radiating heat from the glaring spring sun. After a quick standing breakfast of espresso, jam, and bread and butter we headed off.

I wanted to plan. He wanted to unplan. Neither of us got what Rome would be like on Easter. Klaus hated crowds, agendas, and maps. I just didn't know how much.

We stood in line for hours to crane our necks briefly and marvel at Michelangelo's angels. The chubby cherubs failed to override Klaus's disdain for the crowds and his need for lunch. By now he was grumpy.

"Food. I need food, Susanne."

Klaus's positive mood was reinstated with an outdoor lunch of pasta with smoked salmon and white wine. After a leisurely cup of coffee, I was anxious to get going. After all, I had seen only one thing on my agenda. The Coliseum was next on my list.

"It is disz vay, Susanne." Klaus's thumb was pointing in the direction opposite of the arrow on my map. His certainty didn't come from previous experience of being in Rome or a strong intuitive sense of direction. He had neither.

"No Klaus. The map says it's this way."

This type of interaction never went well. Klaus's belief couldn't be undone by evidence. Words and a map were no match for his stubbornness and conviction.

My memory shot back to a few weeks ago. We were leaving the Stuttgarter Frühlingsfest and headed home. "No Klaus, the subway is this way." Klaus, with a large Lebkuchen heart around his neck that professed in thick pink icing and roses "Küss mich ohne Ende" stomped off in the direction he thought was correct.

When he believed he was right he didn't argue. He just did his thing. Both then in Stuttgart and now in Rome, I was not sure if he expected me to follow him or if he just didn't care. In Stuttgart, I screamed expletives at his silence all the way home on the subway, giving no indications that kissing without stopping would be happening anytime soon.

This time, in Rome, I screamed expletives in German and English, increasing the number of tourists who could understand what I was saying. When he didn't react, I did the only thing I could think of available to me to get his attention. I threw the travel guide at him and stomped off in the direction of the Coliseum.

Scared I would lose him, I only stomped in my direction for a few minutes. When I turned around, I met Klaus coming back towards me. We could never stay mad at each other for very long. We loved each other so much. "I'm sorry, Susanne. You vere right." I fell into his arms, and entertainment for Romans swung to the other end of the relationship continuum. "I vant to make up mit you," Klaus breathed into my ear, the warmth from the cobblestones radiating up through my feet and igniting passion. We found ourselves on a lush grassy hillside from which Romans had watched chariot races, gladiatorial displays, animal hunts, and fights.

The foundations of the Circus Maximus, which in Roman times were a site for mass entertainment, were long since buried. Now the area was green space. As we came up for air Klaus reached into his pocket and pulled out a small brown velvet bag. His deep blue eyes said everything that needed to be said as a small diamond fell into the palm of my hand.

"Vill you marry me, Susanne?"

He had bought a small diamond without a ring so that we could create an original design and have rings crafted by a goldsmith just as he had done with the Yin and Yang pendant from years ago. Always creative. Always original.

"Oh yes, Klaus. I love you. I will marry you." Passion, love, and hope for the future floated us through our last day in Rome and on the bus back over the Alps to Stuttgart where we began ecstatically planning our wedding, aiming for a civil wedding as soon as possible; we just wanted to be married to each other.

In Germany, couples are allowed to marry in churches only after first having a civil ceremony. In 1875 purely religious unions in Germany were made illegal, which made civil marriage a necessity.

We planned a church wedding for the following year when my parents could come.

We told his parents the next Sunday. Fearing my parents' reaction, I wrote them a letter rather than calling them. It was April. We scheduled the civil ceremony for October and planned a trip to Minnesota in September.

My Dad and Klaus hit it off over shared experiences of being immigrants, Karl May books and Westerns they both loved. "Klaus! Trinken wir din Jagermeister?" I would hear as my dad translated Bonanza reruns into English. Although they would never admit it, I believe that secretly both of my parents loved having a German son-in-law. They agreed to come to our church wedding the next year.

Our civil wedding was the Friday morning after we returned from Minnesota. Klaus's family and a few close friends attended the ceremony held at the courthouse in downtown Stuttgart followed by a celebratory meal at our favorite restaurant. While our guests were greeted at the front door with Kir Royale, salmon flown in from Norway came in the back. The salmon came covered in champagne cream sauce with sides of asparagus, wild rice, spinach fettuccine, and boiled potatoes. Dessert was three kinds of chocolate mousse --dark, milk, and white—with assorted fruits.

Planning for the September church wedding commenced. Which church? Who to invite? The meddling from Klaus's parents began.

I couldn't do it. The Susan who felt as if her needs didn't matter came out. The Susan who didn't know how to make her wishes known didn't know what to do.

"Klaus, could we have a baby instead of a church wedding?" Which is exactly what happened. Instead of a church wedding in September, we had Peter in November.

CHAPTER 15

The day after the funeral was a rainy, grey Saturday morning. Even under normal circumstances, getting out of bed would have been difficult. I lay in bed wondering how I was going to spend that long Saturday.

Was it only last Saturday we made four large pizzas for thirteen people? If I took a really deep breath, maybe I could still catch a whiff of garlic or oregano in the air. Our favorite had been a recreation of number 36 on the menu at the Italian place just around the corner from our apartment in Stuttgart: tuna, artichokes, black olives, and garlic. "Numero 36 mit Knoblauch" Klaus would sing into the olive-green rotary phone. Moments later the pizza arrived hot, with a chilled bottle of Lambrusco for us to share and a room-temperature can of Coca-Cola light for me.

Saturdays had always been my favorite day of the week. They began and ended in the same way. In the morning, while the coffee was brewing, I made the sourdough crust with cold water. Time and cold water allowed flavors to develop throughout the day and resulted in a pliable crust with ballooned and blistered edges. Grocery shopping, house projects, lunch or breakfast out, and perhaps a movie were variables throughout the day. Pizza making in the evening was the constant, a coveted invitation for family and friends.

"I wonder if I will ever have people over for pizza again," I mumbled to Gabe as I hauled myself out of bed, roused by nature's call. Gabe, also reluctant to get out of bed, followed close behind. He felt my despair and for the last week hadn't let me out of his sight. The bathtub was piled high with dishes that needed to be done as a reminder that the kitchen sink's pipes were still frozen. So far, the pump outside in the wellhouse had been spared. "I've got to figure out that insulated box he put around the pump," I said to Gabe as if he could provide me the instructions I so desperately needed. It was one of the many house things that needed my attention and that I had no idea how to address.

Flush. Nothing. Flush again. Nothing again.

The toilet was broken.

I sat on the bathroom floor and sobbed. All my pent-up grief from the last days came out, triggered by the fact that the toilet wouldn't flush. Until this moment I never had to think about broken toilets or broken anything.

How was I going to fix the toilet? First my dad and then Klaus fixed everything.

My father had been the consummate handyman and do-it-yourselfer, even filing his own false teeth when the dentist had not made the dentures to his satisfaction. My husband was no different. Asking for help or hiring a handyman was out of the question for both of them.

How was I going to take care of this house? It was not an arena for amateurs. How was I ever going to manage it all? I signed up for the everything-will-go-swimmingly-until-I-die plan. I'd like to speak to the management, please.

How was I going to take care of my family?

Grief and fear overwhelmed me, but the need for a flushing toilet won over going back to bed.

"Ace Hardware. How may I help you?"

"My husband just died, and my toilet is broken."

Was sobbing on the phone my new normal?

"Of all the things to break, the toilet is probably the easiest to fix," a kind voice responded. For me this was a catastrophe as I thought of all the other things in this house, I did not even begin to know how to address.

"Open the tank and tell me exactly what you see," the hardware woman said. I got up off the floor and carefully lifted the tank lid.

At first glance, the array of thingamajigs inside the toilet tank looked intimidating, a bit like the Mouse Trap game that I loved to play as a child. Over the course of the game, players at first cooperate to build a working Rube-Goldberg-like mouse trap. Once the mouse trap has been built, players turn against each other, attempting to trap opponents' mouse-shaped game pieces.

I looked more closely.

"If the water weren't so rusty, I could see better," I said as if someone was listening.

Eventually, through the greyish, misty water, flecked with bits of floating rust and paint, I could make out two vertical pipes. A taller one and a shorter one. In between the pipes was a white plastic lid that was connected to the shorter pipe. The lid looked like the stopper that I used to plug the bathtub drain.

I glanced over to the bathtub to assure myself the drain plug was still where I expected it to be. Klaus's unorthodox ways of fixing things often resulted in finding things where I least expected them.

From the taller tube, a long arm protruded horizontally onto which was connected a large plastic balloon-like thing that looked like it belonged on the end of a turkey baster. There was a chain lying on the bottom of the tank. On one end of the chain was a paper clip and on the other end was a rubber band. I was fairly certain the rubber band and the paper clip were not part of the workings of a toilet.

Klaus's love of cheap fixes made for innovative repairs. Such innovation also came with the fact that Klaus had left me with a home to which only he had the instruction manual.

What on earth were you thinking, Klaus?

When I pushed the toilet handle, nothing happened. I could see that the chain was supposed to be connected on one end to the handle and on the other end to the plastic lid at the bottom of the toilet. When properly functioning, the chain would then lift the plastic lid allowing the water to escape from the tank.

"I know exactly what part you need," the hardware store woman replied. "I will have the parts ready for you."

Getting dressed and brushing my hair were not goals that I had determined as necessary to achieve daily, so I arrived at the hardware store in my winter boots and mismatched flannel pajamas, hair pulled back with a binder. My loud sobbing and puffy eyes likely gave me away as the new widow who needed the working parts of a toilet. As promised the hardware store woman was waiting for me with the parts needed to restore my toilet's proper functioning.

The part did not include a rubber band or a paper clip.

My years of experience assembling the pulleys, gears, and wheels to trap my opponent's mice proved useful as I assembled the new parts of my toilet.

Flush. Whoosh! Eureka! I felt valiant as I screwed the new handle to the inside of the toilet, my hands freezing in the icy water. Gabe sensed my excitement and wagged his tail as I grinned and reveled in the immensity of my accomplishment.

This was my success: tear-streaked and arms wet with toilet tank water, sitting on the floor of the bathroom in my pajamas, I saw, for the first time in several days, a tiny glimpse of a possibility of being able to function. Perhaps I couldn't fix my broken life, but at least I could get a broken toilet to flush.

The momentary feelings of accomplishment I gained from the toilet repair dissipated as quickly as the water dried on my arms. There were no shrieks of eureka or valiant grins as I changed my focus to keeping the water supply to my house from freezing. Arctic cold typical of Minnesota winters was fast approaching. The well was in a drafty shed to the north of the house. Built in 1864, the shed did little to protect the well from frigid Minnesota winds. Klaus had a haphazard contraption that he rigged up in late fall before temperatures plummeted. Clues to the contraption were fragments of insulation, sheets of plywood in various sizes, duct tape, and a small electric heater piled in a corner in the wellhouse.

I needed an owner's manual with diagrams and clear instructions. If Klaus had written the instruction manual, it would have gone something like this:

"To assemble insulated box around well:

Nagging from Susanne will begin in early October. Ignore nagging for several weeks and then grudgingly complete the task as close as possible to the first hard freeze, preferably the night before. Do not wait too long and allow nagging to persist until the first hard freeze because that risks the pump freezing and then Susanne will have been right to nag and you will hate that she was right. Assemble plywood pieces A and C with duct tape. Stuff in insulation fragments randomly. Add electric heater. Do not worry about causing a fire and make fun of Susanne whenever she worries about a fire. To fully close the door to the wellhouse, use heavy object to push against door and insert six-inch nail lying on small window ledge into latch. Reverse order to open door."

Sometimes for a split second, I forgot I was alone and turned to ask Klaus a question, sometimes in my head, sometimes out loud. Questions went like this:

"How do I keep the pump from freezing?"

"How often do you run the heater outside?"

"Is that a fire hazard?"

"Will the insulation burn?"

"How could you do this to me?"

"How on earth does this work?"

"Why didn't you show me this?"

And reserved for the worst days:

"What were you thinking?"

These questions could be asked in the nanosecond before I realized I was alone, before the keen awareness set in of the vast needs of my house and my inability to meet them. It is amazing how long a split second can be and how much pain can be generated in that split second of time.

"What will others think?" My mother's words from the time we had no roof echoed in my present reality. Terror at letting someone else into the world of my house's idiosyncrasies that only my dead husband understood set in, but I was out of my league, and it was time to swallow my pride and cash in on of the "call me for anything" offers. "Could you please help me figure out how to keep the pump from freezing?" I asked Wayne, my meticulous farmer neighbor to the south, who I strongly suspected had experience with quirky old farmhouses. My need for help superseded my embarrassment over the disorder in the wellhouse.

People wanted to help; they just didn't know how. They seemed relieved when I asked for something specific and concrete. "Sure, I'd be happy to help," and within a few hours, Wayne arrived with a fresh sheet of plywood, an intact roll of insulation, and power tools instead of duct tape. "He also can't make sense of the clues Klaus left," I thought. "It's not just me."

Together with Alex, Wayne built a tightly insulated box sure to keep the well from freezing. The box had a removable door so that I could easily access the spigot during gardening season. I no longer feared a too-strong sneeze in the wellhouse would precipitate the box falling into shambles.

A small electric heater set on "auto" was placed inside the box to provide additional security against the most bitter temperatures.

I wished for a similar heater to warm my hands and feet, which were perpetually cold regardless of how many outside layers I piled on. Stress hormones flooded my system and shunted blood to my heart and large muscles to provide energy for running from a ravaging bear that didn't exist.

My physical safety was not threatened after Klaus' death, but my emotional wellbeing certainly was. Stress hormones couldn't differentiate between physical and emotional threats and sent my autonomic nervous system into overdrive. Hormones poured out to prepare me to respond to imminent danger which had already happened. Nausea, dizziness, shortness of breath, and heart pounding accompanied persistent grief, doubt, and fear. My heart ached and there was a sharp, constant pain in my chest that ate at my strength and distracted my thoughts.

Trauma was stuck in the box that was my body, leaving me not knowing which way was up. My masterful mind was stuck in limbo, trying to rationalize emotional and physiological responses. Fear was constant, large, and ambiguous. Without a ravaging bear to focus on, my mind made up colorful tragic scenarios all centered on my not having the skills to make it on my own.

"Umm, Wayne?" I wondered if the neighbor knew what a big deal it was for me to ask for help. "Could you please show me how to turn the heater to auto?" Or if Wayne knew what a big deal it was to put words to my fears and ask for a realistic version of the danger I perceived. "Do I have to worry about a fire?"

I had a new notebook just for house instructions. Thick black marker identified it as "House" and sticky pink post-it flags identified an "inside" and "outside" section which seemed logical until I better understood what other sections might be needed. Wayne's instructions were the first entry into the "outside" section.

I needed help with my emotional box, insulated from the inside out, that was my storehouse of swallowed emotions. I had been tending to that box all my life. It was chained shut, emotions filed away. It didn't matter what I felt on the inside. What mattered was what I showed on the outside. I felt locked into a future I didn't want without the necessary skills. How was I going to manage this house? How was I going to manage widowhood, which was its own job with its own course of study? Like the instruction manual I needed for my house, I needed one for widowhood as well.

I felt strangely without bones. I could float away, and no one would notice. I was the strong one in the family, the one who sorted out everyone's problems. The only useful solution was a practical one, so I focused on solving problems in my house as they arose and envisioned myself wrapped in that protective casing of bubble wrap. And I swallowed. Just swallowed. And carried on.

Obsessive worry was my constant companion as I floated through the days. It was worry fed by fear and fear grounded in the belief that I surely would not survive on my own.

Chapter 16

Klaus's vision of America came from the fictional building blocks of Karl May novels and reruns of the Cartwright family on the Ponderosa Ranch, which he read and watched religiously on both sides of the wall, first as a young boy and later as a young adult. To him, America was the frontier that would transform him into a new person; a free person.

First pregnant and then pushing a stroller, we often sought respite from the city at a small lake close to our apartment. On our way to the lake, we passed by the Birkenkopf, a 511-meter-high hill on the outskirts of Stuttgart. To the inhabitants of Stuttgart, the hill was known as "Mont de Scherbelino" or "Mount Rubble," a place never visited by tourist groups. It was here that thousands of cubic meters of debris from World War II were deposited. Many facades of ruined buildings were still recognizable within the debris, remnants of what people once owned and of what they once lived in. It was a cemetery to the great destruction of the war. We were often quiet passing this spot and reflected on what the war had cost both of our families and the foundation of rubble on which we both stood.

Our walks around the Bärensee always went in the same direction and our conversations always centered around Klaus's dreams of what his life in America would be like and how his life would be changed by leaving Germany behind.

"What kind of a house do you think we will end up in?" He dreamed of owning a small house in the country where he could recreate the cherished memories of time spent on his grandmother's hobby farm as a child.

"I hope our property is long and narrow, like my Oma's," he would frequently say. She lived about 10 miles outside of Erfurt, where Klaus lived with his parents. Here Klaus spent many days helping his grandmother tend a large garden, a pig – one each year – and chickens to supply the family with things not consistently available in markets and grocery stores.

When reminiscing about his childhood it was not the lack of material things or standing in lines that he recalled. It was the simple pleasure of spending time together in the garden.

The farm provided Klaus with freedom and acceptance. At home, his parents glued his blocks into the back of his toy truck to avoid making a mess. At the farm, he was not expected to subordinate to the closely-held German values of obedience and order. Even more importantly, he wanted a home where we would have privacy and anonymity with no one looking over the fence, or his shoulder, to offer their opinions on a better way. Unspoken in this conversation was Klaus's vision of a future free of restraint and criticism, away from those scrutinizing his worth against his material possessions and his ability to be orderly, where no one regulated the arrangement of blocks in the back of his truck. He longed to be able to carry out his dreams of having acreage and being self-sustaining.

He was a lackluster student who never quite fit in. His father had a heavy hand as Klaus desperately tried to complete his homework, but the arrangement of the letters made no sense. He was unable to learn in the ways valued by the traditional German school system and his parents. Undiagnosed dyslexia made everything unclear to his inner world, which was ruled by expansive and creative ideas that did not follow tradition or expectation.

The world made sense to Klaus on his Oma's small farm. Here, he experienced love without condition and acceptance without expectation. He was his Oma's boy.

Klaus grew up in the German Democratic Republic, better known as East Germany, a communist state formed in 1949. The state described itself as a socialist worker and peasant state. The government promised to take care of its citizens, providing for their basic needs. In return, citizens pledged loyalty to the government and its doctrines, but, in reality, it was a country of spies and mistrust.

Trouble was brewing for Klaus's father. Also a Klaus, he was a progressive and liberal thinker. The ruling communist party warned him that if he did not align with their political ideals, his teaching position and family would be in jeopardy. Unwilling to compromise his ideals and risk his family's safety, he made secret plans with his wife to escape to the West.

Items were put into storage or sold carefully so as not to raise suspicion. Friends and family, as well as Klaus and his brother Mario, ages 11 and 9, were told the wooden floors in their apartment were being refinished to provide an explanation for the packing of belongings and the entire family leaving together for a day. "We are going to the zoo in Berlin" the boys were told.

Klaus remembered finding it unusual that his father was carrying a briefcase and that he was wearing two sets of clothes for a trip to the zoo in the peak of summer. His mother only carried a purse. Outside of that, nothing was out of the ordinary. All other possessions were left behind. The family simply stayed on the train past their stop for the zoo and crossed into West Berlin, a gateway to the democratic West.

Klaus's family was not alone. Between 1949 and 1961, approximately 2.5 million East Germans fled to West Germany.

It was August 1961, and an average of 2,000 East Germans were crossing into the West daily.

Many of the refugees were skilled laborers, professionals, and intellectuals and their loss was not having a devastating effect on the East German economy. To halt the exodus to the West, Soviet leader Nikita Khrushchev recommended to East Germany that it close off access between East and West Berlin.

On the night of August 12, 1961, East German soldiers laid down more than 30 miles of barbed wire as a barrier through the heart of Berlin separating the Soviet sector from West Berlin. East German citizens were forbidden to pass to West Berlin. Asphalt and cobblestones on connecting roads were ripped up. It was a Sunday during the summer vacation season. Police and militia stood guard and turned away all traffic at sector borders. A small transistor radio conveyed this news to Klaus and his family in a refugee camp in West Berlin where they received medical treatment, food, identification papers, and housing until they could be permanently resettled in the West.

The West, taken by surprise, threatened to retaliate against East Germany with a trade embargo. When it became evident that the West was not going to take any major action to protest the closing East German authorities became emboldened, closing off more and more checkpoints between East and West Berlin. Barbed wire was replaced with concrete. Houses that were split by the sector boundary were quickly integrated into the wall. Front entrances and windows were bricked up. Residents could only enter their homes from new entrances in the East, the entrance in the West forever closed off to them. More unfortunate residents were evicted from their homes. The wall, East German authorities declared, would protect their citizens from the pernicious influence of decadent capitalist culture.

East German workers began erecting the 15-foot-high concrete walls as East German troops stood guarding them with machine guns. The walls were topped with barbed wire and watchtowers, machine gun emplacements, and mines extending along most of the 850-mile border between East and West Germany.

By this time, Klaus and his family had moved between a few refugee transit camps operated by West Germany for dealing with the great waves of immigration from East Germany. They were settled in Schorndorf, a small town outside of Stuttgart willing to take in immigrants. Klaus's father went back to school to obtain the credentials necessary to teach masonry in a West German Gewerbeschule while his mother worked to support the family.

Klaus and Mario attended school. They were outcasts and teased for wearing the same two sets of clothes and speaking a German dialect not understandable to those in southern Germany. Sensitive and introverted, Klaus internalized the unhappiness of this time, a darkness that emerged intermittently and stayed with him for the remainder of his life. Before and after school, they were under the tutelage of Frau Winkelman, a stern church woman who had volunteered her time. She cooked lunch for the boys when they came home from school, forcing them to eat while holding books under their arms so their elbows did not stick out too far. They did homework until their mother picked them up after work.

Our talks centered largely on Klaus's belief that moving to America would change his life for the better. "Ich will meine Freiheit!" was his frequent emphatic chant. "I want my freedom!" The freedom that Klaus sought, I believe is better described by the word "liberty." More than anything, he longed to be free within society, free from oppressive cultural and familial restrictions.

He wanted to be like those in his novels and on the reruns: people who continually moved West, lived without restraint, faced extremely adverse circumstances, and always made something out of nothing. In reality, he was more like Oliver Wendell Douglas in the 1960s sitcom *Green Acres*. Douglas, a New York City attorney, embraced a long-harbored dream of moving to the Midwest and operating a farm. Instead of being a lawyer trapped in New York City, Klaus was a German national trapped by the rules and policies of the German government and societal expectations, eagerly longing for space and freedom.

On those walks around the lake in the same direction, we also made outrageous promises to each other about our future life together with the foolish confidence of those who didn't know better.

Our return date to America was set for the summer after Peter was born, just after the term of the three-year agreement I had made with Klaus before moving to Germany.

CHAPTER 17

Water from the well came into the house via underground pipes behind the washing machine. From there, the pipes were distributed throughout the rest of the house. I had tackled the problem of the insulated box around the well in the pump house. Now I needed to keep the water from freezing once it came inside the house.

A heat lamp behind the washing machine.

Check.

Keep water flowing throughout the house.

Kind of check.

Get the correct rhythm to the drips coming from the kitchen faucet to keep the pipes from freezing to the kitchen sink.

Epic fail.

Christmas was rapidly approaching, and with it came arctic cold. I did not want to be without water to the kitchen sink over Christmas.

My anxiety reached a fevered pitch, and the energy generated by my obsessive worry could have lit up the Christmas lights for an entire street.

"The roof is going to fall in. Then what am I going to do?" Thoughts of other disasters that threatened my very existence and that were surely just around the corner swirled in my head and alternated in rapid succession. The top three were the roof falling in, the septic exploding, and my water freezing, but there were no bounds to my creativity as I envisioned one catastrophic disaster after the next.

I hated how vulnerable grief made me feel. My head was on my knees, and my arms were wrapped around me in self-defense and pain. Would grief always be embarrassingly raw this way? Life had hurled its ammunition at me, and I was exhausted with worry and fear. Survival was my focus.

The pipes to the kitchen sink ran behind the washing machine along the outside wall and were certainly installed by someone unfamiliar with the frigid temperatures and winds of Minnesota in winter. With the wind from the north and a wind chill below zero, the pipes froze, leaving me with no water to the washing machine or the kitchen sink, my lifelines to survival.

"If I don't fix that this summer, then you kick me in the butt. OK?" How many summers he had made that joking promise? If only I could kick him in the butt, I would I thought to myself as I replayed the frequent conversation in my head. But in the summers, there were so many other novelties to capture Klaus's attention, like building sailboats and moving rocks in the backyard.

"Susanne!" Even in my memory, his voice was German, guttural, and bossy. "Make sure you set duh faucet so that both the hot and cold vater is running." He was chastising me for not turning the faucet to the precise angle at which both hot and cold water would be dripping. I am not an engineer. I am a nurse. I wonder if he can read my thoughts now that he is in the afterlife?

Given that my new attention span was that of a goldfish, I did a lot of dishes in the bathtub. Klaus had keeping-the-water-running-to-the-kitchen-sink down to a science, but the instruction manual existed only in his head. I was failing Survival 101, I thought to myself as I carried another load of dishes up to the bathtub.

Festive Christmas decorations and strains of "I'll be home for Christmas if only in my dreams" seemed to be playing with unusual frequency on the radio, and there was no amount of cookies or swallowing that could dull the pain of that first Christmas without Klaus. Klaus loved Christmas. Planning began in October with ingredient lists and cookie recipes. There were frequent phone calls to his mother to verify his memories and consult on recipes. Nuts of all shapes and sizes, dried fruit, chocolate on a spectrum from milk to semi-sweet to bitter and European butter lined the freezer door for Vanillekipferl, Haselnuss-makronen, Bärentatzen, and Lebkuchen. The older the recipe the better. There were no cookies with glitter, M&Ms, or – the worst of all evils in Klaus's eyes—cookies made with a mix.

Christmas was a time of wistful yearning for his childhood in Erfurt. It was not the place but the simplicity of the time and satisfaction with the little they had that he craved. Celebration of the holiday began officially with Würstchen and Kartoffelsalat on Christmas Eve. "Das muss sein." Hot dogs and potato salad were his way to connect to his past of simpler times.

We fought about when to put up the tree. In Germany, the Christmas tree is traditionally put up and decorated on Christmas Eve. For Klaus, mixing Christmas with Thanksgiving was soulless and seizure-inducing. In Germany, he won. In America, I won, but he wouldn't compromise on the lights. He fought against the overpowering glitz and glam of a Griswold Christmas. He wanted straw stars and real beeswax candles. At the mere mention of Christmas tree candles, Klaus spoke in hushed tones with evocative memories of growing up with them. It only took one year for me to join in his fierce loyalty. A Christmas tree bathed in natural candlelight is heart-stoppingly beautiful. Candles on a tree also make you slow down. You have to focus on the tree. You can't leave the candles burning and run out for a quart of milk.

This year there would be no candles on the tree to symbolize light in the darkness. For me, the darkness held no light. I just couldn't do it. We bought strings of artificial lights, as artificial as my facade of Christmas cheer, to put on the tree Peter had cut down as Klaus died.

Cheese fondue was our tradition on Christmas Eve, beginning with Peter sitting on the kitchen table to be able to reach the fondue pot with his fork. The cheese fondue, from the shopping to the stirring, had always been Klaus's baby. Only certain cheeses were acceptable, all purchased at stores with cheese counters staffed with "experts" to provide advice, not that there was any room in Klaus's ego for advice-giving related to the types of cheese needed. But cheese mongers were associated with quality in Klaus's mind. Two kinds of alpine cheeses were required: a mature and pungent Gruyere and medium-hard yellow Swiss cheese from Emmental to balance the nuttiness of the stronger Gruyere. This time, the cheese was to be sold in blocks without the requisite pieces of tissue paper between the slices. "No slices. Dat vood dry out dah cheese." The cheeses would be grated on Christmas Eve and added slowly under constant tutelage and scrupulous supervision to a slightly sweet and fruity simmering, not boiling, German Riesling. Only small amounts of cheese could be added at a time, "or it vill Klummp." Kirschwasser, with its distinct fruity flavor, was combined with cornstarch and added at the end to keep the cheese smooth and give the Swiss Fondue its required kick. Also known as Kirsch, the schnapps is genuine only when it is distilled from black, fully ripened cherries from the Black Forest, and for Klaus, nothing less than genuine was allowed.

Peter took over making the fondue, and I shopped for the "correct" ingreeDUHments, as Klaus would say when particularly passionate about a recipe's ingredients. Clumping was the reason I could not make cheese fondue. The necessary quota of patience lacking, I would add a little cheese, stir, and then throw in the rest. A large clump of congealed cheese that refused to inter-mingle with the Riesling was the result.

We sat around the tree on Christmas Eve, bathed in artificial light, tears mingled with the cheese that came out in long gooey strings. The hole of Klaus's absence was gaping. His absence filled the room to overflowing. Christmas morning always held my favorite moments of the year. Klaus and I would sit with coffee in hand and wait for excited footsteps to come down the stairs. This year, Gabe pressed his body against mine as I sat alone waiting for those sets of footsteps. Klaus had bought Alex a Christmas present two days before he died, and it was wrapped, and hidden deeply under the tree. "It's from your dad," I told Alex as he unwrapped the little Chinese teapot on Christmas morning.

More tears. This time into my coffee cup. The pain was unbearable.

Somehow, we made it through the day and plunged into never-ending winter. It was an exceptionally cold winter. Snow, ice, and cold dominated both my internal and external life. My feelings, like my pipes, froze intermittently if I wasn't paying attention.

I was not OK. Daily tasks were exhausting, and nothing seemed important. The world no longer made sense. Tasks previously divisible by the denominator of two were now mine alone. I was certain that I would end up eating cat food in the back of an alley. My children were not included in my delusions of sitting in an alley with a plastic fork and Seafood Medley. Someone would have mercy on them and provide them with shelter. But I could not extend this reassurance to myself as the belief that I did not have the skills necessary to survive on my own was firmly lodged in my psyche.

Besides survival caring for my children kept me vertical. "How do people move on?" I asked the confidante of the day. "When you are a mother, you find the motivation to move on. Sometimes the only place you can find it is in your little toe." I began to focus on the energy in my right little toe. What mattered was that dinner was on the table, they felt safe and had the motivation to move forward, and we were together.

A smile from one of them counted for bonus points. They had me, and I had them.

Each day I focused on what needed to be done for survival in this new life in which I was the lone conductor. Many routines were the same, but everything felt different. It all felt like more. Too much.

Meals were a big thing. "What should we have for dinner tonight?" we asked ourselves as we stood in front of the table in our unheated front porch. The table had become an additional refrigerator and freezer, depending on the outside temperature. At any time, it housed an array of breads, cakes, cookies, roasts, pastas, and casseroles, all prepared and left for us magically and daily. I only had to determine which button to push on my microwave: defrost or cook. The Magic Table eliminated the need to think, and I could reserve my limited brain capacity for tasks necessary for survival. While I had often brought food to the bereaved, being the recipient of those meals gave me a much deeper understanding and appreciation for what they provided.

Planning and going to the store was exhausting, so rather than going to the grocery store weekly, I went each day to buy just what was needed to get through the day. I don't know how normal I looked at the grocery store, weaving through the aisles while I absently considered what to make for dinner. The boxes and cans on the shelves looked strangely unfamiliar. My brain felt like sludge. I could not remember how to put these disconnected items together to assemble a meal.

"We've noticed you searching for something. Is there anything we can help you find?" My aimless wandering up and down the grocery store aisles had caught the attention of those behind the scenes watching for shoplifters.

"Nope. I'm good. Thank you." That was what came out of my mouth. In my head, I was screaming, "I need my husband back. I need him to call and tell me what to buy for dinner so that he can cook it when I get home." I wouldn't have needed to say anything if I could just wear a huge "handle with care" sign around my neck revealing my pain.

I plodded along as if my head was in a paper bag thinking of nothing. Occasionally, I took it out to shake the bag around and see if there was anything inside. I put one foot in front of the other in blackness and in metronome fashion. I didn't want to think.

I wished for public rituals of mourning where I could wear black, beat my chest, and wail in front of others, anything to display my anguish and alert the public to my grief or, at the very least, to alert a fellow grocery store shopper to help me remember what ingredients went into tater-tot hotdish.

My tasks and goals were always small, things I could easily accomplish in small chunks of time. Looking too far into the future rendered me useless. The day looming ahead seemed impossible in the early morning hours when I had conversations with Klaus. In the liminal moments of early morning, between wakefulness and sleep, I awaited an answer to questions that plagued me.

Klaus, how do you turn the water to the house off?

Klaus, why do we have three fuse boxes?

Klaus, I can't open the windows on the porch. Why did you solder them permanently shut?

Klaus, how am I going to manage this without you?

Can you hear me, Klaus?

No answer came from the shadows of my house. Quiet. Just desperate quiet.

Then with full wakefulness, came this:

Klaus, I miss you. I desperately miss you. I can't do this without you. I don't want to do this without you. You understood me, Klaus. You understood that I felt different than others. You didn't laugh at me for not being like them.

On particularly difficult days, I wanted to stay in bed with Gabe. In my bed I felt safe; I felt like the ruler of a small, rumpled country. But survival required getting out of bed and being vertical, and I turned to Mother Google to see if an invisible conglomeration of strangers, trolls, and bots could help me get out of bed. "What should I do next?" I typed into the search bar, waiting for the spinning circle of doom to point me in a direction. Surely Google will know what to do. Finally, "the next right thing" popped onto my screen. Much later, I learned this came from Al-Anon. When grief closed over me like a dark veil, "doing the next right thing" became a mantra, and I resolved to do what was needed to move forward and to survive even if the forward movement was only measurable in millimeters.

The familiarity of home soothed my panic. I looked around at my belongings, things that held memories of my years with Klaus: the hand-blown glass vase we had bought when we ventured off the beaten path with Daniel in the Black Forest and found someone who sold vases to Tiffany in New York; the dogeared travel guide that once rode on the car seat between us as we traveled the back roads of Baden-Wurttemberg; the small whisk he gave me in front of the Rathaus in Bondorf.

The grief felt enormous, and my life felt unmanageable. Leaving my home was hard and often required a physical struggle to stuff the grief in a box so that I could do what needed to be done to survive.

Some days it was taking out the garbage or buying milk. Teach a class. Work on my syllabus for next semester. Help with homework. Complete a paper for my Ph.D. Each day, it was brushing my teeth twice and being vertical. My new world without Klaus was vastly confusing. I was confused about how things worked in my house and how someone could at one moment be there and at the next moment be gone. I was confused by how someone could leave things in such disarray when I had been taught to always go out with clean underwear in case of sudden and unexpected tragedies.

Those who filled the Magic Table in the porch moved on to their own lives and their own families. I continued in survival mode. How do I survive this life without Klaus? How do I get groceries on the table? Must I go into the garage to find a drill to tighten that loose screw?

LEBKUCHEN

For me, Christmas without Lebkuchen is like a chocolate chip cookie without chocolate chips – simply unthinkable. Lebkuchen, baked during the Christmas season, is a centuries-old German baked good flavored with spices like cinnamon, ginger, cloves, and nutmeg and sweetened with honey. It is a soft and chewy cookie, also flavored with nuts, and only remotely resembles its American cousin, the crisp gingerbread cookie. As with many things in the German kitchen, the individual Lebkuchen is as varied as its baker. My favorite Lebkuchen are those my mother would make religiously every year at the beginning of the Advent season. Her recipe is one clipped out of a Minneapolis newspaper in the 1970s and labeled as "Maria von Trapp's Lebkuchen recipe."

4 eggs
2 1/3 cups sugar
1 cup blanched, ground almonds
2 ½ tsp. baking soda
3 tablespoons rum
1 cup honey
6 cups flour
2 tsp cinnamon (more if you like a spicier cookie)
1 tsp allspice
½ tsp ground cloves
½ tsp salt
½ cup finely chopped citron

Icing: Lemon juice and sifted powdered sugar to make a glaze.

Beat eggs, gradually adding sugar. Beat well. Blend in almonds.

Combine soda and rum, and stir until dissolved. Blend with honey.

Sift together flour, salt, and spices. Stir in citron.

Add dry ingredients to the egg mixture, alternating with honey mixture, blending well after each addition. Let dough rest in a cool place for several hours or overnight.

Roll on a lightly floured surface to about ¼' thick (important to not roll them too thin!). Cut out with a 2 ½ inch round cutter. Place on a greased or parchment-lined baking sheet, not too close.

Bake at 325 F for about 16-20 minutes, until just turning brown on the bottom. Don't overbake!

Frost with lemon glaze while still warm.

VANIELLEKIPFERL
Viennese Vanilla Crescents

Oma Rose made these cookies every year for Christmas. They ranked among my favorites. The recipe here is a combination of her recipe and a translated recipe I found in *The Best of Baking* by Annette Wolter and Christian Teubner.

Dough:
12 Tbsp cold butter, cut into small pieces
2 cups all-purpose flour
I cup ground almonds or hazelnuts
Pinch of salt
2 large egg yolks
1 Tbsp vanilla sugar*

Topping:
¾ cup powdered sugar
1 Tbsp vanilla sugar*

Pulse the butter and flour together in a food processor until the mixture resembles coarse crumbs. Add the ground almonds, powdered sugar, vanilla sugar, salt, and egg yolks and blend only until the mixture starts to come together. Then dump into a large bowl and knead until the dough holds together.

Break off walnut size pieces of dough and gently shape them into a crescent. Place crescents on a baking sheet lined with parchment paper.

Bake the cookies for 10-12 minutes, until the tips of the crescents just begin to turn light brown. Remove the baked cookies from the oven and let them rest on the baking sheet for 2-3 minutes as you mix together the powdered sugar and vanilla sugar in a shallow bowl.

While still warm, gently roll the cookies and coat them in the sugar mixture. Allow the cookies to finish cooling on a wire rack.

*Vanilla sugar is imported from Germany. Sometimes it can be found in grocery stores in small individual packets in the baking aisle; 1 packet = 1 ½ tsp of vanilla sugar.

You can also make your own by mixing 1 cup of sugar with the pods of 1-2 vanilla beans in a food processor or mixing ½ tsp of pure vanilla and ¼ cup granulated sugar in a food processor and spreading it on a plate to dry.

KARTOFFELSALAT
Potato Salad

I mostly learned how to make Kartoffelsalat watching my "Europa Mutti," Tante Luise. This recipe is an adaption of my memory of her recipe and a cookbook she gave me, *Kochen und Back nach Grundrezept*, by Luise Haarer, the Betty Crocker cookbook of the Swabian Hausfrau. And, of course, made with the addition of the necessary two, not one or three-r "schlurrrp, schlurrp" from Klaus.

The German hausfrau religiously boiled their potatoes first thing in the morning for the noon meal to allow the salad plenty of time to marinate.

2-3 pounds of Yukon Gold potatoes
1 finely minced medium to large onion
2-3 tablespoons white vinegar
1 cup hot broth, preferably beef
Salt and Pepper to taste
Mustard to taste (optional)
2-3 tablespoons neutral flavored oil (canola)

Wash the potatoes and put them in a pot with cold salted water just to cover. Bring the potatoes to a boil with the lid on, then reduce the heat to medium and cook until just tender. This should take between 20-30 minutes.

Peel the potatoes while they are still warm, as warm as your hands can handle. Once they are peeled, slice the potatoes into ¼-inch slices and place them into a large serving bowl. Add the finely chopped onion, salt, pepper, and mustard if desired.

Combine the broth (hot!) and vinegar and pour over the potatoes, mixing carefully to keep the potato slices intact. You don't want to end up with potato mush. At this point cover the salad and allow it to marinate at room temperature, for at least 2-3 hours. Just before serving carefully add the vegetable oil and stir, listening for a 3-R schlurrrp.

Chapter 18

nstead of arriving at the western frontier in a covered wagon, Klaus arrived to the birth of the Rugrats and Sonic the Hedgehog. George H. W. Bush was president, not Thomas Jefferson. And instead of making a big splash as a charismatic cowboy, he was a stay-at-home dad with a stroller rather than a Mustang.

Klaus arrived in America 100 years too late, and to his dismay, everyone spoke English.

English had always been Klaus's worst subject. The only thing lower than his English grades was his motivation to pay attention and learn the language. He'd had a late start, beginning with Russian in East German schools. By the time the family emigrated to the West and he entered the fourth grade, he was already behind. In Germany taking a stab at speaking English had been fun, humorous even. He was less inhibited. Now, in America, when it counted, he was rendered mute when needing to speak in anything other than his native tongue. "Klaus, you just have to speak. Say whatever comes out; no one expects it to be perfect." I was trying to get him to be less reliant on me. "It will get easier; you just have to practice." More than being afraid of failing or fear of looking silly, he hated being told what to do. So I translated everywhere we went.

We were living temporarily in New Ulm with my parents as I looked for work. Peter slept in a crib in my brother's old bedroom while Klaus and I inhabited my old bedroom. The walls were freshly painted in Winter Wheat. The shelves of teddy bears and stuffed pandas were now lined with Reader's Digest condensed novels. New carpet smell provided evidence of my parents' eager anticipation of our return. The Candy Pink of my beloved closet was painted over, but the space stood empty and seemed to be saying, "I am here if you need me."

My parents, remembering the isolation they felt after immigrating to Minnesota, were eager to support Klaus in any way possible. My dad oriented him to the hardware store and took him tool shopping and translated TV shows in real time. Together they watched episode after episode of *Bonanza* and *Gunsmoke*, the adventures of Matt Dillon and the Cartwright family fueling Klaus's vision of living on the Ponderosa in south-central Minnesota. My mom cooked German food and cared for Peter. Baby clothes from my brother and me had been washed and meticulously ironed. Smelling of Dreft and Downy, they were neatly folded in a dresser drawer waiting for Peter. Building blocks, picture books, and wooden toys to be pulled with brightly colored shoe laces, carefully saved over decades and in no way meeting current safety standards, allowed her to relive the time when she found the most worth and validation as a woman.

Our roles were reversed from when I moved to Germany three years earlier and had to learn to drive faster. Now Klaus had to learn to drive slower. Four-way stop signs were particularly problematic. "Vat do you mean dah first to arrive isz dah first to go?" The concept just wouldn't sink through the thick German skin covering his skull. In Germany, drivers yield to the right when no signs or traffic lights indicate otherwise. Rather than acclimating to our rules and paying attention to the order of arrival, Klaus lectured me on why the German rules for right-of-way were superior. "Klaus - go, it is your turn," I interrupted when the car behind us honked.

Klaus was excited about all things shiny and American. Huge parking lots, streets that allowed two cars to pass side-by-side, and wide aisles in grocery stores were sources of wonderment as we shopped for diapers and paper towels, apples, and tomatoes, in stores that were open 24 hours a day, seven days a week. He wandered off, regardless of timetables or the needs of others. His excitement was that of a sticky-fingered toddler left to his own devices in an open-binned candy store. Up and down the aisles I searched for him, yearning for an adult-sized leash to restrain him. Would a leash instill any adult-like feelings of responsibility I wondered? I wished his excitement was contagious, but my over-developed responsibility gene was preoccupied with finding a job and a place for us to live. We needed an income. His excitement insulted my need for security and was fertile ground for building resentment.

"Vare isz da downtown?" Klaus wondered aloud. There was no church to mark the center of the town as was the case in Germany. We wound through the lanes, avenues, and streets of suburbia lined with taupe houses and no clotheslines or birdhouses, looking for an apartment. "And how am I going to know vich restaurant is da best?" Without a central church in town, restaurant quality felt entirely haphazard. I didn't know how to respond. The question so small but so indicative of the cavernous adaptations my oh-so-German husband would have to make to life in America. My insides quaked with fear of the future, and my shoulders caved with the responsibility I felt. I longed for my Candy Pink closet where I had felt safe and protected from the outside world that felt so threatening.

After just over a month of living with my parents, I found a job working 12-hour night shifts in an intensive care unit in Minneapolis. We moved to an apartment amidst those taupe houses with similarly named streets. Klaus's days were spent caring for eight-month-old Peter. "That is the best-walked baby with the fanciest stroller" the woman behind the welcome desk in our apartment building announced as they passed by on their way to a nearby lake.

Before having children, I never knew how complicated the stroller world was. Jogging strollers, umbrella strollers, double strollers side-by-side, double strollers face-to-face, travel strollers. An afternoon of stroller watching on the Hauptstrasse should have provided ample evidence for the world of strollers, but before having children, I am not sure I even knew such a world existed. Germans love flatbed prams with umbrellas and rubber, not plastic wheels, to better accommodate cobblestone streets. Our German stroller looked as solid as a tank, outfitted in brightly colored linen with a matching adjustable umbrella.

For dinner, Klaus often cooked "würstle's soup," a simple soup made with a few familiar ingredients he found at the grocery store that was within walking distance from our apartment: sausage, potatoes, and carrots in a broth seasoned heavily with his holy trinity of onions, garlic, and marjoram. To expand his limited English, he watched cooking shows and Westerns on a small black-and-white television, kept at the lowest possible volume so as not to wake me. Anything with a more substantial plot line was out of the question because of his limited English.

I was desperately unhappy. Resentment that I felt at being the primary breadwinner had traveled with me from Germany. I was resentful of Klaus for the time spent with Peter and despised the tremendous responsibility I felt. My unhappiness was compounded by the lack of sleep from working nights, and it seeped into our relationship. "I promise I vill make disz up to you." No timeline was attached. It would be someday. Swallowing cookies failed to quell my unhappiness.

On my days off, we began looking for a house. We laid a compass on a map of the Twin Cities, its point on the hospital. Our search for a house with acreage was focused on the outside perimeter of that circle.

We looked at house after house, property after property, but nothing met our criteria.

"Could you look in Northfield?" I asked the realtor who knew the town from its motto: Cows, Colleges, and Contentment. Northfield was farther than I wanted to drive, but I had loved the sense of community in the small town that was familiar to me from my college days, and I knew Klaus would feel at home in the small town with a distinct downtown area. The Realtor planned a day with six house visits. Our trip to Northfield fell on that one fall weekend familiar to everyone who lives in Minnesota when trees are at the peak of their color, the temperatures are summery and the sky is brilliant blue. The clarity of the sky is accompanied by the musty smell of leaves that have already fallen. It is autumn's last hurrah before winter takes over. Our house was the last one on the itinerary, and it was already late in the day. We were discouraged by what we had seen and almost skipped the stop to quit early, but the location of this house was perfect. On the north and west side of town, it was just on the edge of the perimeter we had identified that was within commutable distance to Minneapolis. We agreed to extend the day and take a quick look.

Greenvale Township was blooming with ripe corn and bronzed prairie grasses as we drove slowly along behind the realtor, Peter asleep in the back seat of our Honda Civic. I did not yet know the rhythm of the country and farming life, but soon the combine would disrupt the quiet and take down the straight rows of corn in a final fall rush. I later learned that in Greenvale Township, hip-hop was a way a rabbit moved, and a drive-by meant you stopped in the middle of the road and rolled down your window to talk to your neighbor who was driving by in the other direction.

The small one-and-a-half-story farmhouse basked in an autumn glow as we drove up the short driveway. The house sat back from the road, partially hidden by a stand of old maple trees that were at the peak of their golden color. The front porch, shaded by maples, was begging for two rocking chairs and freshly brewed coffee. Several small newly whitewashed outbuildings completed the picture of a charming homestead in the country.

Klaus was in love before we even stepped out of the car. "Disz von is it, Susanne. I know it."

"The original part of the house was built in the late 1800s," the realtor's sales-pitch voice began, magnetic like a cactus. "The design of these houses was simple and straightforward." We parked alongside the one-car garage that split the driveway in half. The house, its mustard-yellow metal siding gleaming in the late afternoon sun, was on the left of the wooden garage, and a large machine shed and weathered grey barn were to the right. "Vee kann hav goats in dat shed, Susanne," Klaus squealed. "And look! A place for our chickens too!" A battered chicken coop revealing years of junk bulging out from the broken windows was directly in front of us. The realtor, also eager to end the day, was directing our attention again to the house. The house's typical A-frame design allowed for a steep roof pitch to help the heavy snows of Minnesota slide to the ground instead of remaining there. The smell of autumn was strong as we moved towards the house, our feet crunching on the dry leaves while those remaining on the two large Maple trees provided a golden crown for the house. "The house has been updated and added on to several times," the Realtor continued. The side door opened into a small entryway, providing Klaus with one of his top home-owning criteria. "Susanne, vee aren't standing in dah living room venn vee kumm in da Haus." The floor sloped gently to meet us as if inviting us into the rest of the house, my novice home-owner's mind perceiving this as a welcoming omen. The first floor was open with three rooms, a kitchen, living room, and bathroom, with few vertical walls to make for easy maintenance. New carpet smell explained why a beige carpet in the kitchen lacked stains or spots. A plastered chimney next to the kitchen sink served as a reminder of the dominant, centrally-located fireplace that had once been used for cooking and heating. Updates had added electricity to the kitchen which now sported the cheapest versions of a refrigerator and stove. Careful not to hit our heads, we took a narrow twisting staircase took us to the second-floor loft that spread over half the house. A small wooden door over the other half provided access to a crawl space over the kitchen.

Best of all, the house was cheap, and Klaus loved nothing more than cheap. He was smitten.

His mind skipped seeing what was immediately in front of his eyes and went to the possibilities the house held. "I can make something out of anything, you know," was his convincing argument.

Why didn't someone tell me a house inspection might be a wise idea?

Despite the house's modest proportions and fairly conventional construction, the lenses through which Klaus saw this house were impossibly complex. In this small house, he saw the opportunity to change his history and create a new destiny for himself. For Klaus, establishing a home for his family was a matter of personal honor as well as an opportunity to break the prevailing rules and expectations that had surrounded him all his life. He saw the potential to create the life that he had lost as a child.

I did not know what I wanted from a house. I lost myself in Klaus's dreams. My needs folded into his vision and I climbed onto the slippery coattails of his excitement and exuberance.

We signed the purchase agreement on the third day of the Halloween blizzard, a historic snowstorm that began just a few hours before trick-or-treaters started making their rounds. The storm dumped more than 28 inches of snow and still holds the record for the highest snowfall total of any single storm in Minnesota. Why did the fact that the realtor made a herculean effort to drive through a blizzard in washboard road conditions to get to us to sign a purchase agreement not provide a warning of his desperation?

"Washboard road conditions" are created from heavy snow falling in a short period, dropping air temperatures, and high winds. The road conditions were bumpy and rough as if predicting what our future would hold.

We moved in the dead of winter.

As I sat on the toilet that spring holding an umbrella above me, I let go of his impossible dreams. I wondered if perhaps the autumn glow had come from our rose-colored glasses.

Summer, 1985, when Klaus and I met. Mausi and me, with my Dad's dark green Volkswagen Fastback.

Visiting Klaus's parents for Sonntagsessen. 1989.

Peter making Rouladen,
Christmas 2019.

The kitchen of our apartment in Stuttgart.

The Schlegel Family, Oma Rose, her parents and five brothers approximately 1914. Oma Rose is on the bottom left.

Oma Rose making strudel.

Left: Strudel attempt. Notice the huge holes, Oma Rose would have been furious. Peter is in the bottom left corner.

Below: Oma Rose in her kitchen making Zwetschgenknödel.

The only picture of Daniel. On our way to the Ammersee the day after we were stopped for non-working windshield wipers. The boat capsized and the film got wet, hence the damaged photo. The car went to a family in Romania, I often wonder if it is still running.

Rome, Easter 1989 between throwing the travel
guide at Klaus and him asking me to marry him.

Shortly after our
engagement, Spring,
1989.

Our first Christmas together, 1988. Note Christmas
tree with real candles, shown on the right.

Christmas, 1988. The living room of our apartment in Stuttgart.

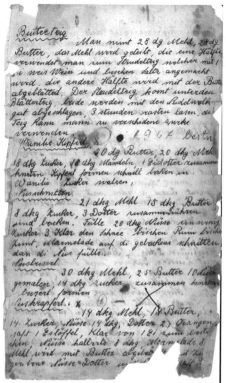

Excerpt from Oma Rose's handwritten cookbook with her favorite recipes. The second recipe in this book is her recipe for Vanille Kipferl, my favorite Christmas cookie of hers.

Lebkuchen made by me using Maria von Trapp's recipe.

Summer 1989: Hiking in southern Germany.

House in 1959, photo given to us by previous owner.

House just after we purchased it. Early winter 1991. The chicken coop I burned down is to the right and the old barn is to the left.

Winter 1992 Outbuildings, the chicken coop is on the right.

CHAPTER 19

Luigi was returning for his car, so today the next task at hand was emptying the trunk of the Honda Accord Klaus was driving on the day he died.

What do I need to do next to survive? To remain vertical? I continued to ask myself these questions throughout the day. Sometimes it was tea. Let the dog out. Buy milk. Take the garbage out. Correct three papers, my concentration flailing by the fourth. Sometimes it was packing lunch and going to work. Sometimes, suddenly and unexpectedly, being vertical was impossible, and an emergency nap was needed. If I wasn't home, I would call random friends. "Can I come rest on your sofa?"

Sometimes the next right thing was to write a section of the paper that was due on Sunday. I was still working towards my PhD one paragraph at a time, one credit at a time, determined to move forward.

There were two remaining cases of champagne strawberry jam in that trunk. It was invaluable to me as it allowed the possibility of prolonging mornings of English Muffins buttered just so and spread with jam and coffee and a conversation with Klaus in my head.

Grief stripped away my protective barrier. I felt like I was once again living in a house without a roof. Unmoored by sorrow, I felt as if I lived in a body without skin, my raw insides vulnerable and exposed for the world to see, just like my kitchen lay open and exposed many years ago.

Intrusive questions from the well-meaning, from everyone and everywhere, only made it worse.

Are you still going to wear your wedding ring?

Do you think I am going to throw away 23 years of marriage A WEEK after my husband's funeral?

Do you need help getting rid of his things?

No, thank you. That will take me a while.

What side of the bed are you going to sleep on?

The same side I have for the last 23 years.

When are you going back to work?

Next Monday. I need structure in my day.

On the days when mental bubble wrap wasn't enough, I switched to envisioning a coating of Teflon.

What are you going to do with Klaus's ashes?

I have no fucking idea.

Some questions required two coats.

They were questions that left the asker feeling more comforted and me more distressed.

The most frequent question by far was "Are you going to sell your house?"

That was a question I could not even consider.

I barely had the energy to brush my teeth twice a day. Could I possibly sort through the sheds that contained years of garage-sale treasures and free items from the curb?

"I don't know," I responded through a clenched smile.

And then the hardest question: "How are you?"

"I'm fine." Did I still have to give the socially acceptable answer?

They wanted desperately to solve my problems. Inside I begged them to just listen.

Previously, when I texted people in grief asking how they were, I wondered why it took them so long to respond. Now I know. Either they were too tired to pick up the phone or their mind was in such a hazy state that they were unable to answer such a hard question.

It was so comforting when people added the qualifier "You don't need to respond."

Some averted their gaze, stuttered "I'm sorry," and changed the subject.

And some just didn't bring up the fact that my husband died. To them, I was a Scarlet Letter D for Death, a reminder that anyone can fall dead unexpectedly and in an instant. They talked about my job as a professor, which I had started three months before Klaus died; about the unusually cold winter; about looking forward to the spring; about anything but Klaus.

"I didn't want to remind you," they sometimes said.

How do you think this goes out of my conscious thought for even a split second?

The knowledge that Klaus was gone rested in the space about two millimeters in front of my face, directly between my eyeballs. Everything was filtered through this invisible third eye.

The many well-meaning in our lives frequently said, "Please call if you need anything," enunciating the word "anything" as if to emphasize its importance. The truth was I often didn't know what I needed. I moved forward moment by moment, focused on supporting the survival of my newly restructured family.

My journey through grief was just beginning. I had no idea how I would last. Would I ever come to terms with losing Klaus? Losing the life I had planned to live?

I had no idea that grief would be so physically exhausting. Fatigue prevented my carrying the cases of jam into the house, nor did I have the emotional stamina to have the jam in my sight and bear witness to the possibility of eating it without him. In my distorted mind, it seemed only logical to move the cases of jam from the trunk of the Accord to the trunk of my Nissan Versa, which took five steps instead of 500. The 48 small jars of bright red jam were carefully snuggled amidst jumper cables and an assortment of reusable shopping bags to keep them safe.

Standing at the gas pump, I wondered who would walk my daughter down the aisle. I thought about how we would never plant sunflowers with our grandchildren and never again have a Bear Hug variety dance in the kitchen. I paid for my gas, got back in the car, and drove out of the gas station with the nozzle still lodged securely in the tank.

JOLT. CRASH. I looked into my rearview mirror and saw the nozzle, thankfully still attached to the hose and the hose thankfully still attached to the pump, bouncing on the asphalt. When I stopped the car an onlooker who had witnessed my absence of mind said smugly, "You're lucky it didn't just snap off." I was embarrassed, ashamed, and most of all in despair. I wanted to scream at the witness, who was surely thinking I was a dingbat, "MY HUSBAND JUST DIED." Please offer me some grace.

Mostly, I thought I was going crazy. I now know that others who have experienced grief recall feeling as if their brain stopped functioning. The problem isn't sorrow; the problem is a fog of confusion and disorientation. The emotional trauma of loss results in serious changes in brain function that endure. That explained why my brain felt like split pea soup on the second day when it was extra thick. The pathways we relied on for most of our lives take some massive detours after traumatic grief, and the brain shifts upside down, prioritizing the most primitive functions needed to keep us alive. Hence my focus on survival tasks. The prefrontal cortex, the locus of decision-making and control, takes a back seat and the limbic system, where survival instincts operate, drives the car. My Grief Brain was certainly manifesting the effects of altered brain circuitry.

Almost two weeks after the funeral, I got a call from Andy, saying, "Klaus's ashes are here. When were you thinking of coming to pick them up?"

Klaus had always been adamant about cremation, but I could not follow through with his wish of flushing his ashes down the toilet. I feared that would cause a malfunction in the fragile plumbing that was beyond my scope of handyman skills.

My Grief Brain could not decide what to do with the ashes after the funeral, but clearly, I couldn't leave them at the funeral home.

Once again, I crossed the threshold into the funeral home with a new personal attendant opening the same heavy wooden double doors with audacious brass handles. I still didn't have the strength to manage the opening of the doors, this time to retrieve Klaus and bring him who knows where. I once again greeted Andy sobbing. This time, we went to his office rather than the beige furniture room. Do I look resilient enough to sit in a hard chair? I sat at the large desk of the funeral director, focusing on his brass nameplate and waiting for him to retrieve Klaus from behind Door Number One. He seemed to be gone a long time. So many questions ran through my head as I waited. "What will they look like?" "Where does he keep them?" "Are they in a closet with others?" "How does he know they are Klaus's?" "What type of container will they be in?" "How heavy will they be?"

He came out with Klaus's shoes and woven belt from the western store that I had bought him for Christmas last year, the same shoes that had been splayed still on his feet in the church basement. I wonder who took them off? They still looked perfectly new. He was also carrying a black velvet bag that he set on the desk in front of me blocking my view of the brass nameplate.

As if to cover the smell of death, an artificial scent stung my nostrils.

"Klaus Huehn," said the fancy brass tag cinching the top of the velvet bag. The bag was clearly marked with Klaus's first and last name, relieving my worry about taking home the wrong person. The black velvet bag resembled the purses I had carried as a young girl, drawstrings on either side that cinched the middle when pulled tight. At that time, when I pried open the tightly puckered middle, the inside revealed a Bubble Gum or 7-Up flavored Lip Smacker, Kleenexes, and some Life Savers or Chiclets, whichever had been on sale at Ben Franklin. Now the inside held the treasures of my husband's remains. Inside the bag was a plastic container about the size of a half-gallon of milk. The math didn't make sense: that so much Klaus, so much exuberance, could be reduced to a volume akin to a half gallon of milk.

Our business done, I carefully collected Klaus and his shoes and belt and carried him out to the car. He was surprisingly heavy resting on my lap. My only context for the weight of ashes came from cleaning out the grill, and Klaus's ashes were much heavier than those. We drove home in silence, my personal attendant and I and Klaus all in the front seat together. Exhaustion had taken over by the time we reached home. Again, agonizing indecision and debilitating anxiety kept me from carrying Klaus into the house, so I put him in the next logical place, the trunk of my Nissan Versa. Here he was safe, but he wasn't in my line of sight. I nestled him carefully among the two cases of strawberry jam, jumper cables, and reusable shopping bags. I wanted to be sure the nest was secure enough to keep him from jostling.

"DON'T! STOP!" I screeched at Sonja the next afternoon as she was reaching for the latch to open the trunk of my car. She was getting ready to load grocery bags as she did every Saturday afternoon. She stared at me with a puzzled expression, knowing better than to ask for the rationale behind my outburst. "Your Dad is in there!" No questions were asked as she quietly loaded the groceries into the back seat around the dog.

We were all working through each day to resume our lives. Memories came and went, brought on unsuspectingly by a glimpse, a scent, or a sound. Sometimes they motivated us; sometimes they weighed us down.

But they always had an impact. They never came and went unnoticed. It had been four months. Sonja and Peter were back in college, Alex in high school, and I was back at work.

The routine of work was comforting. Although new at my job, I had years of nursing experience and could easily and readily teach. At work, I felt competent. I knew what I was doing. At home, I felt unsure.

Given the vulnerable state we were all in, I wanted to know that there were no guns in the house, but I didn't know where to begin looking. Guns had been an unspoken source of contention between Klaus and me. We had many conversations in which I expressed my dislike of guns and adamantly said I did not want them anywhere near the house. He believed that to live in the country we needed guns. The conversations became one-sided: my desires and his silence. I suspected he had brought guns into the house without my knowledge but wasn't sure of the number or location. And, worse yet, if I found them, I didn't know what to do with them. I was scared of touching them or moving them for fear I would set them off.

I found them under a bed. Not knowing what to do next, I called a friend.

"I have guns in my house. I don't know what to do."

"Are they loaded?" he asked. "I have no idea. I barely know which end the bullet comes out of." As gingerly as I have ever touched anything in my life, I grabbed the part of each gun that seemed least dangerous, the part that rests on your shoulder, and pulled them out from under the bed one by one. There were three long guns whose length made them seem particularly ominous. I tentatively placed them onto three comforters and wrapped them loosely, treating them like hand grenades that could spontaneously explode. Sliding them on the soft surface of the carpet made them seem less likely to do something unexpected. They didn't have that particular smell of "a gun has just gone off" like the pop guns I loved to play with as a child, which I took as a good sign. One by one, wrapped in their comforters, I carried them to the most logical place I could think of, the trunk of my Nissan Versa where they nestled against Klaus and the jam.

Inside my Grief Brain, it all seemed perfectly logical. They were out of the house, and I didn't have to see them.

"Be with your guns, Klaus," I thought.

For months, I feared that a routine traffic stop would require my having to explain to a patrol officer why I had three guns, two cases of strawberry jam, and one jar of my husband's ashes in the trunk of my car.

Chapter 20

Klaus used the winter months to make expansive plans for the garden and remodeling. Sharply pointed pencils drew garden beds on graph paper, and brightly colored highlighters circled intended purchases in the multiple gardening catalogs arriving in our mailbox daily. Blue, yellow, green, orange, and pink circles, whichever highlighter was in reach at any given moment, covered the catalogs, which were strewn all over the house. "Susanne!" he would screech from behind the pages of a gardening catalog and come running as fast as purple Crocs would allow. "Look at disz!" He had found a cultivar he recognized from Germany. "We must plant disz von." "But Klaus, it says zone 6, and we live in zone 4." It seemed as if my purpose was orienting him to reality.

I could hear Klaus's footsteps overhead as I sat at the kitchen table drinking coffee and making a grocery list. He came bounding down the stairs brushing cobwebs off his shoulders. "Susanne! Venn vill da Wetter be nice enuff to start to tear duh roov off?"

The sinking feeling that normally rested in my gut rose to my tightening chest.

"Are you sure about this, Klaus?" I asked tentatively. "You have never built a house before." Klaus fit my stereotype about Germans and projects. Once they have made up their minds about something, they don't consider a course just to the left or right of their plan. And woe to those who attempt to alter their intentions. There are no negotiable lines, and Germans prefer not to be shown a different or better way to approach a project. They block any changes, ideas, or alterations to their current thinking. Klaus was no exception. He was unflappable, determined, and living the agency that had been denied him as a child.

"Of course, I am sure," he replied. "Remember? I can make something out of anything." As in Germany when I had begged Klaus to postpone our move to Minnesota for one year so I could stay home with Peter, there was no changing the planned course. His heels were dug in so deep that nothing could sway him from his intentions.

Why is self-confidence so unevenly distributed, I wondered to myself as I tried to breathe.

His certainty only briefly quelled my doubt, but I had an intimate relationship with fear. I grew up waiting for the next bad thing to happen. I knew every nook and cranny of uncertainty, and the thought of not having a roof over my head activated those fears and violated the deep sense of security I desperately needed.

And if I hadn't considered a worry or fear, my dad filled them in.

"What on earth is he thinking?"

"Does he have a clue what he is doing?"

"This is certainly going to fail."

My dad, always orderly and competent, had set the husband bar high regarding home maintenance and repair.

"Susanne! It vill be beautiful," Klaus swooned in his mismatched plaid shirt and plaid boxers, neither of which had a hint of purple to match his Crocs. Excitement and anticipation radiated from his pores and made him skip the step of putting on pants. Klaus took the German stereotype of not caring when wearing socks and sandals together up one notch to socks and purple Crocs.

I was still working nights but with the move had come a new job. I was now working as a labor and delivery nurse in St. Paul and struggling with the inherent sleeplessness of a night shift worker. The mismatch of our rhythms went well beyond my challenged circadian rhythms.

Remodeling plans focused on building with no right angles. Klaus aligned himself with Rudolf Steiner, a German philosopher, who, among many of his ideals, believed that structures should exist organically and in obscure forms as they exist in nature. But Steiner certainly had an architect and building crew larger than one wife at his beck and call. Klaus planned to tear the roof off of the crawl space over the kitchen and downstairs bathroom and then build up, over and down, adding three rooms and over 1,000 square feet. The additional rooms would be a second bedroom over the existing kitchen along with a two-story addition on the northwest side of the house that included an upstairs bathroom and expanded the mudroom, neither of which were in a traditional form with expected right angles. The expanded mud room, in Klaus's mind, allowed for the diligent separation of dirty and clean shoes. Dirty shoes were to be lined up neatly in pairs on plastic mats that could easily be hosed off. For clean shoes, a German-style "Schuhschrank" was imperative, the kind in which shoes are placed at an angle and your daily shoe choice is determined by the shoe's heels. The bathroom was to be a wonder in an acute angle with a sunken tub on a platform.

Tools did not make the cut for shipping from Germany. They were too heavy, too big for the boxes, or were set up for the standard German voltage of 230 rather than America's 120. In early spring, Klaus discovered the American tradition of yard sales. They were the perfect place for him to build his tool supply on the cheap.

Yard sales erupt in Minnesota as soon as warm southerly winds awaken feelings of spring cleaning in its residents and may also be called a moving sale, a rummage sale, or an estate sale. Klaus quickly learned all of the synonyms for one person's expendables becoming another's invaluable treasures. "I luff Amerika" would spontaneously erupt from him as we followed yet another brightly painted homemade sign on fluorescent poster board. Cheap tools! Our car, no matter our agenda, quickly careened in the direction of the arrow in thick black magic marker. From the car, he would scan makeshift tables in driveways or yards looking for tools. Soon he got good enough that the car only slowed; it didn't have to stop if the scan revealed only baby clothes and brightly colored plastic toys.

The other word Klaus quickly added to his limited English repertoire was "free." A "free" box yielded an automatic stop.

The only thing akin to yard sales in Germany is Sperrmüll. The world's recycling leader, Germany has a five-level waste hierarchy comprising waste prevention, reuse, recycling, and waste disposal. There are strict limitations, both of size and amount, on waste allowed from each household. Twice a year, however, all rules are abandoned, and on the designated day you can put your too-big and too-much junk out on the sidewalk. Scavengers, often late at night or in the early morning hours, scour among carpet remnants, old radios with broken speakers, disused vacuums, mattresses, and left-over wood bits for valuables that can be repurposed.

Soon tools, some rusty and well used, others new and in boxes, began to fill our outbuildings. For Klaus, years of living without in the former East Germany gave him the vision of seeing everything as having a possible purpose or a potential use.

"Klaus, do we really need a welder right now?" What I wanted to say was, "you don't know how to weld, and we don't need any more junk lying around."

"But it's soo cheap, Susanne! I vill need it sometime. I am schure ov it."

Things with potential uses began to pile higher, increasing Klaus' sense of security.

As winter turned to spring, the new external walls of the house were marked using a measuring tape and wooden stakes carefully driven into the muddy ground. Orange string was pulled tightly between the stakes to mark the footings. Using a rusty yard sale shovel, Klaus began to dig through the sticky clay soil along the orange string until the footings had a flat bottom and vertical sides. Peter, carefully watching in his high chair, and Klaus together decided the footings were deep enough for the concrete.

Rebar reinforcements were placed in the dugout trenches to support the new foundation.

Our personal foundations were being challenged by the stress of moving to a new country. We both carried threads of war, loss, and immigration in our personal foundations. The historical trauma experienced by our families had similarities that facilitated an easy understanding that brought us together. Yet it was in the reactions to the experiences of our families that Klaus and I differed profoundly.

The main difference between the trauma of our families was choice. Klaus's parents had chosen to leave behind the Iron Curtain out of defiance. Klaus senior, a vocational school teacher, was told that if he did not follow the rules of the Communist Party, he would lose his job, and his family would be threatened. Klaus's legacy emphasized survival and the heroic; his trauma response was one of defiance against outside norms and influences that intended to reign him in.

My father's family had been forcefully displaced following the war and were left homeless and without citizenship to any country. Later, my father was forced by my grandfather to immigrate to the United

States against his will. My mother followed because she had promised my father she would. Regret and guilt came with that decision and followed her for the rest of her life. Both of my parents lived the reality that everything can be lost in a matter of hours. Their story was one of victimization, and this entire legacy was passed on to me at birth. The beliefs that tragedy was certainly around the corner and eternal injustice was my cursed existence were ingrained in me. Fear caused me to doubt myself and doubt Klaus and doubt the entire world.

Neither Klaus nor I had done the necessary psychological house-keeping to recognize how our individual responses manifested in our relationship. Our psychic energy mixed with the concrete as it was poured into the foundation of our house.

Next came removal of the roof. How can anyone make plans for living without a roof?

As the threat of late spring snow passed, Klaus, armed with a reciprocating saw, a rusty crowbar from a garage sale, and an attitude of "how dare anyone suggest what to do or not to do," began to cut off large square chunks of roof.

The century-old nails squeaked and groaned and eventually gave way as the crowbar released them from the wood holding together the framing and shingles. Large pieces of the roof crashed to the ground, representing freedom from the oppressive restrictions Klaus had felt in Germany. The reciprocating saw and crowbar were fueled by feelings of being misunderstood and not accepted, first as a refugee in the West and later as an adult. He was reclaiming his sense of place and purpose.

Peter, sat in the yard in his high chair, far enough away to be safe yet still able to witness the fiasco, which was far more entertaining than anything Big Bird or Ernie was doing. He squealed with glee and clapped his hands as each square slammed to the ground, preceded by a "Vorsicht" from Klaus, who was sharing space with the treetops.

Klaus was fearless. His newfound freedom and liberty emboldened and energized him as the roof continued to come off in huge chunks and expose the raw insides of our farmhouse. For Klaus, uncertainty represented adventure.

I had never received a permission slip to do anything that involved even minimal risk. The result was a debilitating fear of the unknown and an aversion to risk. For me, each descending piece of roof represented an increasing loss of security. My stomach moved in the same direction as the shingles, careening to my feet.

Anxiety coursed through my body on the sidelines, ensuring Peter's safety and waiting to fill whatever demand came from above. I feared I would never have a protective covering over my head again. I wanted to contract myself and revert into my Candy Pink closet.

I had never understood the popularity of horror movies, people sitting together in a state of high arousal, their heart rates elevated, occasionally glancing around nervously, and sometimes jumping collectively in their seats while emitting a high-pitched scream. Working with Klaus on a project was akin to being at a horror movie, except without the popcorn, Milk Duds, or a blanket to cover my eyes.

Finally, the last piece of the roof was on the ground. The raw insides of my kitchen lay exposed. Beadboard existed as the only barrier between the kitchen and potential predators and storms. A roof had never seemed more personal, something to keep out the dark, the storms, and the predators.

For Klaus, the roofless kitchen was bathed in sunlight and possibility. Without a roof, Klaus felt valiant. He was nimble at jumping off ladders while I wanted to hide underneath them.

As a child, I had created play spaces that were small and confined, always with a covering overhead, and an old blanket over a table or the back of my closet with my dearest treasures close by. I wanted to be protected at all costs. Klaus wanted to prove himself to the world and tear off the covers that had been restricting him. What I needed was for him to stop for a moment and recognize my fear and worry. I needed him to acknowledge that my needs mattered.

Klaus's vision prevailed. I remained on the sidelines wordlessly agreeing. For me, the roofless kitchen was a sure sign of impending disaster. I felt unglued.

Our yearning for belonging and being understood had brought us together, but our ways of arriving at our common goal of being understood could not have been more different. We didn't stop loving each other, but we both wanted love in a way the other couldn't give it. Klaus's dreams and my doubts were products of the personal needs created by our individual experiences of trauma. I had buttoned my needs to his dreams and quickly discovered that dreams were simply not transferable. I did not yet know that it was okay to have dreams of my own.

CHAPTER 21

The kitchen cabinet door was hanging precariously sideways. A lot was being asked of the tiny screw whose job it was to secure the door hinge to its framework.

I carefully surveyed the problem and could see that the fibers that had previously held the screw tightly to its hinge were stripped bare. The Phillips screwdriver was not providing a quick fix, and by repeatedly trying to tighten the screw into the same hole, I was only contributing to the increasing severity of the problem.

As a nurse, I used the nursing process to collect and analyze data about the patients in my care. As a professor, I taught students to collect data that is contributing to individuals' lives to provide relevant care unique to them. Now, as a handyman, I found I was applying the same process to the problems in my home. First, look carefully at the problem and analyze the contributing factors to avoid randomly implementing a solution that doesn't address the cause.

Screwed joints get their strength because of the way threads wedge themselves into the wood fibers. When screws stop holding on to the surrounding wood, it is usually because the fibers around the screw threads have torn away. A new approach to securing the cabinet door was in order.

There are numerous solutions when screws tear free from wood. Given the slow evolution of my handyman skills, I tried the easiest solution first, a larger and slightly longer screw. But the necessary drill would require a trip to the outbuildings.

I hadn't been in any of the buildings in years. I had ventured into them when Klaus was out and cleaned, defined as throwing things out. When Klaus saw the garbage can overflowing with his beloved necessities, he wouldn't even come in the house before going through the garbage can and restoring items imperative to his life and wellbeing, which I saw as junk worthy only of the landfill. He was a sentimental hoarder, but the disorder looked like chaos to me. The arguments were never resolved. I determined this was not a cause for divorce and silently decided that as long as he kept his junk out of the house I wouldn't complain. Too much. Every once in a while, though, my insatiable need for order overflowed into an argument.

"Klaus, please. I can't stand the mess. We can't find anything."

"Ok, Susanne. I vill try," he appeased me, knowing his expression of effort would silence me for the time being.

He had every good intention but just couldn't follow through.

I started my search for a drill in the garage. My first mistake was going out after dark. I grabbed the flashlight, which lacked working batteries. Mental note: always keep the flashlight ready in case of emergency. How was I going to survive if I couldn't even keep a flashlight in working order?

Gabe was at my side to build my courage. I flipped the switch to the only working light in the garage, if you could call a few wires loosely connected to a single bulb socket in the center of the double garage a light. The measly bulb did not emit enough light to do more than cast shadows over Klaus's Kingdom of Chaos. Tools lay in disarray on the garage floor, in an explosion of tangled cords.

The garage floor resembled the chaos that was my life and the loose screw my disconnect from my supporting framework.

Dammit, Klaus, I thought. I'm going to break my leg looking for a drill in the dark. And then I won't be able to work. And then I won't survive. My mind only needed a split second to swirl to the bottom.

Was transplanting violets from one spot in the lawn to another spot in the lawn more important than putting real shop lights in the garage?

Crash. Gabe jumped. I bumped into the sharp corner of one of the two metal desks Klaus had picked up on the side of the road. The neon pink "Free" sign in fat black marker was still taped to it.

"I can use disz to organize my schtuff, Susanne," he said proudly as he unloaded the desk from the back of his white Dodge Caravan. The back passenger bench had been removed to make space for impulsive roadside stops that involved free worthless shit and a lottery win for Klaus. It was as if he was preparing for the possibility of again living with the scarcity he had experienced as a child in East Germany. Two toilets. Multiple sinks, all with the plumbing still attached, which significantly increased their value. Three bathtubs were now lined up behind the shed. Yeah, sure, I thought when he described the desk's use. This time it will be different. It won't remain empty like the three metal file cabinets you picked up for the same reason last month.

"Klaus, no more junk. I can't take it."

"Ach, but Susanne, I might need it."

"Please organize what you have."

"It is organized. I can find things."

All I wanted was to stay home with Peter and have another baby, but my life was consumed with working nights, paying the bills, taking care of the house, and managing Klaus's excitement.

Taking him shopping to the PX and commissary in Stuttgart, previously limited to an occasional Saturday afternoon, was like taking a misbehaved toddler on a sugar high to a candy store. Now the arena was everywhere, and he was excited all the time. At stores he ran off without regard for my agenda. I was forever looking for him, and he could be looking at anything: tennis shoes, jeans, rain gear, Dove bars, Mountain Dew.

"Vat isz diss, Susanne?" I found him in the soda aisle inspecting a bottle of root beer. "Is it American beer?" I threw in a bottle for him to try.

"Vate vate Susanne." Still in toddler mode, he grabbed the cart and dug to the bottom of the shopping bag for the "beer" bottle. With the dull edge of his Swiss Army pocketknife, he cracked open the "beer" and took a large swig. German taste buds that expected to be met with a diluted American interpretation of hoppy bitterness exploded onto the pavement in revolt. "Puaaach. Dats duh most awful thing I have ever tried."

All of Klaus's attempts at organization only served to increase the surface area on which to pile tools and valuables from the side of the road that he couldn't live without. The chaos had an order understandable only to Klaus. He was able to find things and recognize when they were moved or, worse yet, gone. Trips to deposit things at the junkyard were an exercise in futility. He left home with a few items and returned with rolls of chicken wire and old windows and doors he was certain he could recreate into masterpieces when, in reality, he trusted most of his work to duct tape.

Maybe, if I could figure out how to get the screw to hold to its hinge, I could find a solution to hold the cabinet door panels in place without the use of the metallic duct tape that was currently doing the job. Shame kept my cabinet doors closed. If only they had wood-grain duct tape matching the birch veneer of the cabinets, then perhaps I could relax my cabinet-closing diligence.

There was a thin line between love and hate when it came to Klaus and his ability to find riches at the roadside or the junkyard. The fact that he could find joy in the simplest pleasures and value in other people's trash was something I also loved about him. "Susanne! Das ist unser Reichtum!" he squealed as he uncovered the huge rocks in the back woods of our property, which he immediately equated with personal riches. "Veee can uze dem in da garten." He would giggle with glee and clap his hands over one Ferrero Rocher I brought home for him from the box someone left at the nurse's station or a piece of smoked pork belly from the Asian market.

To preserve what little sanity I had, I didn't enter the garage or the outbuildings. Until now. I looked at the years of accumulation. Now his chaos was mine alone, and I was left to find order in the explosion of tools on the garage floor.

I needed to find a drill, a screw a bit larger than the one I was holding, and a drill bit to match its head. I tried to channel the joy I felt when going on a childhood scavenger hunt in my neighborhood on Jefferson Street, using clues to find the hidden treasures that were drawn on my treasure map.

Some tools lay on the edge of the Farmall H precariously close to falling, and some were in a heap in the shell of the workbench Klaus hadn't finished building.

Gabe pushed against my leg. At least he had confidence in my ability to survive. I longed for an orderly garage, one in which all of the tools had their place, either in a drawer or on a shelf or, better yet, on a pegboard with an outline in thick black Sharpie. I looked at the screwdrivers, hammers, and saws strewn about and wondered how I was ever going to create some order in the garage. In my life.

The drill was in the middle of the heap, its cord tangled with tools I had never seen before and did not know their purpose.

Next, I needed a drill bit and a screw. I found loose screws in a Cool Whip container.

Klaus had a special love affair with Cool Whip that began with early experiences of American products I brought home to our apartment from the grocery store at Robinson Barracks. "Klaus, what's wrong?" I had just come home mid-afternoon to find Klaus, green-tinged, sitting on the sofa in the living room, and moaning. "Vat was dat in da refrigerator?" When he particularly savored something, he would eat it directly out of the container, leaving tracks of concentric circles made with the smallest spoon he could find. With Cool Whip there was no restraint on Klaus's part and tracks were never left. The only evidence of a Cool Whip binge was the extra-large one-pound tub in the recycling bin and a green Klaus.

I dug through the Cool Whip container looking for a screw that was longer and slightly larger in diameter than the one I was holding in my hand.

Check.

I found the drill bits in a small Tupperware container with dried Ranch dressing. So that was where that container had gone!

Why the hell are there so many different kinds of drill bits? Twist bits. Brad Point bits. Masonry bits. Rivet bits. Bits with a snowflake. Auger bits. Countersink bits. Klaus always said that having the right tool for the job was the most important part of getting a job done. I searched for the one that matched the head of the screw.

One after another, I tried them out until I found the right one.

Just as Klaus was always striving for order but never achieved it, I longed to fit my emotions onto an orderly pegboard with a distinct outline around each one. Emotions I never knew I had were surfacing. I didn't know their purpose or where they were coming from. Sometimes they scared me, and I struggled to put them where I thought they belonged—into the linear tidiness of the five stages of grief.

Number 1: Denial. There is no denying that your person is gone. It is a constant painful reality.

Anger, useful in that it gives energy but not useful because there are so many feelings underneath the anger: fear, pain. Anger initially gives temporary structure to the pain. On some days it was directed at the person failing to go at the stop sign. On others, it found an outlet in thinking of my friend's husband who was going to walk their daughter down the aisle. Anger at Klaus? Never. No one is allowed to speak ill of the dead. After death, they become a saint with no faults or flaws.

Number 3: Bargaining. I do not get this one at all. I will do anything if Klaus comes back to me? If I devote the rest of my life to helping others, will I wake up to find this was only a nightmare? Perhaps I should bargain to stop feeling this pain.

Number 4: Depression. After bargaining, the attention shifts to the present, and depression moves in. This intense sadness includes wondering if there is any point in going on alone. But these steps never occurred in a linear fashion, the beginning of one signifying the completion of another. My feelings were everywhere, and I flipped in and out of one and then another.

Number 5: Acceptance. Life has been forever changed and I must adjust. I donwanna.

I wanted a syllabus for my grief work and expected learning outcomes just as those I planned for my students. I was looking for tools to fix my life. Just like the drill bit, I needed tools that fit just right. Maybe there was a special wrench somewhere? It was like shopping for shoes, some fit well and some didn't.

While the duct tape in my toolbox served many purposes in home improvement projects, it was not a viable tool for patching myself back together again. Among the most important early tools were outfits that included scarves to mop up unexpected tears and hide my face if needed. I was also looking for a grief group.

"Who do you anticipate joining this group?"

I was calling the social worker at the retirement home about the grief group that had been recommended.

"Grief is grief, you know. It doesn't matter the circumstances that bring us together, we all have the same feelings," she said patronizingly during the intake.

The only time I attended this group I spent the entire two hours trying not to make funny noises because I was crying so loud. Everyone there was a manifestation of what I wanted my life to be. They were all in their eighties and had lost their spouses after 60-plus years of marriage. That one downright hurt.

Books on grief began to collect on tables, chairs, nightstands, or any flat surface that would hold advice.

But I needed a person, not a book. I needed a person who could teach me coping skills that weren't found in a bag of Pecan Sandies.

"I just want to move to Kansas," I told the therapist I began seeing, Nancy. This time it was a teal couch that seemed to be swallowing me up. Never mind that I had never been to Kansas and did not know a single soul there. My only connection to Kansas was Dorothy and Toto. Perhaps what I wanted was a place like a leper colony but for the grieving, where we could live away from the expectations of mood and pressures of a polite wellness-obsessed society in which we are told that psychic suffering should be relieved just as a broken bone should be set. We live in a society that privileges positive thinking over negative realism and we are expected to be chipper, industrious, extroverted, and calm. When we can't do that on our own, Prozac is there to help.

"Why Kansas?"

"I just want to move away and start over."

"But what you want to be changed won't be changed by moving to Kansas."

Oh, yeah. Klaus will still be dead even if I move to Kansas. That round goes to Nancy.

Nothing could have prepared me for the overwhelming experience my grief would be. There was nothing linear or tidy about it. It was as if the grief had a life force all its own, and I was subservient to it. It breathes, provokes, and teaches; it aggravates; it wants attention. Some days it kept me on my toes, and some days it knocked me off my feet. I could never anticipate or predict when that would happen. Like so many other things in my life, my emotions didn't come with an owner's manual, and they were as frayed as the cords of the tools on my garage floor.

Was I supposed to be in Denial? It had only been a couple of months. I would regularly check in with myself seeking to find a tidy home on the pegboard for my feelings. Denial may have offered a momentary reprieve from the despair I felt. My feelings weren't anywhere close to the pegboard. They were all over the garage floor, and I tripped over them unexpectedly.

I must be doing something wrong. Did I miss the denial stage?

I did not yet know that love transformed into grief would defy timetables and predictable stages. Grief would be complicated and messy with unexpected storms and no syllabus, instruction manual, or pegboard to provide order.

Chapter 22

ife was complicated without a roof, and spring storms hadn't even begun.

The word "storm," from the word "sturmaz," meaning noise and tumult, describes a disturbed state marked by significant disruptions to normal conditions. Living without a roof was a significant disruption, and abundant noise and tumult resulted.

Warming temperatures during late spring in Minnesota bring severe storms. Just when you feel like the humidity will suffocate you, a cool front collides fiercely with the warm moist air, creating extreme conditions that include horizontal rain and strong winds, sometimes hail and tornadoes. I could feel a similar storm brewing in my psyche. Dread of storms was my faithful companion. The morning's air was thick and heavy. As the temperature rose throughout the day, the air coalesced and felt charged. Without a roof, my senses became exceptionally keen to impending storms: inherent stillness in the air, increased chatter of birds, slight changes to the wind, and an indescribable smell I knew as well as I knew the smell of lilacs.

As the winds increased, I watched the storm unfold to the west with nervous anticipation. Klaus was on the roof waging a war with the blue construction tarps he purchased to provide a protective barrier for the exposed sections of our house. I fretted as the storm clouds marched towards us.

Construction tarps are classified based on a variety of factors, such as material type, thickness, and grommet strength. The greater the weave count, the greater its resistance against ripping in high wind conditions. Klaus, of course, purchased the cheapest ones.

"You didn't tell me that Minnesota has such terrible storms," Klaus said after a long night on the roof trying to keep the tarps secure. "I didn't think you would tear the roof off of the house," I thought. Saying something wouldn't have made a difference, so I kept the thought to myself.

Klaus worked desperately to secure the tarps, but they didn't stand a chance against the storms that spring. Sometimes the storms came while I was working nights delivering Storm Babies. Any labor and delivery nurse will swear that a drop in barometric pressure brings on labor despite the lack of scientific evidence to support this. After a particularly long night of grueling storms, I arrived home from the hospital to an exasperated and soaking husband and Peter eating scrambled eggs and toast in his highchair. Surrounding him was every possible water-holding vessel we owned. They were spread across the whole first floor of the house, each associated with its individual steady drip or stream. Klaus rushed among the teapots, plastic pails, mixing bowls, and our largest stock pot to keep them from overflowing with rainwater. There were no words. Holding an umbrella with one hand and brushing my teeth with the other, I sobbed with exhaustion and exasperation. My house and my soul were drowning. I wanted to paint the entire interior of the house Candy Pink. Did we have excessive wind and storms that spring? Or was I feeling especially vulnerable from the absence of a protective barrier?

Not only were the blue tarps failing to provide necessary protection against the elements, but the weave count in our relationship also failed to provide resistance against the outside conditions. Neither of us had the emotional intelligence to look outside the vortex of our own neuroses. Both of us were struggling for security and seeking validation, things we had never received as children from those important to us. Both of us wanted desperately to understand and be understood, but we did that in vastly different ways, unable to recognize and name our individual emotional needs. He was surrounding and smothering me with his dreams while all I wanted was a roof over my head, an orderly house and yard, and to feel safe and cared for.

Our methods of communication vastly differed for individual and cultural reasons. I had grown up with the understanding that feelings were hidden and left unspoken. Secrets were kept. Germans, on the other hand, Klaus included, say what they mean and mean what they say. Communication is clear, direct, unambiguous, and without euphemisms. "Vat are you asking, Susanne?" was Klaus's way of saying "get to the point."

I did the only thing I knew to do with my worry, fear, and insecurities. My feelings were washed down with Pecan Sandies, which also filled the empty rectangle inside me. I also worked harder and harder to make Klaus's dreams a reality. Maybe then I could be happy too?

Mostly I just wanted to light the house on fire. It was the only way I saw out, but it was too wet to ignite.

As spring storms gave way to summer heat, Klaus waged fewer battles with blue tarps and ropes on the roof, and the summer heat began to dry out the house.

Sheets of plywood and construction beams were delivered from the lumber yard, and with that delivery came new hope and more momentum. Klaus stood on the roof of the kitchen, and I pushed the materials up the ladder until he could reach them and pull them to the top of the house, plywood sheets first and then beams. These innocent piles held big expectations: to restore order to our house and harmony to our relationship.

Klaus strode with purpose on the roof, his steps ringing confidently in the kitchen below as he assembled the outside walls for the new second story. Swinging his yard sale hammer with solid faith in his capabilities, he was announcing to the world "I am here. I am alive. I am capable." In eight-foot sections, the studs were placed at 16-inch intervals, with spaces for windows interrupting the pattern. When the time came to erect the wall, I crawled out onto the roof from the inside of the house, avoiding the scary ladder. I held the new wall while Klaus used a 4-foot level to check that the stud edges and faces were plumb. He moved the level and used a hammer to tap the wall into place until it was perfectly vertical. When satisfied, he fastened it into place against the floor joists.

"Get me some skverrels," he screeched impatiently from the rooftop. Could I have misheard? Or was this his limited command of the English language getting in the way of his requests?

To those around him, Klaus could seem impatient and obnoxious, bordering on insulting at times with his Germanic method of communication. I operated on American rules, approaching topics cautiously, using euphemisms to transmit messages, and aiming to be polite, sophisticated, and effective. When he screeched at me, my first reaction was often hurt and silence.

Squirrels? What the hell? A pregnant pause ensued as I considered the options, afraid to ask for clarification. What could he possibly need? I was considering how rodents could fit into the picture. A pause of anything longer than a nano-second was far too long for my impatient German husband.

"SKVER-RELLS, Susanne!"

Rodents were, for me, an unexpected addition to a move to the country. Opossums in dog food bags on the porch left me afraid to feed the dog. Chipmunks and mice burrowing into the house when the weather turned cold elicited screaming from me that could wake the dead. Klaus knew I hated rodents with a vengeance and that any jokes played on me that involved a rodent would be cause for divorce.

"SKVERRR-RELLS!"

He seemed to think that an elevated decibel level would hasten my comprehension of the mishmash of German and English. After several highly anxious moments and flagrant hand signals holding a drill and an empty box, I determined it was screws that he needed. I sighed with relief that squirrels were not being integrated into my home renovation after all.

Window spaces weren't the only thing interrupting Klaus's building pattern. Also interrupting the building rhythm and momentum were Klaus's Big Garden Plans. His vision and dreams, which had been evolving in his head for years, were diagrammed during the dead of winter onto the quarter-inch graph paper. Four boxes equaled a square foot. Thick black marker to identify the fence was drawn around 640 little graph paper squares. The planned garden was a template for order, remarkably rigid and traditional in design, especially considering the current state of my house. Inside the black lines, there were five garden beds, four evenly shaped rectangles, and an oval in the middle.

"Disz von is for da herbs, Susanne," he said, pointing to the round garden. The garden beds were separated by tended paths to provide easy access for watering. Currant bushes for Träubleskuchen held places of high honor to the right and left of the entrance to the garden. In Swabian, any word can be made diminutive by adding the suffix "le" to the noun. Thus, a car, an Auto, becomes an Autole, a little car, and a house, Haus, becomes a Häusle, a small house. Red currants look a bit like small grapes, Trauben in German, hence in Swabian they are called Träuble. In all other parts of Germany, they are called Johanissbeeren.

Träubleskuchen, a tart and sweet meringue-based cake laced with either hazelnuts or almonds and served with whipped cream on the side, was a favorite for Klaus with afternoon coffee.

Four apple trees for baking and two elderberry bushes were planted outside of the garden fence. Elderberries were planted to make Holundersaft. The thick elderberry concentrate is mixed with hot water, honey, and lemon to ward off ailments during the winter cold season.

A rented manual sod cutter came in to take long narrow strips sod of sod off in low straight ribbons to reveal thick red clay soil, which looked as raw and vulnerable as my insides felt. Manure, compost, and peat moss amended the soil, readying it for the small transplants that were thriving on the kitchen table.

Next came the picket fence to keep out the deer and rabbits. We carefully measured and marked where each post hole needed to be dug. Every eight feet would hold a 4x4 inch post to which fence post panels would be screwed. The sod cutter went back to the rental store, and a two-person auger came in its place.

Holding on to my side of the power auger was a trust exercise similar to being on a merry-go-round at the playground. I had to trust the person spinning to not spin too much or I would lose control. Augers are very powerful with a lot of torque that could throw either one of us like a sack of potatoes if the auger hit a rock or root. Together we eased the auger into place. Klaus pressed a heavy boot against the bottom ledge and advanced the throttle slowly until the auger began to spin. He let the huge drill bore into the ground and throttled up as needed to dig a three-foot hole while I held to the other side and made sure the auger was at the exact point we had marked. He learned to push the throttle more slowly so that I could hold on. I practiced trusting him to not push too quickly or push too much. As we moved around the perimeter of the garden, we found our groove, working together in a rhythm that allowed us to dig all of the holes before Peter woke up from a nap. Wooden picket panels were leveled and screwed onto fence posts, and eureka! The thick black marker line was turned into a charming picket fence, and within that fence, we were going to create something growing and beautiful together that could sustain us in the summer as well as the cold, dark winter. We dreamed of eating fresh tomatoes with basil in late summer and canning them for the winter.

"Next summer we can get goats and make goat cheese for the salad!"

"And I can make soap with the milk," I added.

Chickens for fresh eggs were also on the wish list. "But not until we have a roof over our heads, Klaus." A literal roof. This time I drew the line. I came before chickens.

What our relationship was missing on the roof we gained in the garden hoeing, planting, and dreaming of plans. Tomato seedlings, potatoes, onions, green peppers, and yellow and green beans from colorful seed packets gave us new life and hope. Planted flowers gave us beauty. We walked the garden paths, anticipating the heady scent of the rosebushes we had just planted. Everything was in bloom. Bees were buzzing around the roses. Their roots in the garden held fast to our own, anchoring us to our dreams of a beautiful life together and hopes from those long-ago walks around the Bärensee.

"Klaus? Could you work on the roof today?" The garden was planted and the threat of spring storms no longer so acute. The rafters were up, but we were far from anything close to a protective covering. We were on a timeline. Klaus's parents were making their first trip to America. And now the stakes were much bigger than the blocks being glued on the back of a toy truck.

CHAPTER 23

Winter seemed never-ending. It was as if the snow, ice, and perpetual cold were protecting me from too much interaction with the outside world. I continued to focus on survival, dealing with life's demands in small increments. I focused on small decisions like "What should we have for dinner" and remained unable to make large decisions such as where to put my dead husband's ashes or how to respond to the most frequent question of all: "Are you going to sell your house?"

With the arrival of the gardening catalogs that spring, I developed a fear of the mail. The first catalogs made it across the road from the mailbox to the garbage can, where they landed unopened and unadorned with highlighted pink or yellow circles. They felt so heavy and threatening in my hands that, had the garbage can not had a lid, I would have thrown them in from across the road.

The mail was just too scary. Too much energy was needed to go through the stack of letters. I marveled at the resilience of my dad who opened the mail every day at the oval kitchen table made of fake wood on Jefferson Street. He would arrive home from his factory job daily at 4:07PM and sit down still in his grey Dickie work clothes smelling of perspiration and hot metal and, with a letter opener, cleanly slice open every envelope, reading its contents carefully. The mail would then be sorted into a "keep" and "discard" pile.

The black metal mailbox affixed to the house on Jefferson Street could not possibly have held mail as overwhelming as what was in my large dented rusty rural mailbox. My mailbox contained dangerous reminders from the outside world of life without Klaus: letters from my bank, doctors, insurance companies, social security - both German and American, and the IRS.

It was the handwritten note addressed to Klaus from the hospital that had pronounced him dead that made me stop checking the mail altogether. I sliced the small colored envelope open, the kind that contained greeting cards, thinking a sympathy card would slide out, like the one the vet sent when your pet died. Simple and to the point, it came without fail the same week a pet was put to sleep. "We are so sorry about your tragic and sudden loss," followed by numerous signatures of people I didn't know but wanted to show they cared.

Instead, the card read like this:

Dear Klaus,

Thank you for seeking care at our hospital. We would appreciate your feedback regarding your recent visit to the emergency room.

Please answer the questions on a scale of 1 for extremely satisfied to 5 for extremely dissatisfied:

_____ Did you feel like you got good care?

_____ Were you cared for in a timely fashion?

_____ Did you feel heard?

_____ Were the discharge instructions adequate?

Signed.

By someone who did not do their homework and check the hospital death records before sending the follow-up survey.

What the fuck? WHAT THE FUCK?

This one rendered me unable to walk the short distance from the mailbox to the safety of my house. I broke down sobbing about halfway between the apple trees and my back door.

After that, the letters stayed in the darkness of the mailbox and the darkness that was my mind.

Soon, the mail carrier had to hang a plastic bag on the hinged mailbox door for the overflow. The bag even had an imprint of a target as if to draw extra attention to my shame at being unable to collect the mail.

"Look at that crazy person" screamed in my head as I drove as rapidly as the gravel would allow past the mailbox with the taunting red target flapping in the wind. Recognizing the irrationality of my ways, I turned quickly into my driveway to avoid the shame and inadequacy I felt over not being able to empty the mailbox.

My Grief Brain's ability to track information wasn't keeping pace with the proliferation of mail. Just as snow blindness outside was keeping me from distinguishing between a snow drift and a shoveled path, information blindness kept me from absorbing data that was too much to take in.

Finally, the anxiety of anticipation outweighed my fear of the unopened mail. With a racing heart and sweaty palms, I carried bags of mail into the house. Haphazard piles from both sides of the Atlantic covered the kitchen table. Fear of the unknown contents drove my generalized anxiety about things over which I had little control.

I finally tore open the envelopes. It was nothing like the controlled and clean mail duties modeled by my father at the kitchen table. Sometimes I even committed the cardinal sin of damaging the contents of the envelope. Once I had opened all the mail and dealt with the contents, relief engulfed me, and I was certain the memory of this liberating feeling would carry over to the next time, tomorrow even, emboldening me to take a different path, one that didn't involve a red and white plastic bag of overflow mail.

But not so. The next day, certain there was bad news inside an envelope, I quickly passed the unopened mailbox and turned into the driveway. I didn't want to deal with life's problems that made me feel powerless, my irrational fear of the mail rooted in the deep belief that I couldn't make it on my own. "I'll start tomorrow" I promised myself. But the next day and the next my paralyzing fear prevented me from opening the mailbox and the cycle began again.

My fear of opening the mailbox rivaled my fear of opening the trunk where Klaus was still safely nestled amidst the jam, guns, and unused (but reusable!) shopping bags.

Psychologists call them triggers. They are a stimulus—such as a sight, sound, or smell—that triggers reminders of past trauma. Sometimes they are accompanied by crying jags caused by inanimate objects that held great meaning. The gardening catalogs were only one of many reminders of Klaus everywhere. I most acutely experienced a trigger in the operating room with a patient having an emergency Cesarean section shortly after my return to work. In addition to being a professor, I was still working part-time as a bedside nurse in labor and delivery. The metallic smell of blood combined with the rhythmic beeping of monitors and urgent voices making commands in the operating room took me back to Klaus's side in the emergency department. It appeared without warning and hit me like a lightning bolt. Hard, hot and unexpectedly, I was back at Klaus's side willing him to take a ride in the helicopter.

Denial was nowhere to be found in the gaping hole left by his absence. I tripped over reminders of him everywhere. Shoes by the front door which I nudged so they were lined up, side by side. Sometimes I put his shoes on, feeling the empty shapes of his feet. I tied and untied the shoes. I held his toothbrush by the sink. I smelled the chocolate cake he loved. The reminders were incalculable and unpredictable and were like shards of glass piercing my soul. I did my best to stuff them away so that I could remain vertical. Slippers found in a corner and books found hidden under sofa cushions were shoved into a small closet with his clothes, shoes, belts, and jackets. Soon, opening the door more widely than a small crack risked a dangerous explosion of evidence from Klaus's life. A quick sharp thrust of my left hip helped to close the door against an emotional barrage.

The well intentioned offered to help me to get rid of Klaus's clothes. Details varied with the person.

I will come and help you bag things up.

I don't want you to come and help me. I can't deal with bagging up his clothes while they still smell of him.

I will come and help you sort and label Klaus's clothes.

Sort and label? They have been stuffed into drawers for years without being sorted.

What is the purpose of doing that now? Isn't that the thrift store's job?

Be sure you search the pockets.

Why? To find more painful evidence of his life?

I will help you with mending them before you get rid of them.

Mending? I never did that while he was alive.

I wanted to write those well-intentioned would-be helpers a letter.

Dear person wanting to help,

Please show up, but call first. I will be really happy to see you. Don't say "call me if you need anything" because I don't have the energy to figure out what I need so I won't call. Just say I will come and wash your car before the funeral or I will bring dinner on Tuesday.

Don't say God only gives you as much as you can handle or that there is a bigger plan for you. That makes me want to kill myself.

Just come and sit with me and let me tell the same stories over and over again. If seeing Klaus's picture bothers you, please sit where you don't have to see it. Or take a deep breath and say, "It is so hard to see his picture." It helps to know that you miss him too.

And, for the most help of all, say you will take my son fishing. Do anything that will bring a smile to one of my children's faces.

And please don't leave me. I need you.

Love, Susan

"You need to get rid of his stuff to move on" was the universal underlying message delivered in various forms, but always with urgency. But I couldn't do it and kept stuffing them away in the closet. Until Alex went looking for a belt.

"Mom? Do you still have the braided brown belt Dad got at the western store?" His hand reached for the knob on the dangerous closet door before I could stop him. The stuffing of Klaus's life instantly came out in an avalanche and, with it, my facade of holding things together.

"Do not break down," my internal voice commanded when I found a flannel shirt that still smelled of Klaus. I was lost in the collar of the shirt, imagining his earthy, musty smell, breathing in his scent. I could almost persuade myself that he was still here. I felt my body stiffen and my feelings freeze as I held it next to my cheek. The warmth of the flannel and the familiarity of the smell thawed my core. Crying was rhythmic and repetitious. It began in a low moan and quickly reached a shrill pitch, then receding to the original moan with a complete loss of energy. Remarkably, I found that I cried in twenty-minute cycles. After the current cycle passed, I swallowed and steadied myself, trying to force myself into believing I would survive, and I stuffed the evidence of Klaus's life back into the closet.

I wanted to be less sad. I wanted to feel less pain. I wanted to check the mail every day and resemble a sane person. I wanted to understand my house and know how to fix things. And I wanted to be able to put groceries in my trunk again.

The guns were now stored at a friend's house and the jam was in the cupboard, but Klaus remained tucked among the jumper cables. Should I scatter him in the garden? What if I move? What about a cemetery plot so my children have a place to visit? Klaus would hate being surrounded by a sagging chain-link fence. He loved the water. Maybe I could scatter his ashes in a lake?

Klaus's parents still called several times a week about the ashes. I told them he was still at the funeral home; I couldn't bring myself to tell them he was in the trunk of my car.

His struggle with his parent's control was now transferred to me.

"I just want them to leave me alone."

I was holding my weekly rant about them to Nancy.

"Do you want to do that? They're your husband's parents."

Anger was the antidote to sadness; it gave me energy. Anger does not grovel; it is pure power.

Weekly, she tried to direct my anger to understand that my control over his ashes did not solve the problem.

But the ashes and their disposition remained a source of contention and I just didn't know what to do. So, for now, Klaus continued to ride in the trunk, and Gabe shared the back seat with the groceries.

Chapter 24

hey came with a scrutinizing lens and a healthy dose of German judgment and expectations from the unwritten Code of Correct Conduct embedded in their DNA.

The Code of Correct and Orderly Conduct read like this:

> Houses should be built of stone, not "a better version" of cardboard.

> Toilets should have brushes at their side, not umbrellas.

> Toilet brushes are religion in Germany. A toilet brush is next to every German toilet and you shall use it.

> Walking paths should be paved, not covered in gravel.

"The gravel hurts my feet."

> Coffee should be served in cups with matching saucers and demitasse spoons for breakfast and afternoon coffee, with coordinating table

linens and elaborately folded napkins. China selections should preferably not be repeated twice in one day. Klaus's mother had numerous sets
of china with matching table linens. I did not own a matching set of
china and I did not know what a demitasse spoon was. Sometimes I had
my shit together enough to use Chinet napkins. Mostly I used paper
towels folded in half.

> Table linens should be ironed. I did not own an iron.

> Bed linens, towels, and underwear should also be ironed.

What the hell?

> No elbows on the table. If you placed your elbows on the table, you
would be required to hold books under your elbows to remind you of
proper table etiquette.

WHAT THE HELL?

> House shoes must be worn at all times.

> Slippers were for winter for keeping your feet warm, not a manda-
tory part of your daily dress regardless of the season.

> Children should be demure and not talk back and tolerate having
their blocks glued onto the back of a toy truck to not make a mess. Not
up for discussion and definitely not an option.

Klaus Senior came ready to work with serious work clothes, gloves, and
boots. The roof pitch was decided, the rafters went up and the decking
was nailed under his tutelage in the six weeks they were here. Conversations on the roof went like this:

"How could you do this?"

"Things in Germany would be so much better for you."

On the roof, Klaus quickly reverted to being the young boy trying
and failing to sound out words from a reading primer with his father
looking over his shoulder, fearful that the chair would be pulled out
from underneath him when he stuttered over the sounds unable to
make them into words. He wasn't understood then, and he wasn't
understood now for moving to America and buying an old farmhouse

when concrete walls and slate tiles, and a social net would have safely secured his future in Germany. However, he was still trapped by the flypaper of their expectation and his need for their approval. Each nail that was pounded and screw that was driven was a breadcrumb on an invisible trail that tied the present to his history as an obedient boy. And as much as he hated it, that was whom he became while they were here, a young boy desperately seeking their approval and understanding.

Klaus hoped the span of an ocean would change his reaction to the shaming, but the old defensive tapes were loud and deeply ingrained. Anger was directed inward, towards himself, and fed his paralyzing self-assessment and fear of evaluation. On the outside, he worked for their approval. The wounds and shame were deep even though it was decades later, and they laid the foundation for his belief that he was fundamentally flawed. Some things do not change no matter the size of your body and its geographic location. It turned out, the noise lay between his ears and had traveled with him across the Atlantic.

Inside the house, when I wasn't sleeping during the day after working a night shift, I was busy attempting to meet the high expectations of Klaus's mother, who came to help me whip the household into shape as defined by her German standards. She was a career homemaker, who tied a woman's worth to the cleanliness of her home, the number of sets of china she owned, and how crisply the shirt creases were ironed. Cooking lunches, baking cakes and bread, keeping the bathrooms spotless, never leaving a dirty dish in the sink, and scrubbing the kitchen floor every day after lunch were the standards to aspire to. There was constant criticism to deflect, like when I used too much water to clean the tray of Peter's high chair as well as time spent defending my American heritage and cleaning practices. It was a full-time job for a National Guard troop, yet it was just me as Klaus was waging his own battles on the roof. I balked at ironing towels and underwear.

"See how I am doing this better?" was her mantra. It was working. Underneath that statement was "See? Your lives would be so much better in Germany." She didn't understand the economics of our household, that I was shouldering the responsibility of wage earner, and that her expectations were impossible.

I felt woefully inadequate as both a housewife and a working mother.

"I feel sorry for any child whose mother has to work," was the comment of Klaus senior one day during dinner. I wonder if he knew how that comment burned like a hot poker into the vast pool of resentment that festered just below my surface. I wondered what he would do if he knew that I had begged Klaus on my knees to stay home when Peter was born.

Reality and expectations clashed on multiple planes: the roof, where Klaus was working with his father; the kitchen where I was working with Klaus's mother; and the kitchen table from Jefferson Street, refinished but still holding the memories of my childhood, where we all now sat with Peter in his high chair four times a day for three meals and afternoon coffee.

Peter, almost two years old, was the joy that connected the four of us. A happy toddler, he giggled and laughed as he planted nails in the garden and entertained us at the table with his infectious smile.

They left after six weeks. The roof was up, and we had shelter from the outside storms. I no longer had to use an umbrella to go to the bathroom, but I still needed to climb a ladder to get upstairs. I hoped that the momentum on house projects would continue after they left, but Klaus had his fill of living up to expectations and following orders and quickly reverted to living the childhood he never had in which he was unconditionally loved and not subject to harsh judgment.

Forward motion on the house projects was no longer interesting. There were so many other things to focus his intention on, which, in my opinion, were a worthless waste of time.

He was building the playground he never had, where creativity was valued and the blocks in the back of the dump truck were allowed to remain in disarray on the floor.

From the beginning, I was drawn to his exuberance for life and all of its possibilities, and I longed to make that enthusiasm my own. I remembered the outrageous promises he made long ago on our walks around the Bärensee pushing Peter in the stroller and how, during those walks, I had found his traits charming and enviable. Could that have only been a few short years ago?

"Susanne! Veee vill haff a beuoootifull life in Amerika. I can't vait."

He would fix up whatever house we bought and make it beautiful; he would stay home with the children and do the housework; he would bake bread while building a root cellar and starting a furniture-building business. "I vill make it up to you, Susanne. I promise." I swallowed my fear and doubt and latched onto his dreams. I believed him and wanted his dreams for my own because I didn't know what my own were. I focused on his needs because I had learned my needs didn't matter. I wanted to pursue all of his cool hobbies. I wanted, like him, to grab life by the horns. Yet I had grown up in a world where my long blond hair was divided into equal thirds every day, with no room for a loose hair, an emotion out of place, or any disarray. Everyone was out to get me and I would be sure to fail at whatever I tried my hand in. "Life is going to get you," was the underlying mantra. I wanted, like Klaus, to trust that things would be okay, that using an umbrella to go to the bathroom was exciting and wasn't the end of the world. I wanted him to show me how to trust life rather than fear it. I longed to be seen and to know that I mattered. But the traits that had been charming behind the stroller were less so once life got going.

After living with his parents, I became more aware of Klaus's arrested development so I felt the responsibility I carried more acutely than ever. I hermetically packed my emotions inside myself and sealed them tightly. I handled this realization the way I handled all difficult things: I filled the large empty rectangle in my soul with cookies and worked harder. I held fast to the hope—or was it belief?—that more work would save me and make me happy. I continued to work nights and tried to sleep during the day. In between, I pretended it didn't matter.

What about my needs for order and security? I was desperate for a decrease in the chaos that surrounded me, which meant finishing the sheetrock and trim and building stairs. I wanted to make a home, but instead, I was sweeping up sawdust and working around power tools while working nights. The more I pushed him, the more impenetrable he became. Ultimately, he would go to bed and pull the covers up to the bottom of his nose, leaving a crack just large enough to allow for adequate oxygenation. I prodded and pleaded, but to no avail. He was immovable and unreachable.

Silence drove me crazy. Having suffered the silent treatment from my father for weeks on end, there was nothing that triggered me more. I wanted to retreat to my Candy Pink closet in those moments for some respite from the silence that was unwilling to address problems, the silence that made me feel like I was at fault, and a closet where I could stay as small as I needed to be, surrounded by my most treasured possessions and covered with my security blankets. But hiding in a closet was no longer an option. Showing up for life was a requirement.

I had been schooled to be the responsible one and always take the safe route. I was The Responsible Wife, and I was parenting my husband. That realization poured gas on the resentment living just underneath the surface of my skin. He was living his dreams. He got to stay home with Peter. I had to work. I had to make sure we had groceries on the table and the oil was changed in the car and the bills were paid. What about my expectations? My needs? Would he ever finish the house?

I lived his childhood firsthand during his parents' visit and learned where his need to be free of expectations came from his acute reaction to any kind of evaluation or criticism. I now more deeply understood his need for liberty and to be free of restrictions, demands, and critique because I witnessed his parents' coldness first-hand.

Mostly I was scared he would never grow up.

Being the sole wage earner was difficult, and I was insanely jealous that he could be home with Peter when that was what I wanted. I resented Klaus for taking that away from me even though I had agreed to it. I desperately wanted another baby but, for that to happen, Klaus had to get a job.

Somewhere in the wake of the absent roof I disappeared; my needs and wants went into hiding.

We had conquered the external storms without a roof. That was just the beginning. It was the internal storm inside me that I was worried about.

CHAPTER 25

When you lose someone, you don't lose them all at once, and their dying doesn't stop with their death. You lose them over and over again, a thousand times in a thousand ways.

Winter's final hurrah came on May 2 and dumped sixteen inches of wet, heavy snow onto the back of my barn, collapsing it in the middle. Zoe and Abby stood in the pasture that bright, crisp morning staring at their broken home as I stood on the snow-covered doorstep in my pajamas and Sorrels staring from mine.

I felt like my barn, fragile, slumped with grief, and broken in the middle by the weight of my fear and worries.

"Mom, what do you want to plant in the garden this year?"

Peter was home from college for the summer. Gardening was something we had always done together from the time he could walk. He was now interested in planting edible and ornamental corn and apple trees instead of the nails he had planted as a toddler.

I walked through the garden every day to get to the back fence where Zoe trotted up to meet me for the treat I always had ready, mostly carrots or apples. But on some days I had a Mr. Freezie popsicle, which was her favorite.

As she nuzzled into my neck and whinnied, I wondered how would I garden without Klaus. I couldn't. I wouldn't. I didn't want to. I wanted the garden gate to stay closed. I could see the hops he planted to brew beer just beginning to sprout along the back fence.

"I don't think I have it in me to plant a garden this year, Peter."

"Mom, can't you just be happy that you had Dad and not be so sad anymore?" He was desperate to cheer me up. "You should remember how much you loved to garden together."

Gardening represented normalcy and family togetherness, and normalcy was something they --we all--were desperate for. But could we regain our old sense of normalcy, or was there a new normal to build?

"Maybe I should just start over and make the garden mine instead of mine and your dad's," I thought out loud. Peter was willing to do anything that might feel normal.

Finally, the snow and ice of winter melted and gave way to spring sun and wind, new growth and possibilities. Siberian irises in deep purple and bright yellow were blooming on the banks of the creek Klaus had dug so many years ago, each one a reminder of Klaus's love for beauty and of his prioritization of things like digging a creek by hand over everything else.

"Mom! Did you see what I did today?" Peter asked excitedly as I came home the next day from a shift at the hospital. I hadn't seen, so I went back outside. Remnants of the picket fence Klaus and I had put up together decades ago were smoldering in a pile.

"You said you wanted to start over."

"But that didn't include burning the fence!" I thought.

Sometimes I would just put myself in a time-out because I was afraid of what would come out of my mouth. This time-out lasted until the next day. I couldn't bear to deal with the naked fence posts and I couldn't possibly hurt Peter who had every intention of helping me. The next day, I stood looking at the pile of ashes and felt as if I might disintegrate like those fence panels. Everything felt shattered. Holding on to the remaining fence post with both hands looking at the gardening beds felt like the only possible course of action.

"Could we just go and look at gardening stuff, Mom? And then you could look at the lawn tractors too." He knew that I had decided this was going to be the Year of the Lawn and that I wanted a lawn tractor.

Klaus loved many things about America and Americans, but one thing he never gained an appreciation for was a neatly mowed lawn. He lived his life governed by rules such as "The best place to go camping is the spot marked 'No camping'" and was certainly not going to assimilate to the American ideal of a manicured lawn.

I wanted the type of lawn that was mowed in straight rows and trimmed around bushes and trees; a lawn that was a bright deep green color because it was regularly mowed and tended to. I wanted the kind of lawn that required a working lawn mower or, better yet, a garden tractor. Klaus attempted to understand, but he didn't. And he certainly was not going to agree to spend money on such frivolity.

Lawnmowers, on a spectrum from a push mower to a lawn tractor with a sickle bar attachment to mow down especially high grass, were all in a corner of the garage in various stages of disrepair. Most had been found at garage sales.

In the brief periods that I could mow, Klaus, assuming I could hear him, would chase after me in his unique blend of German and English, yelling "Vorsicht! Duh vi-o-lets." He loved the tiny purple flowers with yellow faces that grew wild in the lawn and was always careful to mow around them, leaving behind little tufts of grass that challenged my vision of a neatly manicured lawn and frankly drove me crazy.

When I couldn't mow, he would come home with another lawn mower with a large colorful "free" sign that he had picked up from the side of the road. "Not another lawn mower, Klaus. Can we please just buy one lawn tractor that works? I want a nicely mowed lawn."

"No Susanne, I can fix the lawnmowers in duh garage. Veee don't need to schpend money."

"What will the neighbors think?" This was a prompt that did not elicit any response. Klaus had spent decades hearing what the neighbors think and couldn't care less.

Klaus had a vision of himself as a mechanical genius. After two years of driving Daniel Dusentrieb, I already knew this wasn't true, but there was no amount of evidence that would invalidate Klaus's self-inventory, even when I presented him with facts that his dreaded enemy, the mosquito, hid and rested in the tall grass.

"If we mow the lawn, the mosquito population will decrease," I said, thinking this bombshell would surely result in some mowing action. Again, no response. He never got around to putting the disassembled mowers back together, and the corner of the garage became the Island of Misfit Lawn Mowers.

This year, I was the only one making decisions about my hobby farm, and I had twenty years of pent-up lawn-mowing frustration inside of me longing to get out. To say I was excited to mow the lawn was an understatement.

Peter and I walked up and down the aisles filled with gardening paraphernalia among the last remaining cheerful jelly beans and bright yellow and pink Peeps from Easter on clearance.

Grief overwhelmed me next to the Gladiola bulbs on my way to the lawn tractors.

Susanne. Can veee pleesz plant Gladiolas in dah garten disz year?

No Klaus. I hate Gladiolas. They are only for funerals.

But dey are so beautiful Susanne.

This was one time my wish prevailed. We never had Gladiolas in the garden.

Until now. Klaus, I will plant gladiolas in the garden every summer from now on. Just for you. I made the promise as I threw red, yellow, and pink ones into the cart. The tractors were in the next aisle. I could feel my heart beat a little bit faster.

There were yellow ones, green ones, and orange ones. "I need a heavy-duty lawn tractor," I told the salesperson from the seat of the lawn tractor closest to me, my skin itching with excitement. Visions of myself mowing through twenty years of grass and growth were dancing in my head. I bought an orange one.

I could barely contain my joy when the tractor was delivered. It was multiple Christmases rolled into one. I marveled that no special tricks were needed to start the engine. A simple turn of the key and the tractor, along with a corner of my soul, roared to life.

Finally, I could mow. I began to cut clean swaths in twenty years of grass and pent-up desire. I did not mow around the violets.

How much time is there for remembering in a day? Sometimes it worked to envision me as a Teflon surface, letting images and memories slide off of me resisting the pain without allowing the memories to get hung up: just awareness and letting go. Walking alongside the seed packets, hoses, and pruners, the memories felt like torture.

Clunk. Crash. Bang. Klaus's chaos and disarray were not contained only to the garage and sheds. As if Klaus was mocking my desire for a manicured lawn from above or expressing his dissatisfaction with the mowed violets, I ran into wrenches and shovels, pitchforks, and car jacks all over the yard. Each crash threatened my goal of a neatly mowed lawn and the integrity of the tractor.

Clunk. Crash. Nothing. A spool of fencing wire buried in the tall grass had brought my tractor to a screeching halt. The wire was now partially wound around the tractor blades, with the remainder emerging from beneath the mower deck in a 15-foot Slinky. Cursing Klaus, I put the tractor in neutral and sheepishly pushed it into the garage.

"Keep your mom away from the tractor?" the guy at the local small engine repair asked my son as he presented with my newest tractor casualty.

Piling twigs and branches into a spring burn pile the next day, I contemplated my intense longing for an orderly house and yard, the kind with only working machinery and tools and that coveted tool pegboard. I also contemplated the constant reminders that stunned me into facing the irrevocable truth that my life with Klaus was over. I couldn't force myself into thinking that these memories were buried. They were always lurking close to the surface and ready to jerk me back into my new reality.

My attempt at a fire smoldered and smoked; any possibility of a spark suffocating underneath the large pile. I carefully removed the large logs and began again. Small twigs and paper first, working from the ground up to ignite a spark. One at a time, I carefully placed the larger logs to allow for enough air to move between them so as not to suffocate the spark.

Finally, success. Watching the roaring fire, I reflected on my emotional state. Fire was the oldest rite of catharsis and brought cleansing by smoke and prayer. The logs would undergo a chemical change from wood to ash. Could I too, through grief, undergo a similar transformation?

Spring peepers were chirping in the background to declare the end of winter. The air moved around the logs, which began their transformation. Spring symbolized new beginnings. I thought about giving my insecurities to the destructive property of the fire and allowing them to burn along with the refuse from my yard. I thought about making spaces between my thoughts, similar to the spaces I created when I stacked the logs at first, so they wouldn't swirl so quickly into a tightening downward spiral. Could I learn to give rise to my feelings and emotions before I swallowed them?

Water was sloshing behind me. The washing machine's rinse cycle had begun, and the dirty water flowed into the septic tank. Maybe the septic system wouldn't explode after all? Maybe my fear of the septic exploding was irrational, and the constant wet spot of sludge around the outside of the tank was just going to dry up and go away as spring unfolded into summer?

I knew the septic system was held together as innovatively as the toilet I had repaired months ago. But this was beyond paper clips and rubber bands. Holding Klaus by the feet as he hung into the septic tank "fixing it," I had asked, "Is this legal?"

Let it go, Susanne, I thought as I looked past the septic's drain field to the sun setting over the rows of corn beyond the gravel road. I thought about the irrational fears that were refuse in my mind, fueling my anxiety and suffocating my soul. I needed to untangle the knot of emotions and make space to breathe. I couldn't keep hiding from my mailbox. Klaus needs to come out of the trunk. I needed to move forward.

The septic pump kicked on with a low rumble. A large fountain of soapy water erupted next to me. A fountain of this magnitude belonged in the center of a city, but at this fountain, there were no passersby throwing coins, and the water had the scent of Floral Spring. With this geyser, any spark of hope I had gained by looking into the fire disappeared. I did not need an owner's manual or an experienced handyman to tell me something was seriously wrong with the septic system.

Chapter 26

"Everything OK, ma'am?"

A police officer knocking on the car window startled me awake. I had stopped at the Rainbow Foods parking lot after working a 12-hour night shift for an emergency nap.

"Yes officer, everything is fine. I work nights and pulled over for a short nap so I could make it the rest of the way home."

There was nothing comparable to the fatigue I felt after working a 12-hour night shift. "Oh, Gromboboolee" Klaus would say when I stumbled through the doorway, invoking the cozy nickname he had given me while we were exchanging letters over the Atlantic. All that I had left was a quick snuggle with Peter before I headed upstairs to bed.

"I'll be right there." Klaus followed close behind to tuck me in. These were the most tender moments in our relationship, rare moments when

I felt Klaus's deep care for me and perhaps associated guilt that I was working when all I wanted was to stay home with Peter.

He started by stroking my hair away from my face and then tucked the blankets in firmly on both sides, finally folding the blanket under my feet. A small kiss and he was gone. I was asleep before he got back to the kitchen.

I woke a few hours later to bright noon sun shining through the room-darkening curtains in our bedroom, not fully rested but unable to fall back asleep. Klaus and Peter were in a far corner of the yard, both in rubber boots, Peter's red, Klaus's black. Peter was splashing and stomping through the mud while Klaus was engaged in his specialty: doing something simple in a very complicated way and doing something that addressed Klaus's internal agenda items rather than mine.

Some progress had been made over the winter on the inside of the house, but our understanding of "done" was still light years apart. We had stairs and the sheetrock was up. I didn't need an umbrella to go to the bathroom or a ladder to get upstairs. There was electricity and some mud covered the cracks on the sheetrock, but it was far from finished and even farther from homey.

This spring brought a full-on war against mosquitoes; annihilating them took all his time and attention. Rather than sanding sheetrock, Klaus transformed into the intrepid mosquito hunter and, with a vengeance, went to battle.

Last summer there had been no time to wage this battle as his parents were there, consciously and subconsciously directing his actions. But, in the intervening months, Klaus had collected a great deal of evidence about this unexpected side effect of immigration to the United States.

Klaus HATED "MoszKWEEtoes" as he called them. He hadn't had time as a youth to build up resilience and, as a result, his tolerance level was ZERO. It was as if the mosquitoes mocked him; either that or German blood was more palatable. They swarmed him when we were outside together, leaving large nasty itchy welts while the rest of us were left alone. He was my best mosquito repellent.

Mosquito repellent in the forms of sprays, creams, and oils lined our shelves. They came in packages of bright orange and a particular shade of dark green as if somehow the colors were specific to mosquito demise. All of them were pungent and strong-smelling, and offensive to sensitive cilia in the nose. Some came labeled "natural," others with a caution about toxicity.

"Klaus, you just have to get used to mosquitoes in Minnesota." My observation came from a place of frustration and built-up resentment. He responded with silence, as always when he was convinced of the merits of a project with which I disagreed. I repeated myself, more loudly this time, perhaps with an accusatory tone. "There is nothing we can do, Klaus." More silence. Inside my mind I was screeching, "Could you please get some groceries or take the car for an oil change?" The bar for my expectations had dropped. What I wanted was a house that was "done," a house I was not embarrassed to have people visit. He was unreachable when the silence came from the place of "you won't tell me what to do and what not to do." My need for a working door on the bathroom flashed before my eyes as he walked away with a gallon tank of insecticide in his left hand and a pump sprayer in his right.

Deep fatigue that came with the recognition that Peter and Klaus were demonstrating the same developmental milestones for toddlers settled in my soul.

"Where are you going with that shovel?" I asked, frightened of the answer.

I had envisioned him spending the day sanding sheetrock so we could paint. Maybe hang pictures after that? Buy some plants?

"To dig a creek."

Water collected in the northwest corner of our property, forming an excellent spring vacation spot for visiting wood ducks. It also became the perfect haven for mosquitoes laying eggs.

"To do WHAAAT?"

"Dig a creek, Susanne. It vill drain da vater from da schvammp." It was part of his battle plan in the war against mosquitoes.

I was speechless. "So that you can stand in it with bare feet and splash?" I thought. I remembered the story his mother told over and over again of Klaus as a three-year-old dressed for a wedding in a white suit with matching patent leather white shoes.

In communist East Germany, nearly all clothing was mass-produced and functional rather than fashionable, leaving little room for things like suits and patent leather shoes. Fashionable clothes were risky and provocative as they represented capitalism and a rejection of socialist ideals in favor of the West. Such bold moves could affect your ability to find a job or an apartment. Klaus's mother, always concerned with outward appearances, had spent months securing the wedding outfit. On the day of the wedding, after her final inspection for perfection, she sent Klaus, the ring bearer, to the street to wait for the rest of the family who was following closely behind. But the muddy creek across the street called to him, and that was where they found him, jubilant and immersed to his knees.

"Duh creek vill run disz vay, Susanne."

The creek was to run across the back of our property in front of the woods, leading either to or from the swamp, I don't know which. Regardless, the result was to have less standing water, which in theory made perfect sense.

What didn't make sense was doing that digging by hand when your wife was working and managing most other household responsibilities. Exhaustion was constant, from working nights and caring for two toddlers, one of them in an adult-size body. My saving grace was that at least one of the toddlers was potty-trained.

Slowly and methodically, he dug and dug. Small mounds of dirt formed creek banks on either side of the slow, steady, trickle of water that followed him.

I just wanted to bulldoze the trees and bring in a dump truck of dirt to fill up the hole and hire someone to sand the sheetrock.

I get it, Klaus. You didn't get the opportunity to be a kid when you were growing up. But could you be a grown-up at least intermittently? Could you do the dishes and wipe the countertop? My internal despair was growing. And the worst part of the despair was that I couldn't share it with anyone for fear of them saying, "Well you brought him here, didn't you?"

"Loooook Susanne! Siberian Irises vill be perfect along duh creek. It vill be so beautiful."

In between the hours and hours of digging there were the twelve Buff Orpington chicks to get ready for. The golden beauties, chosen to match the illustrations in one of Peter's favorite picture books, were scheduled to arrive any day by mail. For them, the old chicken coop had to be cleaned, which hadn't been done in decades.

Cleaning the old coop was a task more easily accomplished by two. I stayed in the coop, shoveling the highly-prized dried chicken manure into a wheelbarrow that Klaus would transport into the garden and quickly return. Or such was the plan in my head. I could not stand straight in the chicken coop, so a prolonged return translated into acute back pain.

Standing knee-deep in dried chicken manure, shovel in hand, I was waiting for the wheelbarrow to return.

"Klaus, wo bist Du?" The decibel level in my request reflected rising anger in direct proportion to the pain in my lower back. He had left with a wheelbarrow headed for the garden but now was nowhere to be seen.

No response. Unfolding myself out of the chicken coop, I found him kneeling on the lawn looking at a newly emerged crocus.

"Susanne! Look at dat!"

How could I be angry at a grown man kneeling in wet grass relishing in the beauty of a tiny purple crocus, barely discernible among the new blades of grass? Even in my frustration, I remembered how I loved his ability to find beauty in the simplest pleasures. My anger was quickly forgotten and, after both admiring the crocus, we finished cleaning the chicken coop together.

Before the chicks were large enough to go outside, they would live in the kitchen for four to five weeks. A large Rubbermaid container was lined with cushy paper towels for litter in the corner of the kitchen.

The feeder contained protein-filled Grubby Little Pecks starter feed. Chicks also need supplements added to their water during the first few days of life to give their immune and digestive systems a good start on fighting off disease. The bottle with a dropper to count twenty drops per quart of water was ready at the kitchen sink. Once they arrived all we needed to do was turn on the heat lamp.

Together with Peter, we followed their route via the US mail system. The excitement was no less than following the Santa Tracker on Christmas Eve. Finally, the phone call came. "Your chicks are here! They can be picked up at the rear door at the main post office on Saturday between 1-2 pm."

We arrived at the locked back door of the post office at the designated time and rang the bell to announce our arrival. For Klaus, the excitement could not have been greater had we been redeeming a winning lottery ticket.

"Can I help you?" came over the intercom.

"Veeee are here to pick up duh baby chicks." Oddly, Klaus was able to speak English at this time. He often delegated speaking to me, saying "I can't speak good enough English, Susanne." But in matters of great urgency to him, such as the delivery of his first flock of chickens, his inhibition was nowhere to be found.

Perhaps he feared that if he left the talking to me, I would turn the chicks away and lock him in the bathroom to sand the sheetrock?

A man in a grey post-office-issued uniform arrived carrying a chirping box that, had it not been labeled "Live Animals," might have warranted suspicion.

Peter grinned ear to ear from his car seat where he held the chirping box on his lap. Once home, we carefully lifted each downy chick into its new home. Klaus and Peter carefully tended to their needs and watched for any sign of illness. Daily they fed and watered them and watched as the down turned to feathers.

Secretly, I wished Klaus would pay this much careful attention to my needs, that he would watch me this closely for signs of distress. Klaus, please see the hairline fractures that are occurring in my composure, I begged inside my head. I need you. I need your help. I need you to be a grown-up. I'm pregnant.

Klaus and Flicka, spring 1992. Klaus building the foundation for the first addition.

Fall 1992, first addition.

Knocking the chimney out of the kitchen.

Klaus, Peter, Sonja, and Alex.

Peter, Sonja, and Alex at home in Northfield.

Klaus, Peter, Sonja, and Alex with my Mother's Day gift from Klaus... a Farmall H.

House after three additions by Klaus, winter 2012.

Sonja and Gabe.

Klaus at the Farmer's
Market in Northfield.
2012.

Wedding Photo, October 20, 1989.

CHAPTER 27

"Can I help you?"

What are they going to think of me? My house?

I was scared to death to let someone into the world of my house and all of its idiosyncrasies. But the seismic activity that exploded from my septic with as much predictability as Old Faithful began to loosen the tight core of shame that prevented me from asking for help. I was out of my league. There was no special wrench that would fix the geyser.

Securing his feet to a tree with a rope, Klaus would hang into the septic to fix the pump every few weeks. His fetid smell would arrive in the house moments before he did letting me know to get out of his way.

"Klaus, I don't want to risk having the septic back up into the house. Could we please have someone come and take a look at it?"

"NEIN." Flying spittle added emphasis and translated as "LEAVE IT." Pride and emotion clouded the definition of "fixed" for Klaus. For ster, and also for me, being fixed means fastening something securely in a permanent position. For Klaus, being fixed meant doing something yourself and not asking for help no matter the circumstances.

Years ago, following a hailstorm with tennis-ball-sized hail, I watched as the houses around us got new roofs one after another. "Klaus, maybe we should call the insurance company too? May we can get a new roof?"

I knew the roof was a mess less from the hailstorm and more so from Klaus's inability to finish it from the upstairs addition. My repeated questions regarding the status of the roof were met with silence. I feared again having to use an umbrella to go to the bathroom. But, at the time, the roof was watertight, and Klaus was not interested in attending to the necessary details related to finishing.

Why did I think I would get anything but a "No vaay" from Klaus?

The hailstorm was my opportunity to have something that was completely done, and I wasn't letting go. Imagine, something done from beginning to end, by a professional who followed code? The possibility was a dream come true for me, and I was giddy at the thought. Three days later I called.

"Klaus?"

He was out back, clearing a fallen tree in the woods. Knowing this wasn't going to go well, I found him outside to keep the argument from the children.

"An insurance adjuster is coming tomorrow to look at the roof."

He froze in place and didn't speak to me for days, staying in bed with the covers pulled up to the bridge of his nose. I know now it was paralyzing shame over his inability to complete a project that prevented him from getting up, speaking, or addressing the problem. Having the insurance adjuster look at the roof was taking him back to the dark musical chairs game his father played while Klaus tried to make sense of the hieroglyphics on the page.

Occasionally I would rant at the bedside but then realized it only served to further deepen his silence.

"Your roof is a mess," the insurance adjuster reported as he was coming down the ladder after only a few minutes. "It will be completely replaced." Ed McMahon could have been on my doorstep, and I would not have been more excited.

Once Klaus realized the house would not be pulled out from underneath him, like the chair by his father, he was eager and onboard, willing to do anything to get the project completed.

Glee at having someone else complete the roof unfortunately did not transfer to other projects needing finishing, and Klaus quickly reverted to digging his creek and fixing the septic every few weeks.

Anger is a normal emotional response when one feels scared or powerless. I felt both. Dammit, Klaus. The anger I felt at him for leaving me with unfinished heaps of messes both inside and out, bubbled dangerously close to the surface. Yet the anger didn't have enough energy to erupt. I had bigger things on my mind.

Hindsight and emotional disconnection have brought some clarity about what prevented Klaus from finishing projects. Was it the fear of failing to impress? Or perhaps subconsciously prolonging the completion of a task or project was one way of avoiding his fear of being harshly evaluated? Or, almost too scary to think about, was he afraid I wouldn't need him anymore after project completion? Or that I could sell the house and move away? Those questions will forever remain unanswered.

Although I couldn't see into the dark septic, I was fairly certain that it, like me, was being held together by a flimsy paper clip and rubber band. Or duct tape. Unwilling to hang headfirst, I was left to deal with the problems of an errant geyser on my property that did not make money with entrance fees.

"I think there is something wrong with my septic system," I said to the man on the phone. My knees were shaking along with my voice. I was certain he was going to laugh at me and tell me there was no help for me.

"My husband just died and my septic is exploding and I'm not sure what to do," I gushed.

"I will send someone out to take a look."

"I am having someone come and take a look at the septic," I announced at dinner. The shoulders of Sonja, Peter, and Alex visibly dropped with relief that a professional was coming out and they would not be involved in the repair process.

Sonja, Peter, and Alex answered the question of "why to live" without a doubt, which made me search for the answer to the next question, "how to live."

The answer to that question came rumbling down my driveway in the form of a large septic truck. "You were really lucky, lady. The whole system was close to breaking down. It's good it came spouting out here rather than backing up into your house."

Knee-deep in shit took on a whole new meaning.

I stopped questioning the meaning of life. I stopped searching for the meaning behind Klaus's death. Searching for answers only increased my desperation.

Instead, I found I was being questioned by life daily. Hourly. Fate had given me an assignment.

It was a miraculous revelation that I could make a call and someone would come and repair something completely, without duct tape, paper clips, or rubber bands, all in one shot, and clean up after themselves to boot.

I lay in my bed and giggled.

Chapter 28

his time the pleading paid off, and Klaus reluctantly left his playground to work in a cabinet shop so that I could have a maternity leave. Or maybe it was the added guilt I had available to me this time around? "You promised to make it up to me, Klaus. Remember?" I invoked the memory from Stuttgart, on my knees and begging him to take a job so that I could stay home with Peter.

Some progress had been made on the house before Sonja arrived in late winter. We were able to move into our bedroom above the kitchen, and Sonja and Peter shared the loft space. There was no carpet, but the roof was tight, there was heat, and it was painted.

I was blissfully happy during my stint as a stay-at-home mother while Klaus reluctantly made fixtures for department stores and salons. His broken English made communication at work difficult. Maybe it was that or the structure that he was expected to conform to that contributed to his unhappiness, but I didn't care. The relief I felt at not being the sole breadwinner was immense, and I was home tending the chickens and doing crafts with Peter, baking bread, and reading about how to use the herbs and edible flowers I would plant in this year's garden.

"I vant goats, Susanne."

Goats were part of Klaus's re-imagination of his grandmother's farm. Making soap and cheese with the milk provided multiple uses for the herbs from the garden, so I was on board. We did our homework and selected French Alpines, a breed that originated in the Swiss mountains and was known for their tolerance of colder climates and the quality of their milk.

"We haff to buy two, Susanne. One goat vill be unhappy."

I wondered if Klaus connected my current happiness to his working an outside job? I wondered if he was as concerned about sustaining my happiness as he was about the happiness of a goat.

So that spring, as Peter and I planted sweet corn seeds along straight lines marked by string pulled taut between two wooden stakes, we were watched over by Sonja, a few months old and sitting in a car seat wearing a floppy purple hat, just outside the garden fence. Sunning themselves alongside her on the picnic table were Pipkin and Buttercup, our two new snow-white French Alpines.

Contrary to popular belief, goats are quite finicky and do not eat anything and everything. Pipkin and Buttercup sauntered past grasses and alfalfa and found the single tree or shrub Klaus had just planted and gnawed off the bark. His cheap fixes had met their match. No matter what Klaus jerry-rigged to keep them contained, they taunted him and crawled over, under, or through, eager to get at the one succulent rose bush or juicy herb he had just planted and mulched.

Pipkin and Buttercup were everywhere, but mostly they liked sitting on the front porch, which offered them opportunities for sun or shade. They shared Peter's favorite spot, the three of them atop the porch wall where they scanned the fields around the house and watched the comings and goings of combines, tractors, and farm implements.

They weren't on the porch on a particularly hot day as Sonja, Peter, and I returned from the local wading pool. "Where are Pipkin and Buttercup?" Peter asked from his car seat, accustomed to them running to greet us as we pulled into the driveway.

We couldn't see them anywhere. Ominously silent, there was no bleating as we got out of the car. I had learned to check on Peter when there was longstanding silence, but I had not yet transferred this knowledge to raising goats.

"I don't know," I responded as I scanned the garden and then Klaus's prized fruit trees.

Perhaps they were behaving for once and staying in their enclosures? Or, even better, perhaps Klaus's latest fence improvements had kept them contained?

Arms full with Sonja in her car seat and wet swimming paraphernalia, I suspected the worst when I saw the front door slightly ajar and a large package just inside. Klaus and I knew to keep the front door tightly closed; the mail carrier didn't.

The porch apparently hadn't provided enough shade on this hot summer day, so they had made themselves at home on the living room furniture. Pipkin, the slightly larger of the two, was sprawled out on the large couch while Buttercup was relaxing in the recliner. Both had lop-sided grins, the kind that only a goat can have. They greeted us with a friendly bleat, taunting me as if to say, "would you like some ccc-oooo-ffffeeeee-e?"

Peter chuckled with glee that the goats had moved in. Sonja, sleeping and unaware, was startled awake by my "GET OUT" shriek and began to cry.

Chairs were tipped and flowers spilled out of their vases as Peter and I chased the goats out of the living room and around the kitchen table before they finally exited through the back door.

The next morning Klaus was out of the driveway before I could ask where he was going.

"Dad must be going to get new fencing material," I said to Peter over waffles. I had been reading about building the best fences and told him about a wire fence that was strong and durable enough for goats.

"You can run an electric wire over the top and bottom to increase the security of the fence," I told him the night before over dinner while Peter regaled him with the story of the goats moving in.

He returned a few hours later, the back of his car full of hoses of all shapes, colors, lengths, and diameters.

My heart dropped to my stomach.

Alongside the hoses were PVC pipes of various lengths but all with a half-inch diameter.

I cautiously asked, "What are you doing Klaus? I thought you were going to work on the fence."

"I hate hauling around duh hoses. I am going to make an irrigation system." He began pounding holes in the hoses with an old hammer and rusty nail. "Do you know there are irrigation hoses that you can buy with holes already in them, Klaus?"

"I von't schpend da money." With that, I put myself into a time-out to keep myself from saying something I later regretted and besides, I already knew that screeching obscenities and laying on guilt didn't work.

I felt trapped in a quagmire of hoses and PVC pipes, all punched full of holes.

A four-spigot faucet was attached to the spigot coming from the well. From each spigot, a hose was attached that directed water to a different place in the yard. Hoses with holes in them were laid in the garden beds. The spigot farthest to the left flowed to the gardens on the south side of the house. Spigot number two went to the chicken coop. It was connected to a hose that went across the lawn and under the clothesline. At the garden gate, the hose garden was attached to a PVC pipe. The PVC pipe went along the top of the picket fence around the perimeter of the garden until it reached the far side of the garden. Here it was attached to another piece of hose (without holes) that permanently hung in the chicken yard.

Spigots three and four went to different areas of the vegetable garden where they were attached to more PVC pipe and hoses that were laid in the garden beds.

All of this existed in Klaus's head without an accompanying diagram. Instructions came out in bits and bobs of English and German mixed together, and it was up to me to organize them into an understanding of how his system worked.

"Klaus, there are irrigation hoses that do the same job in America," I suggested sheepishly.

"I von't spend da money."

The PVC pipes were carefully cut with a hacksaw so they would seal to T-connectors or hoses without leaking.

"Klaus, which way do I have to turn the spigot so it is on?"

"Klaus, why is there no water coming out?"

"Klaus where does this PVC pipe go?"

His mind was expansive with ideas that were crystal clear to him and flowed in as many directions as the water.

"It is disz vay, Susanne. Don't you see?"

"No Klaus, I don't see," I thought silently to myself. You're cutting me apart with a hacksaw, and I'm leaking all over the place. I wondered where the water was going to emerge. I couldn't keep it straight which went where and which way to turn the spigot so it was on. I was forever running to the other end of a hose to see if water was emerging.

My mind was wired for order and a desire was a thriving garden, but I didn't know where the water was going to come out. I wanted things to be as expected. Righty tighty. Lefty loosey. Water on. Water off. Like the long straight rows of corn surrounding our property, I wanted a predictable path for the water with an expected outcome at the end of the hose I was holding.

"Susanne. You can't turn on da vater in all four directions or da flow will be too weak."

It all looked like an astounding riddle to me. I dared not ask my questions and especially dared not laugh. Just like the numerous house projects, the flow was going in all directions, but the force was not enough behind any single one. I was being pulled in as many different directions as the hoses. Sometimes it felt as if the water just stopped in a swampy bog at the edge of a desert and was in danger of drying up.

Our love became tangled in a labyrinth of spigots and hoses going in all different directions, pieces that fit together in ways that made perfect sense to Klaus yet made no sense to me. Sometimes the hoses were leaky. Other times not. Mostly the pieces were put together haphazardly and in ways that I couldn't anticipate.

Our love was on a journey moving through a circuitous Rube Goldberg contraption with individual curves and dangerous hairpin turns. Could someone please remind me where the source of the water is and in which direction it should move? It's important because I am expecting another baby, and I feel like I am breaking.

CHAPTER 29

Electricity. Electrons. Charge. Current. Amps. Resistance. Ohms. Volts. Voltage. Conductors, semiconductors, and insulators. This was the vocabulary of a foreign language I learned Easter morning when the power went out in half of the house.

As a handyman, my job in the electricity department was limited to recognizing deficiencies.

The movement of electrons from one place to another brought up memories of Mr. Gieffer who wore houndstooth-checked gabardine pants while talking in the high school physics lab about what made lights turn on.

I went upstairs to Sonja's bedroom, stood in front of the metal box, and looked at the switches.

"Whenever electrical wiring in the house has too much current flowing through it, the circuits cut the power," Mr. Gieffer's monotone recited in my head. "This protects houses from fire."

When the electricity went off, Klaus flipped the switches back and forth until the lights came back on. He did this many times and still had hair on his head. There was no reason mine was going to be burned to a crisp by doing the same thing, right? I cautiously flipped the first one and ran downstairs to see if any lights had come back on.

Nothing. Connectivity was something I always took for granted. Flip a light switch, and the flow of electrons commenced. The lights turned on without my stopping to think about the complex networks of wires, servers, and circuits that kept bits and bytes flowing. Same thing with the stove and the coffee maker and the pump outside in the wellhouse. Without electricity, there was no water to make coffee or flush the toilet.

With a bit more confidence, I flipped the second switch back and forth. No sizzle coursed through my fingers to the top of my head. Nope. Not that one. The alarm clock was flashing in my bedroom.

I continued flipping switches and running to see if the electricity was restored. The breakers in the same metal breaker box on Jefferson Street were all neatly labeled by my dad with numbers in neat handwriting with a fine-tipped permanent black marker. A corresponding map on the back of the door labeled the location as "downstairs bathroom" or "back bedroom."

Might have been a good idea, Klaus.

Breathless from flipping and running, I stood in front of the breaker box wondering what to do next.

"Hey, Siri. The electricity is off in half of my house." I had equal faith in a credible response from Gabe, but, given that Gabe was now hard of hearing, I waited for my phone to answer.

"Just a minute."

The all-knowing Siri took me to the "Virtual Electrician."

Put some pressure into moving the switch first to OFF. Wait a few seconds and then flip it back into ON.

"That must be it!" I excitedly reported to Gabe. "I'm sure it is going to work this time."

Flip. Push. Wait. Flip again.

Twice for good measure.

Nothing. Nothing. Nothing. The extent of my handyman skills exhausted, I considered whom to call for help.

It was Easter Sunday. Even people who routinely didn't go to church were in church now.

"Now what?" I mumbled to Gabe.

Without electricity, I had no heat or water, and my connectivity to the outside world was equivalent to the length of the life of my cell phone battery which was ominously flashing a "low charge" warning.

For good measure and lack of other ideas, I tried all of the switches once more to see if maybe I hadn't pushed hard enough or waited long enough.

Still nothing.

I wanted my grief to be as neatly ordered and predictable as the breaker box on Jefferson Street. But, all year, sometimes too much current flowed through my wiring and I needed to flip the switch. Not having a map to these stupid switches increased my voltage, and I was reviewing a list of transgressions in my head, which made me furious with Klaus.

How come you didn't label the switches and make a map?

How can you leave behind such a mess to clean up?

How can you leave me behind to grow old without you?

Who is going to plant sunflowers and collect eggs with our grand-children?

How could you not allow me to say goodbye?

Anger at Klaus for those transgressions was fleeting. Mostly I was angry at unsuspecting others.

Why do they get to live?

Why do they get to grow old together?

In the first year, I was focused on filling the hole that was the absence of Klaus. Anger left me feeling depleted and took necessary energy away from my primary focus of survival. What I wanted was to forget the things my heart had committed to memory: the look from Klaus's steel blue eyes, his smell, the feeling of his beard against my cheek, his warm hands that begged to be held to warm mine, his creamed leeks, and his passion for violets that sprouted randomly in the grass. My suffering formed a seal around me and left me no place to go except inside myself where I could safely consider my distress. I wanted to put my truck in forward and not look into the rearview mirror.

Five stages with a beginning, middle, and end were no longer an end goal, and there were no more questions like "Am I in denial? Bargaining?"

Even my previous experiences of death with my parents were different. Their deaths after a long illness were expected. They were my parents and were supposed to die before me.

My mother died over eight long years after being diagnosed with breast cancer, leaving time to go through her clothes and relive memories; time for her to give away her cherished costume jewelry accompanied by a story to provide context; time to breathe deeply into her Lavender-scented hankies with hand-crocheted edges to imprint the familiar smell into my long-term memory. My father died four weeks after being diagnosed with lung cancer, which was still time enough for him to remind me that the Chevy Lumina needed an oil change, for him to recall that he hadn't always been the father he wanted to be, and for him to say "I'm sorry."

Perhaps our brains protect us from that initial shock of grief in year one. Entering the second year, I had survival down pat. I could plan dinner, get groceries and sign permission slips. I made progress on my Ph.D. In the second year, losses I never saw coming startled me. The outside world came creeping in like a low tide asking me to adapt to my new reality. Missing Klaus was going to go on forever, wasn't it? I had floated through year one and now had to get back to the land of the living. I had to figure out how to go to dinner parties alone. Sit in the church pew alone. Go to my childrens' graduations alone. I crashed onto reality shore. I had taken my wedding ring off months ago, signaling to the outside world that I was no longer a Mrs. But who was I now that I was no longer part of a couple?

I wanted my external world to be safe from danger and mishaps. Previously I had looked to Klaus for this. I relied on him for my confidence because I did not trust myself, and the more I relied on him the more self-doubting and insecure I became.

"Do you think Klaus died so that I would have to learn to depend on myself?" I asked Nancy. Nancy rolled her eyes. I had crossed Nancy's therapy boundary.

"You aren't that powerful," she replied.

Would I integrate into my new reality of moving forward in my life? Would I recognize that life would be different without Klaus? Or would I keep dealing with the absence of Klaus rather than returning to the activities of living and establishing life as a single woman?

An electrician couldn't help with my circuit board, but an electrician could help with the half of my house that was without power.

"I know it's Easter Sunday, but I need help."

"I'll be right over."

He had more experience flipping switches than I did and solved the problem in under five minutes.

With that problem solved, I needed to consider the implications of a life without Klaus and ask myself what would my future look like. It was time to answer the looming question: "Are you going to sell your house?"

Klaus's love for this house and property was in my blood. Its idiosyncrasies were warped to my body. I now knew the answer was, "No, I am not going to sell the house."

"You charge by the hour, correct?"

"Yes."

"In that case, could you spend the remainder of the hour teaching me about my house and electricity?"

I began to learn the foreign language of connectivity and groundedness. I began to learn the special language of my house. If I was going to stay in this house, I better learn about circuits and breakers.

KLAUS'S CREAMED LEEKS

This was hands down, my favorite thing that Klaus cooked. I loved them so much I had difficulty stopping. I can still hear Klaus saying, "Susanne, schtopp eating!"

4 tablespoons butter
¼ cup all-purpose flour
½ cup dry white wine (optional)
1/3-1/2 cup heavy cream
Thinly sliced ham (optional)
8 medium leeks, whites, and light green parts only; trim dark green
        ends and save for stock
*cut leeks in half horizontally and rinse thoroughly several times to
        free of sand and grit that gets trapped in the leeks

Once cleaned chop the leeks horizontally into approximately one-inch chunks and simmer in salted water for 5-7 minutes, until tender but still firm. Keep the braising liquid!

While the leeks are simmering, in a shallow pan melt the butter and add the flour making a roux. Slowly add the white wine if using. If not using wine add braising liquid from the leeks. Whisk in enough liquid to make a creamy sauce. Remove the leeks from the cooking liquid with a slotted spoon and add to the sauce. Finish the sauce with cream, salt, and freshly grated nutmeg. Stir in sliced ham if desired and serve over boiled potatoes.

Chapter 30

lowly we inched forward with our house and with our lives. I worked half-time, and Klaus continued to be a reluctant, time-clock-punching employee who followed someone else's agenda. We expected our third baby at the peak of summer.

I worked one week on and one week off. During my stretches off, I loved baking dense rye bread that I started the night before with a sponge to develop deep flavor. Together Peter, Sonja, and I watered the tomatoes, picked green beans, and made goat cheese and goat-milk soap laced with herbs. In the afternoons, I drove Peter to preschool and classes at the zoo while Sonja went to ballet classes or had play dates with friends. I envied the stay-at-home moms and longed to be one of them.

On bad days, I lashed out verbally at Klaus. "If only we had stayed in Germany and you had gotten a job, I could be a stay-at-home mother."

This may or may not have been true, but my unhappiness fueled my resentment. I felt like my parents, longing for what could have been on the other side of the Atlantic. He was unhappy too, working long shifts for little pay and feeling misunderstood as an immigrant.

Klaus's English was improving with the help of television mentors like Martin Yan, Julia Child, and Bob Ross. The largest improvement came from the fact that his coworkers didn't speak German, and he was unable to rely on me to translate. Frustration was deep when his coworkers tried to make him understand by speaking louder rather than showing him or explaining it in another way. Frustration was especially deep when he lacked the vocabulary to respond to questions like "You don't have to pay taxes do you?" He rarely spoke of his unhappiness as it provided fodder for my resentment at having left Germany.

Maternity leave was inching nearer. I anticipated driving Peter to kindergarten every morning and making play dates for Sonja without regard to how well I had slept the night before.

I sensed an impending storm when Klaus's idea of staying home to help me after Alex's birth was building an addition to the house.

"Susanne. I vill make two bedrooms upstairs."

I couldn't argue with that. With another baby coming, we needed another bedroom. But what I wanted now was someone to coddle me a bit after having a baby and a bedroom door hung. Coddling and finishing were not in Klaus's wheelhouse.

The old porch would be torn down and a new porch added, this one with windows so that we could use it earlier in the spring and long into the fall. The loft space that Peter and Sonja were sharing as a bedroom would be extended out over the new enclosed porch and divided down the middle to make two large bedrooms.

Hugely pregnant and still working, I was once again fretfully observing Klaus's idea of a sporting event. He began to tear the old porch down piece by piece. Turns out only a few pieces needed to be removed as the entire thing easily crashed down. The pillars were rotten at the top and held on by a nail or two at the bottom. With a few well placed blows of a hammer and a sneeze from Klaus, the porch was in a heap.

Klaus's blows to the house were soul-crushing to me, and I felt as if I was close to falling into a heap. Klaus, could you please do the laundry and perhaps rub my chubby, swollen feet that I could no longer see? But we still lacked the relational skills to negotiate what we needed.

My water broke in the school supply section while considering the value of a 32-pack of crayons versus the 64-pack that came with a sharpener. I was thrilled with Alex's early arrival which extended my maternity leave by three weeks.

Klaus took two weeks off work and rented a backhoe to coincide with my discharge from the hospital.

Instead of seeing the need to support my foundation, he saw the need to pour a new foundation.

"I haff to pour duh concrete, Susanne, while I am at home mit you."

While Klaus was focused on digging footings twelve inches deep, the cracks in my foundation were in danger of splitting open.

Peter was thrilled to sit in the backhoe and was kept busy with Klaus digging the foundation for the addition while I adapted to my role as the mother of three. The cement truck came the day before Klaus was going back to work. At least when Klaus went back to work, I was able to get some rest and respite from large machinery.

Outside walls quickly went up on the weekends after Klaus went back to work. Windows purchased from a salvage store were lined up and ready to be installed.

"Klaus, they are predicting an early winter. When will you get the windows installed?"

"Jaja, Susanne." The rest of the unspoken sentence was "I will get it done in my way and in my own time. Don't push me."

The inches we were moving forward turned to millimeters when Klaus decided to move the garage.

"You want to do what?" His head was in the car trunk removing the nuts that held the jack in place, his urgency to get started so great that he hadn't taken the time to remove the PVC pipes from the trunk. The red flag tied on the end of PVC pipes, meant as a warning for fellow travelers on the road between our house and the hardware store, was taunting me. What danger was it predicting?

Mumbling with a pronounced German accent came from the trunk. I thought I heard the words "garage" and "move." I could not possibly have heard him correctly. After all, his head was inside the trunk.

I had been talking about getting rid of the old, single-car garage that was awkwardly situated in the middle of the driveway. It was in the way, and we weren't using it, except to store junk. The garage also had bad juju. Rumor had it that someone had left the car running in that garage and taken their life decades ago. Hard to believe now that the garage was once that airtight. We could get rid of the junk. Someone down the road collected old buildings and resold them, so it would be easy enough to get rid of the garage, except, of course, that Klaus was emotionally attached to the old trampoline poles and wide gauge wire fencing that was stored there. And innovative projects that cost no money and kept him from making progress on the house were a source of vital energy, for Klaus. If only he was so urgent and passionate about projects that were important to me, I thought.

"I am going to move the garage." That eliminated all possibility of my having misheard. This would have been perfectly fine had we needed the garage and Klaus had nothing else to do, like creating trusses for the roof so that we could open the wall to the new addition and make the space livable. My heart sank to the center of the earth. But I was walking the tightrope of knowing that if I was too vehement in speaking my wishes, that would make Klaus's heels dig in even deeper.

He wanted to singlehandedly move the garage to the other side of the driveway. "We can use it someday. For storage or a workshop." That was what he said, and those were his honest intentions. Inside my mind, I was screaming, "To store more shit you bring home from the junkyard? and "Do you spend your time dreaming up projects that will infuriate me?"

"Are you kidding me?" is what came out of my mouth as liquid comes out of a funnel. "Let's burn it down. It has bad juju."

"I can use it to store my tools."

"It's in the way."

"It's still a good building. We can't just get rid of it."

"There is someone up the road who buys old buildings and resells them."

Nothing. Klaus won. I succumbed. The story of my life.

I fumed. I just wanted things organized, or at the very least a path through the chaos that was my life.

The roof was somewhat completed and the porch windows fused shut to save time, Klaus began to empty the garage, moving his treasures to another outbuilding.

My insistence only fueled his indignation. When I felt external uncertainty and discord, I wanted to burn things down. When Klaus felt external uncertainty and discord, he dug in deeper. When I felt inner discord, I ranted. When Klaus felt inner discord, he went to bed and pulled the covers over his head. Neither one of us was able to listen to the other. What was in our power to change?

"You are never going to be able to pull this off, you know."

My doubt only fueled his indignation and commitment to the challenge. I began to acknowledge the powerlessness I felt and started looking for ways to fuel my fire.

"Would you like a career in teaching?" the small postcard said. Teaching would allow me to practice my profession in its ideal form, which appealed to me as I became more and more disillusioned with the healthcare system. I was also worried about my future. With Klaus's inconsistent employment, I had to be sure my financial future was secure, and I wasn't sure that I could keep working as a bedside nurse until retirement age. Apply now and you can start in two weeks, the card teased. I had never considered a fully online educational program, but I called for information and in two weeks found myself logging on to a master's program in Nursing Education.

As I was learning to use the drop box and participate in online discussion forums, Klaus began using a car jack to elevate the single-car garage, held together by hundred-year-old nails off of rocks farmers had picked from their fields, which served as the foundation. PVC pipes of various diameters were placed underneath, and the garage, now nicknamed Inchworm, was pushed to its final destination about fifty feet away.

We were both inching forward in our realities. Klaus started a handyman business. I started advancing my education.

CHAPTER 31

My life had a steady escape of gas with an extinguished pilot light. Dread of a future without Klaus eclipsed the ability to find joy in the present. Headaches and extreme fatigue were daily physical responses to Klaus's absence. One day, when the fatigue was especially bad, I was lying on the couch when Sonja came home.

The question "How was your day?" had long since been replaced with "Can I do anything for you, Mom?"

"Could you please get me a couple of Tylenol and a glass of water, Sonja? Could you also check the refrigerator and see what smells in there?"

I felt as if I were suffocating. I wished I could open the windows, but they remained fused shut. I made a mental reminder to figure out how to open them and add the necessary hardware so they could stay open. The fresh air would be welcome.

Klaus's death was sudden, harsh, and disorienting. I was working to understand what had happened. It was not the kind of death that occurred over a wide threshold that granted time to prepare for death, honor wishes, and anticipate life without the loved one as my mom's had.

Klaus's sudden death was translated by many into a comfort.

"At least he didn't suffer."

"He died doing what he loved."

"He didn't know what hit him."

While that was all certainly true for Klaus, I was dealing with the trauma of how he died. Suffering formed a seal around me and left me nowhere to go except inside myself, where I could safely consider my distress from all angles.

"I'm so tired," I told Nancy at my weekly appointment from the teal couch. "I just can't seem to find any energy." It didn't make any sense. In the final stages of my dissertation, I no longer worried about milestones and approvals. It was the peak of summer, and I wasn't teaching. There was no physical explanation for my extreme fatigue.

Did I have complicated grief? Prolonged grief? Did I experience profound impairment after the loss of my husband? Or did I just have garden-variety grief that needed time?

Or was I depressed? Did I need to be medicated? I checked my list of symptoms against the Diagnostic and Statistical Manual for Mental Disorders as I prepared a lecture on depression for the coming semester.

Grief: There is a recognized loss.

Depression: There may or may not be an identified loss.

Answer: Grief. Klaus was exuberant, a void that I struggled to fill and a void for which denial was never an option. For months after his death, my physical body reacted to his absence with pain on my right side which is where he should have been standing.

Grief: There is physical exhaustion. The body is allowed to collapse and the grieving admit to exhaustion.

Depression: Often accompanied by unnecessary physical risk. Increased vulnerability to illness due to lack of sleep.

Answer: Grief. I was exhausted and wanted to sleep all the time. Sometimes I just couldn't make it another five minutes without a rest, and I called on our good friend Hortense, who lived just down the hill from my office. "Can I come over, Hortense?" was code for "I need an emergency nap on your overstuffed dark red couch." It took just about the same amount of time to go down the hill as for water to boil. By the time I arrived, tea was steeping next to the sofa. Hortense's presence was enough. All I wanted was to collapse without someone telling me how strong I was.

Grief: Focus is on the preoccupation with the deceased and the implications of the loss and the future.

Depression: Focus is on persistent, distorted, and negative perceptions of the self.

Answer: I don't know. While I focused on the loss of Klaus and fear of my future—how would I take care of this house alone—everything came back to me beating myself up for not having the necessary skills for surviving and, dare I say, thriving.

Grief: Moods are ever-changing; moving from anger to sadness to equanimity in the same day.

Depression: Withdrawal and despair; being stuck.

Answer: Depended on the day.

Grief: Focus on spiritual connection.

Depression: Focus on the unfairness of the loss and persistent failure to find purpose; why me?

This was a tough one and elicited the least helpful responses from the well-meaning around me: "There is a purpose in everything. You may not know it now but someday you will find meaning in Klaus's death."

Not helpful.

"Think of the wonderful Christmas Klaus is having in heaven with Jesus."

Not helpful.

Answer: I have no idea. But one thing was for sure; I would not go down the slippery existential slope of looking for a purpose in Klaus's death.

I posed the question to Nancy.

Do you think I am depressed? Or just grieving?

Do you think I need anti-depressants?

Picking the dry skin on her foot was Nancy's way of quickly getting me to extrapolate in hopes of diverting her activity.

"Tell me what you have been doing."

Nancy skillfully began tracing the breadcrumbs in my mind, following them toward possible causes of my fatigue.

"I am cleaning out the outbuildings."

Nancy knew about the chaos that existed in the outbuildings and my inability to deal with the disorder.

"It is no wonder you are tired!" came from Nancy's chair on the other side of the room. I always appreciated her clarity when something was really serious.

My strong "do not ask for help neuroses" motivated by the false belief that anti-depressants would mask feelings and prolong the grief process, were still on a ridiculous mission to work through the grief process to "be done" and "move on."

"You're dealing with Klaus's emotional baggage and the effect that baggage had on your relationship." When Nancy said impactful things, I just wanted to lie down on the couch and close my eyes instead of sitting in my usual position, legs crossed and hugging a small pillow. A loud roaring took over inside of my head, Nancy's voice now far away.

"I'm doing that thing when I have trouble hearing what you are saying," was her cue to slow down and give me time to focus on her voice rather than the voices in my head.

"Two metal desks. Free." I made a sign.

Four simple words started the cascade and brought me into the world of metal collectors. Two dump trucks full of stuff from the outbuildings went to them. All I had to do was say yes or no to what they pointed at. A group of college men advertised as "hunks hauling junk" came next. This time, I was doing the pointing, and, without even an abracadabra, whatever I pointed at disappeared.

The hunks followed my pointing index finger to the garage, the machine shed, the wellhouse, and the basement. The trampoline poles, the hospital bed, and the old pipes were gone. All gone. It was nothing short of a miracle.

I dutifully swallowed the three Tylenol that Sonja held out in her palm. "Umm, Mom. There is nothing rotten in the fridge. You left the oven on and the pilot light is out. No wonder you have a headache."

Chapter 32

*S*itting next to the window in a Pizza Hut on the Rotebühlplatz, I
nursed a dark beer and watched bundled Germans hurriedly tending to their Christmas errands. Thick mittens, hats pulled over their
ears to prevent ear infections, and scarves tightly woven around their
necks to cover any bare skin left at the closing of their warmest winter
coats, it was just cold enough for my Minnesotan self to be wearing a
mid-weight jacket and thin gloves to walk down the Königstrasse from
the Stuttgarter Weinachtsmarkt. I was in Germany with Sonja and Alex
visiting Klaus's parents.

The Christmas Market in Stuttgart is one of my favorite places. It is
not only one of the most beautiful Christmas markets in all of Europe
but also one of the oldest. It was officially mentioned for the first time
in 1692, but its roots stretch back farther. The elaborately decorated

wooden huts wind through the downtown cobblestone streets of Stutt-gart with intoxicating smells of sugar-roasted almonds, Lebkuchen, and smoky sausages twisting among the many visitors.

I was feeling nostalgic and melancholy from the Glühwein. My favorite hut from which to buy the hot mulled wine was on the Schil-lerplatz where it was ladled from large copper vessels with sliced oranges studded with whole cloves floating on top. The heady scent was enough to intoxicate. This stand was well known by locals. Businessmen in long wool coats stood next to the large statue of the poet, philosopher, and historian for whom the square was named. Cigarette in one hand and mug of hot wine in the other, they huddled together, brainstorming business deals with Fredrich Schiller looking over their shoulder.

Sonja was under the table, still in her embroidered wool cape, matching beret now thrown on the short red bench next to me, boots kicked off. She was exhausted from the crowds and excitement of riding the children's train and small Ferris wheel on the Schlossplatz. Potato pancakes and applesauce failed to sustain her, and we were waiting for the familiarity of Pizza Hut. Alex had stayed back with his Oma and Opa, playing with blocks and trucks and being schooled on how not to make a mess. Klaus had stayed in Minnesota with Peter, who could not miss school. I hoped Klaus was working on finishing the kitchen floor project that had been ongoing that fall. Lord knows he had the time. He was laid off again. I hoped I didn't have to deal with mismatched plywood underlay, unopened tubes of grout, and stacked tiles for Christmas.

"I have a surprise for you when you get home," he had said on the phone just that morning, fueling my hopes that he was making progress on at least one of the unfinished projects.

"Mochtest Du auch Käse Pizza?" Sonja asked her new stuffed animal in her child's German.

She was sitting under the table with the stuffed toy I had just bought her at Spielwaren Kurtz. Sonja was the same age as I was when I made my first trip to the multilevel toy store on the Marktplatz to climb the stairs to the third floor which held the Märklin model railway supplies. We were visiting my mother's mother; that time, however, it was summer and I, with three braids and red lederhosen with hearts for pockets, was exhausted from the heat and from dancing to polka music at the Sommerfest. My Dad needed Esbit fuel blocks to run his steam engines at home and became lost in nostalgia looking at the model railways. My Oma Barbara took me back down to the first floor and bought Pustefix and together we stood on the Marktplatz blowing bubbles and waiting for my parents. It was one of the only opportunities she had to make memories with me.

Now, thirty years later, I was filled with nostalgia and had my own four-year-old in tow. Sonja and I stayed on the first floor with the dolls, Pustefix, stuffed animals, and hand-carved wooden toys. She had seen the stuffed Dalmatian puppy and fallen in love. There was no leaving the puppy behind.

"Mama!" It was Sonja calling me back from my daydreams to place and time.

"We got a cheese pizza, right?"

"Yes, Sonja. Plain cheese."

Looking into my beer, I thought about my life. I was unsatisfied. My needs and wishes lay so deeply buried that I could barely access them. Shame kept me from identifying my needs and asking for them to be met. I was stuck in the toxicity of my frustration.

Klaus loved me deeply; there was no doubt about that. But neither he nor I could see out of our whirlwind of neuroses to meet the other's needs.

I loved Klaus but wasn't being taken care of in the way that I needed in a relationship. I wanted to know what it was like to share financial responsibilities in a relationship. Klaus's choices made him feel better instead of meeting my needs for safety and security. I can only assume that my choices felt similarly selfish to him, but those are questions that I will never be able to ask and problems I will never be able to address.

I had waited years for him to reach out and say, "I see you." Our love was trapped in his steady diet of dreams that I did not share. How could I love this man so and yet feel like the ocean that once separated us was again sloshing between us?

I returned home and, instead of progress on the kitchen floor, I found an extended greenhouse built onto the old window that was facing south in the kitchen. Additional old windows from the junkyard were propping up a wooden box filled with dirt and ready for spring seedlings in a few weeks. "Look, Susanne, vat I did!" Proud as a five-year-old, he was anxious to receive a gold star for a job well done. I tripped over a tube of grout on the way to admire the window garden. On the outside, I pretended everything was okay and feigned excitement to start tomato and bell peppers well before the outside gardening season. On the inside, I mourned that my kitchen floor wasn't finished and tubes of grout stood between the Christmas tree and the kitchen.

Instead of voicing my discontent, I buried it and went on. The large empty rectangle inside myself was growing and bumping against my insides.

CHAPTER 33

Standing between me and a cozy reading corner on the front porch were the three walls of fused windows and the boat Klaus had started to build years ago. The unfinished dinghy lay upside down filling the porch. A blanket of heavy air and old intentions suffocated me every time I needed my hiking boots. It was time for fresh air and ventilation. Peak-of-summer humidity levitated from the door when I opened it, and I squeezed through the crack to get to the windows, careful not to trip over the boat. I feared that soon my shoes would start baking their own bread.

Klaus didn't share German enthusiasm and national devotion for crisp air circulation and lüften. Germans are obsessed with lüften, the art of ventilating their homes. Considered a key measure for good respiratory hygiene, Germans often crack open windows to let nasty, stale air out and fresh air in, even in the dead of winter.

To open the windows, I first needed to know what secured them firmly to their casing. Putty? Paint? Nails? Screws? Sheer German determination and will? A crowbar seemed too aggressive. Maybe a putty knife? I carefully slid a putty knife between the bead and the window sash to cut through the paint seal and carefully peeked into the dark crack. No nails or screws. Maybe just glue? Or were they painted shut?

I pushed a little harder and the window gave way, loosening its hold on the casing. Working my way around the window, I pushed and pried against the old adhesive and paint as allowed fresh air to pour into the porch.

Was it retribution that I kept Klaus locked in the car trunk this long?

Nancy had, finally, after many months, convinced me that hanging on to Klaus's ashes would not solve past hurts. I was leaving in the morning for Germany and giving half of Klaus to his parents. That meant I had to get him out of the trunk.

Fraction of an inch by fraction of an inch I carefully opened the trunk of my Nissan Versa, half expecting Klaus to leap out at me like a Jack-in-the-Box and screech at me for burning his half-finished boat.

There he was, snuggled in between the jumper cables and the reusable shopping bags just where I left him, the velvet bag barely dusty. I carefully lifted him out of the trunk and took him to our beloved garden to separate him: half for Germany, half for America. The Germany half went into a transparent Rubbermaid container with a screw-on lid to hold him securely in place. Silvery fragments of Klaus scattered in the garden and landed on the blooming gladiolas. The Germany half went into my backpack. The America half crossed over the threshold of the house. I tucked him safely into the bathroom closet.

I could feel the weight of Klaus's ashes pushing through my backpack as I passed through airport security in Minneapolis and then through German customs on the other side of the Atlantic.

The end connected to the beginning as I took the ashes out of my bag and passed them through tears and over cake and fine china to his parents. Lifelong knots deep inside me loosened, and I realized that grief is an intimate connection to the expression of love for the person who is no longer there to express it. I left Germany and wondered what else I was leaving behind. Perhaps I was also freed from a version of the truth I had carried inside me for so long that it defined me.

I returned home and as I sat down with a book on the front porch, I reflected on how I had changed while I was gone, fresh air from the open windows lifting my spirits.

Chapter 34

the recession was making a dent in Klaus's handyman business, which led to a dangerous surplus of free time. Fall was usually his busiest season, but this year the phone rarely rang requesting the cleaning of gutters or sealing of windows. Limited by his promises to not tear off any more sections of the roof or cut holes into our house, he dreamed of other possibilities. The numerous unfinished projects failed to garner his attention or fascination. I now knew that begging him to finish a project most often backfired.

In hindsight, perhaps we should have completed a prenuptial agreement defining "done" in terms of house projects. The contractual agreement would include components required for a project to be considered completed along with timelines. Initiation of new projects was prohibited without meeting the contractual requirements.

His self-esteem plummeted along with his outside income. "Klaus, you have made so much money by doing things in our house. You can't make money any faster than when you do something yourself." I was trying to bolster him up and let him know it was okay to not start a new project. But before I knew it, he was planning a renovation of the downstairs bathroom.

Germans love bathrooms, and Klaus was no exception. After creating the upstairs bathroom according to his vision, it was time to recreate the downstairs bathroom to his rigorous German expectations.

The first order of business would be getting rid of the bathtub.

"Showering in da bathtub is a veerd American dhing. I hate dat." In Germany, showers are tile or glass stalls, and there is always a squeegee somewhere inside the stall that comes with the expectation that you clean your shower stall before you towel off to prevent dreaded water spots. Doing chores in the nude first thing in the morning: only in Germany.

Bathrooms in Germany also don't have fans. Instead, they all have windows that open. Regardless of the season, you open your window while showering or risk having a dank black mold-infested bathroom. The breeze that is pleasant in summer can get a little arctic in January in Minnesota, especially considering the German expectation that while showering you turn on the water, get wet, then turn it off. Lather up, turn the water back on, and rinse. All of this is done quickly to use as little water as possible. Water is expensive in Germany. American showering was a practice Klaus never adopted.

"Turn off da vater," he would yell from outside the bathroom door. "Can't you go and empty the dishwasher instead of lurking outside the shower?" I screamed in my head. In reality, I kept my mouth shut and the water on, pretending I didn't hear him. It was an ongoing contest of wills that remained a conflict and never reached a solution, a problem we never worked on, like so many areas of our married life.

"Klaus, can you finish up the trim in the stairway and fix the sagging ceiling tile in the bedroom before you begin another project?" The sagging ceiling tile, along with the insulation drooping out, was interrupting my transition to peaceful sleep. The amount of internal energy I used up being angry about the sagging insulation so far exceeded the amount of energy it would have taken to push it up and screw the ceiling tile tight. I had asked so many times that "please" was no longer included in the sentence, hoping that my request sounded stern enough for him to finally get a ladder and drill and follow through. "Maybe we could start with the bathroom next spring." I was up to my eyeballs in a master's thesis, student teaching, and two jobs. "I would like to take the winter off, Klaus."

Was it ironic that my master's thesis was on active learning? Could I transfer similar principles to active home repair?

"Ach, but Susanne," he pleaded, eager to demonstrate his worth by starting yet another project. I looked at those bright blue begging eyes. It was as if my five-year-old was begging for a Ritter Sport bar at the German import store.

I was also worried about my dad.

"Could you come over during fall break to help me with the yard?" My dad might as well have been a matador waving a red flag in a bull ring to alert me to danger. It was the first time my father had ever asked for help. "Of course," I responded. "We'll be there on Friday morning and stay for the weekend." He had been complaining of feeling tired and short of breath for a few weeks but nothing serious enough to ask for help. Was it his heart? It had been more than ten years since his bypass surgery. Or was it a recurrence of the depression that he had suffered on and off for much of his life? It had been four years since my mom died. His depression had worsened after her death, but now he seemed to be doing well, outwardly at least. He was cooking, cleaning, and driving my mother's friends to their weekly hairdresser appointments. Just a few weeks ago he had lifted his shirt in my kitchen. "Look!" He proudly showed me darts he had sewn in his pants to take them in. A threat of a diabetes diagnosis had put him on the straight and narrow with no carbs or no sugar.

Klaus remained insistent on beginning the bathroom remodeling.

"It vill be fine, Susanne." Those were fighting words. I had heard the same words before standing at the top of an Alp in southern Germany before we were married. "Disz vaay," he yelled over his shoulder. He was already ten feet ahead of me, excited about the possibilities that lay ahead. The sign "Trittsicherheit und Schwindelfreiheit unbedingt erforderlich," stopped me. "Klaus," I yelled after him, already not dizzy-free from the height and reading the sign. "I am not an experienced climber, and I am not sure-footed."

"It vill be fine, Susanne." Off he ran. "They alvays say dat," he yelled over his shoulder. So, I followed him. Within ten feet, I was clinging to a cable on the side of a mountain, my feet barely touching gravel, screaming "FUCK YOU" into a canyon.

After this many years of marriage, I no longer had the energy to scream expletives at Klaus. But I thought them as we rocked the old and crusty bathtub out of the corner.

"I promise I will have the bathroom done in a few weeks." The plan was to complete the demolition, help my dad for the weekend and then begin work on rebuilding.

He didn't intend to disappoint me. He wanted me to be happy. He intended to finish projects and keep his promises, and he felt bad when he didn't. But he was a victim of his creative mind, which kept hijacking his attention to other new and shiny projects and objects, and nothing could divert his attention faster than a sailboat. Currently, there was a boat building project underway in the front porch and a sailboat renovation going on outside the back door. Neither was finished. The furniture I bought for the front porch remained boxed up and pushed against the wall, along with my vision of rocking in the wicker chair while drinking coffee and watching the sunrise.

In the papers waiting to be organized and my student teaching, I found my passion, my voice, and a vision for my future. I could not allow those dreams to be punctured. They were my lifeline.

"Shouldn't we turn off the water, Klaus, before we remove the bathtub? And maybe the electricity too?"

"You always vorry too much, Susanne." True. I was an expert worrier. But things like uncontrolled water and the potential for electrical shocks in the same place and possibly at the same time seemed to warrant worry. This time he complied. Forward and back on the creaking flooring, we rocked in sync with each other and the bathtub. Forward and back. Decades of caulk holding the bathtub in place loosened, tearing the striped wallpaper. Forward and back. Cracking of tile. Dust from the grout. Forward and back. We paid careful attention to the rhythm so the bathtub would come out straight from the wall rather than be wedged in the corner. Finally, with a large surge of bathtub energy, a cloud of dust, and a combination of smells I never wanted to smell again, we were thrown against the opposite wall. It seemed to me that this is what decades of death would smell like if the smell could be contained in place and time, perhaps under a bathtub. Thankfully there were no petrified squirrels to be found. Sneezing and gagging, we carried the bathtub into the yard.

The water heater came out next, a new one was on standby so we would not be without hot water for more than a few days. Next came the toilet. I started by flushing the toilet to get the water out of the tank, holding down the handle until the water stopped draining. My mind was often like this, thoughts swirling tighter and tighter the closer the swirls got to the drain. My thoughts would descend along with the swirling water, and I would not have the motivation to lift my finger off the triggering handle. With a sponge, I soaked up any remaining water to prevent nasty spillage. Klaus was often the one to pick up the nasty spillage when the spiral of my thoughts swirled tightly in an ever-downward spiral. "It vill be okay," he said into my ear, knowing the exact spot to stroke at the base of my skull to provide primal reassurance.

"Be careful!" Klaus admonished as we disconnected the water supply from the tank and the tank from the bowl. "We can maybe use disz again." I could practically feel him thinking, "everything will be ok if I keep a lot of stuff and have it piled high around me."

"Susanne, disz vill be our Masterpiece!" He always had big ideas, but his excitement at the beginning of a project was no longer contagious.

The flooring came out; mirrors and vanity were detached from the wall. We measured for a custom glass door for the shower so Klaus wouldn't have to fight with the flimsy shower curtain, something he hated almost as much as showering in the tub. An inch wider and the glass door would have hit the opposite wall when we opened it.

The bathroom was bare and ready for construction, which would begin after helping my dad for the weekend. We headed to New Ulm on Friday morning, stopping as was tradition, at Casey's gas station for donuts for us and a *Star Tribune* for my dad.

He was standing at the stove as we came in the back door. "The box says cook for seven minutes, but the spaghetti isn't done yet. What should I do?" He was making lunch for us. The canned sauce was stove side and ready to be heated as soon as the pasta was done. "Just cook it a little longer, Dad."

After lunch, we began raking and mulching leaves. Dad tried mowing the lawn but then sat in a lawn chair, too short of breath to continue. By Monday morning, the shortness of breath was accompanied by pain in his right shoulder so severe he could not pull his shirt over his head. I called my brother as we headed to the local emergency department. "I am worried about Dad." Instead of heading in for hospital rounds, he met us at the emergency department in New Ulm.

My brother and I exchanged places with a short hand-off report. Klaus and I returned home so Sonja, Peter, and Alex wouldn't miss the entire school day. I was scheduled to student teach my first class, "Care of the Laboring Patient," that afternoon. And we were down hot water and one bathroom. Just as I was walking into class, my brother called. "They're transporting Dad to Abbott Northwestern. They need to do more tests."

The phone rang again just as I was walking in to teach my second class, "Care of the High-Risk Laboring Patient."

"It is lung cancer," my brother said.

"What did you just say?" I asked, not sure I heard correctly over the chatter from the students heading into class.

"Lung cancer." My dad, who had quit smoking before I was born over forty years ago, had lung cancer? This wasn't possible. We had all assumed it was his heart. Lung cancer had never even crossed my mind.

"Are you still there?" my brother asked into the silent phone receiver. I was dumbstruck and devastated. A squeak provided the necessary evidence of my existence on the other end of the phone line. "The prognosis is not good." My dad was dying.

I taught my class and then went home to absorb the news and tell Klaus and the kids before heading up to the hospital. I found Klaus just finishing up the installation of the water heater. He had also ordered the drywall and tiles, vanity, and toilet for finishing up the bathroom.

It seemed there was no component of my life in which there was some semblance of order or control.

"My dad is dying. It's lung cancer." He bundled me up in his arms so that I could snuggle in and cry. I got the first round of tears out before the kids got off the bus. I told them their Opa had cancer but spared them the gravity of his diagnosis. Better to hear it over some time, I thought. As soon as we got them settled in at home, we headed up to the hospital.

"I want to go home" were my dad's first words as we walked into the hospital room. "I can get treatment in New Ulm." The plan was for radiation to control the pain and then chemotherapy to shrink the tumors. The care was palliative. Cure was not part of the discussion.

He could return home the day after tomorrow.

Throughout the years, my dad had said over and over, often enough that it was ingrained in me, "no matter what, I am going to die in this house." My brother and I committed to this plan and agreed we would do whatever was necessary to make this happen. As both of us had incomes that were depended on, we turned to Klaus, who was currently without a job.

We made a plan to care for my dad at home, Klaus being the primary caregiver and my brother and I, providing relief.

The bathroom would have to wait.

Anticipating my father would die, I was working frantically to finish my master's thesis, due just before Christmas.

The day before Thanksgiving, I was relieving Klaus at my dad's. My Dad was in hospice, but still getting up to go to the bathroom, eat, and converse. My paper was done save for final edits. The strewn-about papers were organized into a folder. I wanted to be able to focus on my dad.

Gabe, accustomed to special treats as soon as he came in the back door, rushed into the house looking for my dad. The medicinal smell from my childhood home-turned-hospice burned my nose as I walked through the door. Gabe ran from room to room, looking in all the usual places. He wasn't expecting to find my dad in the back bedroom in a hospital bed. Gabe, who had long been unable to jump onto a bed because of arthritic hips, found it in himself and took a long leap, and snuggled in at my dad's side. "Oh, Gabe," was my dad's response as Gabe greeted him with a slobbery wet lick across the face. Gabe pushed his 20-pound body against my dad, absorbing what energy and pain he could. "Hallo Susile," my dad said, reaching for my hand. I bent to kiss his warm cheek. "You look good!" And he did. There was color on his face and a small smile.

"Klaus kommt morgen mit die Kinder" I said. The plan was for Klaus to join me tomorrow with the children, bringing Thanksgiving dinner in a magic box from the grocery store. The box included all of the necessary components of the meal in heat-and-serve packages. I wanted to have Thanksgiving Dinner together, likely our last one.

Thankfully, the hospice nurse diverted my attention before I broke down crying. I didn't want my dad to see me cry.

"How are we going to manage until the spring?" I asked her.

"This isn't going to last long," was her response. "He's going downhill fast."

I could and couldn't believe it. A month ago, he was sitting outside watching us mow the lawn. But he wanted to be with my mom, and he wanted to die in his home. He had had enough and told us so after his first chemo treatment put him in the hospital with severe side effects. "No more," he said resolutely. "I know what's coming, and I am ready."

I settled into the Lazy Boy next to my dad and Gabe to watch a *Gunsmoke* rerun and knit. I opened the window a crack to exchange unusually warm, late autumn air with stuffy, medicinal air. The late afternoon sun was shining in through the window. My dad woke up looking for Klaus.

"Wo ist Klaus?" He needed to go to the bathroom. His pride intact he wanted Klaus to help him to the bathroom rather than me. "Klaus kommt morgen wieder."

I helped him to the bathroom a few steps away and safely returned him to Gabe's side. I put some drops to ease his breathing under his tongue along with some pain medication.

The cuckoo clock ticked in time with the regular breathing of someone in a deep sleep. With each episode of *Gunsmoke*, the cuckoo clock's ticking became drowned out by the breathing that was becoming louder, raspier, and irregular.

At some point in the breathing, cuckoo, and perpetual *Gunsmoke* cycle I fell asleep. When I woke in the wee hours of the morning, the TV screen was static and the only audible sound that remained was the ticking of the cuckoo clock. My dad had died. His last spoken words had been asking for the man he had so vehemently opposed having in his life.

CHAPTER 35

"Mom, there's a loose tile." Sonja made this seemingly innocent comment after a morning shower. What could be wrong with a loose tile that was only 1 inch in diameter?

After all, Klaus had redone this bathroom not long before he died. My memories and the scars of his innovative approaches to home repair had faded enough to prevent me from even considering what could be lurking behind that tiny tile.

It was just before Christmas.

Only half listening, I postponed attending to the loose tile until after the prime rib had been served and the holiday dishes were put away.

"Just put it back, Sonja, and we'll deal with it after Christmas." How bad could it be?

Each Christmas was getting a little easier. This was the fourth one without Klaus. The memories were not quite so vivid or painful. With each Christmas came decisions about which traditions we would keep and new ones would we make. We no longer lit real candles on the Christmas tree on Christmas Eve, Christmas Day, and New Year's Eve. We no longer had a bucket of water in the living room for a possible fire resulting from burning candles on a live Christmas tree. The small weighted holders full of drips from the natural beeswax candles we specially bought at the Stuttgart Christmas market were still safely tucked into a box from Klaus's last Christmas in case we changed our minds.

After Christmas, though, I turned my attention to the tile. Surely this was an easy fix with a little glue, a simple adhesive that prevents things from falling apart. I just had to be sure the others would stay put too. Surely there was some special waterproof adhesive made just for this. I would buy the most expensive one to insure a long intact life for my shower floor. The tile was still in good shape and could be reused. Using my sharpest kitchen knife I chipped away at the old adhesive.

Ah, but I can't forget the grout. Once I glued the tile in place, I would have to refill the cracks around the replaced tile to make it watertight. Such a small amount was needed that I decided it warranted a trip to the basement to make sure there was no leftover grout that I could use. A trip to the basement was not taken lightly; it had been close to a decade since I had descended into that frightening place, even scarier than The Mailbox. Going To The Basement was close to the top of the List of Things That Scare Me. Descending the narrow cement stairs required ducking to avoid hitting the ceiling and a constant sweeping motion with my left arm to prevent running headfirst into cobwebs. My bent right arm shielded my face from the monsters I was sure were lurking there.

Found it. All of the grout was included in a Klaus Organizational System: a Rubbermaid container without a lid. "Without a lid" is significant as it means there was the possibility of a dead mouse that had searched the container for food and had been tragically trapped in its contents and unable to climb out. A quick large breath through my mouth, to avoid the musty basement and possible dead mouse smell hitting the sensory fibers of my nose, and I shuffled through the plastic tubs. No mouse, thank God. Also, no tan grout. My trip to the scary darkness having been in vain, I quickly scrambled up the stairs and, in my haste to leave The Scary Place, I forgot the imperative sweeping motion and found cobwebs tangling with my hair.

Pre-mixed grout in tubes resembling large tubes of toothpaste would save me time. I could rely on my many years of experience of squeezing just the right amount of toothpaste. "I hope they still have grout that matches," I thought. At that point, mismatched grout lines on my shower floor were my biggest concern. A little adhesive and a little grout and voila! An intact shower floor done in one afternoon with only one trip to the hardware store.

Therapy was providing the necessary adhesive to hold my pieces together. There was no easy path forging through the darkness, but I could feel my positivity increasing. Therapy focused on solving the day-to-day issues of raising my children as a single parent. But I was still so tired. A couple of years had passed; I had car keys; the bank account had no "and" behind my name; I paid the bills; food was in the refrigerator and on the table. These all proved to the outside world that I was surviving. When I doubted my abilities, I would mentally check off these manifestations, which provided the necessary assurance that I was doing this on my own.

But what about my inner landscape? Daily I questioned my ability to keep moving forward in a life that felt so scary and uncertain and entirely altered. Comments like "I could never do what you are doing" or "I don't know how you are doing it" shone a spotlight on how undesirable my life and circumstances were to the outside world that was creeping in like a low tide.

Until now I had been focusing on the tasks necessary for day-to-day survival in my now family of four. Filling the hole that was the absence of Klaus. The flashbacks, the sleepless nights, the emptiness in my bed. The endless tasks now divisible by a denominator of one rather than two.

A one-inch square diameter tile just off-center from the shower drain. This couldn't be a big deal. Right? What darkness could lurk behind the darkness underneath such a small shift?

But questions began to grow inside me. Who was I without the physical presence of Klaus? Who was I as a single person? I had been living in unyielding fear with a smile on my face that now, after a few years, only occasionally moved off-center. What was lurking behind the facade of survival I presented to the outside world?

It was a weekday, just after the hardware store had opened. The pros went shopping on weekdays, not Saturdays, and had a look of confidence and certainty about them. They were mission-driven and carried lists on clipboards and wore tool belts. I lurked by the tiles. It didn't take long this morning to find someone who met the criteria. I waited until he was off the phone and made my move.

"Excuse me. What do I need to glue a tile back into place?"

Until now, pros I stalked at the hardware store and on YouTube videos had provided me with ample handyman skills to complete minor repair jobs. I trusted this job would be no different.

I pulled the tile out of my pocket to show him. I had taken my sharpest kitchen knife and scraped away the old grout and adhesive to make the tile appear good as new. The old grout and adhesive had come away with my fierce determination to make this an easy fix.

"Oh, boy." That's never a good opener from a home repair pro. "Do you know what's going on underneath the tile that made it loose?"

"The tile is in good shape. Can't I just reattach it?" Surely with a little adhesive grout, no one would see the difference. The facade would be intact.

"You better look underneath that tile to see what is going on before you just glue it back in place. You need to see what made it come loose. And make sure you have a firm foundation to glue the tile onto."

Damn. This was not going to go as planned. A firm foundation made sense, for both me and the tile. But I didn't want to look into the darkness.

I returned home and peered into the small hole behind the tile. What could be underneath? The crack was visible to the outside, but there was only darkness underneath. I saw nothing visible onto which I could glue the tile. The same was true behind my own facade when I looked: only darkness. Where should I glue my tile? Where was I going to plant my feet? Klaus had been my foundation. He was the one who held firmly to my kite string, tethering me to place. He was the one who shone light on my self-doubt, anchoring me in the belief that I could pursue graduate school and become a full-time professor and doctor nurse.

In grief, manifestation on the surface can be small as life goes on and problems are not attended to. During the day I was a nurse. A professor. A mom. A handyman for small home repairs. But where was Susan? There are many reasons we don't attend to our problems. There are things to be done. Groceries that need to be bought. Homework that needs helping with. We just can't find space to attend to the bigger underlying issues.

But I shone my brightest light into that dark hole. The light bounced back, reflecting something shiny. It was a pool of standing water.

My mind pleaded with my circumstances.

How much trouble can be behind a one-inch square? A lot.

How much can be hidden behind someone's façade? A lot.

How much pain can be behind one loose square inch? The pain can be bottomless.

I had to explore deeper to see the root of the problem. A crowbar helped to remove tiles that were firmly stuck to the shower floor.

Soggy layer after soggy layer revealed layer upon layer of wet. The pool of water that was intended for a drain pan got larger and larger. As it turns out, a lot can be behind a small crack in the surface. Klaus's DIY prowess had failed as he installed the shower drain. It had slipped, and water had been pooling underneath the shower for who knows how long while the facade was firmly glued in place.

When we are in grief, we desperately want to return to the old and let it define us. We don't have the energy for new or different. It is easier to put energy into staying with the past. We peel back layer upon layer, each one revealing new damage, new and unexpected pain. How can grief affect yet another layer of my life? How much can be underneath that small one-inch tile? We may look great on the outside, but inside we are a turbulent mess or a bottomless pool of tears. Life also wouldn't stop crying. My grief seemed to be going on forever. There was no bottom to missing Klaus and no end to figuring out how to do life without him.

I was lost and still running. But where? I had to make a choice: build up my life as a single person? Spend time looking back and trying to recreate the past? Dealing with perpetual wetness, anger, and resentment?

I remembered Klaus putting up the now soggy drywall and cement board designed to withstand water without falling apart the winter after my dad died. "Dis vill be beautifell," he said as he slid in the shower insert and finished up the surrounding tile. His goals were always enormous and unattainable. All of it now seemed so pointless.

Finally, the dirt floor had been reached for my bathroom and for me, both vulnerable and stripped bare. The layers of wetness had been removed, and all that was left was dirt. The house and I had reached the bottom, and I wondered how we would both get back up, my bathroom and I. How would we reproduce ourselves from the shattered pieces of our past? Would I find a way out of the endless middle of grief? Or would I stay at the dirt floor forever, choosing bitterness and resentment?

Was it time for "out with the old?" Staring at that dirt floor, I knew that my fear was getting me nowhere. My doubts were keeping me fixed to place and time. Living with regret meant living with the disappointment of not growing old with Klaus. What would happen if I let my fears go and chose something else? I had to rebuild from the dirt floor up. This was an opportunity for a new bathroom. A new relationship with life.

New green foundation timbers were laid. A new subfloor was built to provide a firm foundation for the tile. On what should I glue my tile? Did I ever think life must be bigger than what I saw here? "Be brave," I whispered to myself, "or at least pretend to be." It was time to build up.

Chapter 36

It was a bittersweet moment as I stood balancing on the stage of Orchestra Hall in my new pink velvet high heels, three straps holding the shoes fast to my wobbly feet. They were a gift from Klaus.

Many years ago, when I emptied the trunk of the Honda Accord of the last remaining strawberry jam, I also found a cash box holding 680 dollars in jam-sale proceeds from the Farmer's Market. The mostly bills were carefully folded in half, all facing the same direction and ordered according to denomination. His billfold, first holding Deutschmarks, then Euros, then dollars, had been an unusual constant of order and predictability since I had known him. At the time, I carefully counted the money and resisted using it towards buying ham sandwiches and fruit cups to accompany the holy soup at his funeral. My grief-stricken brain set the money aside to use it to buy one last gift from Klaus. Now, years later, the first $29 went towards the pink velvet high heels I found on the clearance rack.

The loud clicking of the heels competed with the old tapes and voices in my head as I walked across the stage toward the Dean of the College of Education. "Did I walk weird?" and "Did I look funny?" were playing in one ear and "Congratulations Dr. Huehn" was playing in the other ear as the hood slipped over my head. The moment was sweet because I had finished a PhD, a huge milestone and perhaps the biggest accomplishment of my life; bitter because Klaus's absence was palpable. In moments like this, I missed him terribly. Klaus's encouragement had brought me to this place, both the hood and the high heels.

The tapes that played in my head originated when I first stumbled up and down the hallway on Jefferson Street experimenting with high heels as a middle schooler. The themes were few, but they played on repeat at varying intervals:

"You walk funny in them."

"They don't look good on you."

The messages were so well ingrained that by the time I was in high school I didn't even consider the possibility of wearing anything higher than a clog. Flat shoes, jeans, and loose fitting, plain colored t-shirts –long sleeve for winter and short sleeve for summer—were as adventurous as my wardrobe got; the loudest message of all was "Do not attract attention to yourself."

Klaus loved fashion and worked to mute those beliefs by helping me to find clothes I felt beautiful in. "Dat's it, Susanne. You haff to buy dat," Klaus said as I came out of the dressing room that day so long ago when we were shopping for clothes to wear to our wedding. It was a magenta pantsuit with a matching vest and a long coat and lapel with zig-zag edges.

"I look like a ringleader at a circus." Just looking at the pantsuit on the rack had started the old tapes rolling at a rapid clip. My skin also took on a familiar itch as anxiety and self-doubt rose.

"You haff to try it on, Susanne." Both Klaus and the salesperson worked to convince me.

"I'll look silly," I said over my shoulder as I disappeared behind the curtain of the dressing room. The salesperson was waiting for me as I came out of the cubicle with a pair of dark purple satin high heels matching the pantsuit's lapels. By now, the voices were yelling full-blast, and the tapes were playing on repeat. I wobbled as my feet slid into the high heels. A perfect fit. Channeling Cinderella, I strained to hear the external voices convincing me I looked beautiful over the din in my head. As I turned in front of the three-way mirror, the voices muffled and I smiled at my reflection. "I do look beautiful," I thought. "And yes, I can wear this," I said to myself as I carried the packages out of the store. I wore them on our wedding day feeling glorious.

More of the jam-sale proceeds had gone towards the regalia I was now wearing and the hood that was being slipped over my head. To-morrow the remainder of the money would go towards the wurst and a keg of beer for the party.

For my Ph.D party, we resurrected Klaus in the form of his beloved Thüringer sausages. The relish table daringly had ketchup as an option as Klaus's spittle-infused commentary was not a threat to our pleasure in his resurrected form.

German potato salad accompanied the sausages. "Real" German potato salad is nothing like American Potato Salad or the German Potato Salad made by Americans and called German. This was a lecture Klaus had at the ready for those within earshot, interested or not. "Real" German potato salad is started in the morning by boiling potatoes in their skins. As soon as they are boiled just right, not too hard, and not too soft, the potatoes are peeled, sliced, and seasoned with salt, pepper, beef broth, chopped onions, garlic, grainy mustard, and vinegar. The potatoes are left to steep in the seasonings with an occasional stir until just before serving time when a few tablespoons of a neutral flavored oil are folded under the potatoes. "Venn you stir da oil into the Kartoffel Salat, it has to go schlurrp schlurrp" Klaus would explain. "That's how you know there is enough oil." The potatoes were stirred with a special emphasis on the "r:" One "r" in schlurrp was too short and three "r's" too long.

So much grief has been metabolized in the time since Klaus last lectured me on the proper way to make potato salad. Grief rarely returned to me any longer in its original raw form. Peter, Sonja, and Alex were moving forward. Peter and Sonja had finished college and Alex was well on his way. What journey was I on, and where was I headed? I had reached my educational goal, but what would come next? Sometimes I felt as if I were still perched on a comma, a punctuation mark at the baseline of a sentence, curving towards the past and away from the future. Was I, too, curving towards my previous life and the narrative I had told myself that prioritized Klaus's dreams rather than my own? Was I not bending forward to a life that was yet unwritten?

The empty rectangle still lived inside me, its corners bumping up against my edges. Would I have to live with that space inside of myself forever, or could I release the beliefs I held about myself?

Summer culminated with my 50th birthday. How was I going to cross over into this new decade? I did not want to become a soap opera of personal battles. Memories were a gift. I could look at old photos and not be enslaved by pain. I also stopped asking "How do you want this?" and instead became a pioneer in mapping my own desires and destiny. I imagined a different me, one that didn't include outbuildings.

I wanted to get rid of the outbuildings for a long time, but in the background, I heard, "But vee can't burn dat down Susanne; vee might need it." Dismantling buildings requires careful planning and a competent professional to avoid unplanned structural collapse. Anxious to dismantle Klaus's playground and restore order, I did not want to deal with the complexities of taking them apart piece by piece.

"Just burn them down," was the only answer I needed when I asked my neighbor how to get rid of them.

First Inchworm. The dry decades-old wood went up in one huge flame of black smoke, leaving hundreds of nails in the grass. A rolling magnet over the area protected the integrity of my tractor tires and ensured my precious lawn tractor would keep moving forward.

Next came the old chicken coop, which had long been inadequate in keeping out chicken predators. Now it was stuffed with chicken wire that Klaus had determined was essential for a project he had not yet identified. It held more chicken wire than anyone could possibly use in several lifetimes. Sonja was leaving as I went out with a gas can, matches, and a crazy fire-starter look in my eyes. "I am going to burn down the chicken coop." She only hesitated a moment, wondering if it was okay to leave me to my own devices, before backing down the driveway.

I wanted a new boundary to the outside world, one that considered new possibilities. Could I form a narrative that was all about asking myself what I'm going to do rather than what do you want me to do? I began asking what I wanted rather than what the world wanted from me.

I returned to the question that arose most frequently after Klaus died. "Are you going to sell your house?" This was now my house, and I was working to make it my own. And, dammit, I was going to learn to really do home repair.

A little gas, not too much, and in just the right places. I built a trail of paper that would carry the flame to the gasoline. I didn't want things to get out of control. The hose was nearby and at the ready. I struck the match.

"Whoosh." The chicken coop went as soon as the flames met the gasoline. This time, I didn't have to worry about laying the logs just so to allow spaces for the fire to burn. The old dry wood burned quickly, leaving behind charred remnants of chicken paraphernalia and chicken wire.

Fire plays a crucial role in nature, allowing a species to emerge and flourish by creating necessary gaps to let sunlight in and for new species to compete. What necessary gaps was I creating? Where was sunlight entering now that it hadn't before? More and more of the cement platform that had been the foundation of the old coop emerged each week as I shoveled charred chicken coop remains into the garbage can.

It had been nearly five years, a milestone. Distance lends perspective. In the past years, I had survived the tumultuous and messy work of grief.

Until now, the journey had been focused on the unraveling of my life with Klaus. I began to see how my life could move forward with the pieces put together in a new and different way. It was time to shine a light on the dark rectangle at my core.

CHAPTER 37

I looked out the kitchen window surrounded by American-cheese-colored molding and wondered about the story I had told myself. Was it a myth of my own creation? Was there a different story I could tell? The molding did little to hide the weathered wood that held the window in place. Peeling caulk failed to keep cold drafts from seeping in around the edges. Remnants of the window garden that Klaus had built years ago were still on the ground under the window. Windex had long failed to return the sparkle to the old panes, which were cloudy and shaded, making the view to the outside blurry and easily misinterpreted.

The window was moved from the living room to the kitchen years ago, changing the view to the outside from sunrises over the mailbox at the end of the driveway to a wide expanse of either corn or alfalfa fields, depending on the farmer's crop rotation.

Grief can dramatically shift our perspective. At some point, we must make a choice. Do we remain in our grief, choosing continued suffering and viewing the world through dark glasses, or do we choose to let our grief experience transform us as we move forward? There had been nothing noble about my grief journey thus far. It was dark and dismal. The suffering felt destructive and caused me to reach a bottom I did not know existed. And when I crashed through what I thought was the bottom floor, I crashed through again, only to find another dark cavity.

The suffering took me out of the routine of life, and I found myself not who I believed myself to be. Finally, looking out that clouded window, I realized that I had some ground under my feet and could choose my view to the outside world. And while I didn't want to change it entirely, I did want it to be brighter, with more sparkle.

The window needed to be replaced. Was this something I could do myself? Until now, my handyman skills had been an unprecedented experiment of simple home repair. Had my skills evolved enough to take on the task of replacing a window?

Klaus was whispering in my ear as I armed myself with a crowbar. "Careful. Don't push too hard. Vee can use dis molding und da vindow somevare else."

Oh, Klaus. I would have given anything to see him again, even if for just a moment. There were so many things I missed.

The scratchiness of his beard against my cheek.

I missed him for Sonja.

Planning out the garden on graph paper and then working side-by-side to bring it to life.

I missed him for Peter.

Challenging me to think outside of the box and dream big.

I missed him for Alex.

Bringing my thoughts back from the downward spiral into the toilet.

I missed his warm hands.

However, at this moment, I was glad he wasn't at my side telling me how to correctly hold the crowbar to remove the molding. I wanted to rely on my own ability and learn to do these things for myself. I was certainly glad that the molding and window wouldn't be stacked in the garage among other things he considered invaluable treasures. This was now my house, and I was craving order and organization.

My fingers felt around the window for areas in which the molding was not quite flush with the wall. I carefully inserted the flat end of the crowbar into the first gap and began to push slowly and cautiously on the rounded handle at the other end. The 100-year-old nails creaked and, with a little pressure, released themselves from the molding, the window frame, and the surrounding wall.

Carefully, I moved the crowbar around the rectangle, the molding coming loose in satisfyingly long pieces. Soon the window was laid bare, its rectangular frame openly visible. It appeared more vulnerable and shakier without the yellow molding securing its edges.

Life's crowbar had removed the framework around my world and myself. I had found the gaps. I pushed tentatively on those gaps, creating tension and exposing cracks. I was careful not to apply excessive force and wondered what would be released and what would be exposed. Perhaps even the cracks would be avenues for new light.

Our mouths shape easily into a smile, faking a bright yellow mood. We do it automatically out of politeness. I had done it too many times to count in the past years.

"How are you doing?"

"Shitty," I thought.

"Fine," I said.

"I don't know how you do it."

What is my choice? To stay in bed all day and let my house and our lives fall down around me?

"With the help of others, I move forward." I said the right words, but inside, I was utterly alone.

When people fake a smile, they usually forget about the eyes being windows, the giveaway to the soul's pain. When we are truly happy, we not only smile but also crinkle the corners of our eyes. I wanted to replace that old rectangle in my soul or, at least, give it a chance to fill with light and have eyes with crinkles.

I jiggled and pushed the window sitting in the wall. The window held firm to the frame of the old house, reluctant to release its longstanding hold on familiar surroundings, reluctant to let go of its long-held view to the outside world.

What was I holding on to? Could I let myself release from my old frame? My long-held views? What would I do with the empty rectangle inside of myself?

To remove the window from the house, I needed more and different tools.

I armed myself with my reciprocating saw. When the universe promoted me to CEO of handyman projects, the reciprocating saw was a gateway to the world of power tools. Relatively small, it was easier to handle than other power tools and not as heavy. With the blade clearly visible, it was also less frightening.

With a rechargeable battery, there was no restriction of a power cord. The saw had been used to slice through long-neglected garden weeds and volunteer trees. It also came with exciting accessories that I had used to scrub away stubborn stains and rust and scratch out tile grout.

Could I use it for a real handyman job?

"Make sure you get the right kind of blade," my advice-giving neighbor instructed as I headed to the hardware store. "You need a blade that will cut through nails and wood."

I thought back to how frustrated I had been with Klaus when any home repair job required multiple trips to the hardware store. "I'm sorry, Klaus," I whispered to him hoping he would accept my much-too-late apology.

"Make sure you don't cut through any electrical wires," were my neighbor's parting words.

I was afraid to ask how I would know if there were some wires in the wall.

As if preparing to cross a dangerous intersection, I looked both ways before I inserted the blade between the wall and the window frame. I slowly pushed the on button. The sharp new blade sliced through the resistance it encountered: framing lumber, sheetrock, plywood, and the ancient nails that served as the last connection between the window and the wall. The window became looser with each nail that gave way. I peered past cobwebs into the dark interior of the wall for hidden electrical cords. There were no electrical cords, just an empty beer bottle, and a perfectly petrified squirrel. Were these casualties of that summer so long ago that we had lived without a roof?

As I moved around the window, crowbar in hand, I worried that the panes of glass would shatter, just as I had worried in the past years that grief might break me open and shatter my soul. What I had once thought would keep me safe was no longer there. Traveling the Candyland palette to the pink closet was also no longer a possibility. I had worked to choose vertical over horizontal; growth over fear. I wanted to yield to changes imposed by the sharp saw blades of life, not remain resistant and unyielding to changes inherent to loss. What inside me could give way to sharp new saw blades?

Could I step into the present moment without attachments to what I had known before or what I had expected or wanted for my future? Could I open myself to new joy? I didn't want to step forward by denying my loss and feelings of grief and despair. Rather, I wanted to step forward in a way that acknowledged these and also opened me to the possibility of joy. Grief, despair, and fear had taught me so many lessons. It was time for lessons from hope, joy, and courage.

Finally, I cut through the last nail holding the window in place. With a great deal of sweat and grit, as well as a firm jiggle, the window finally was freed from the house. Light, unencumbered by clouded panes, poured into the kitchen.

The first thing I found was a calm and gentle sadness, the kind that hits you in your heart. Sometimes the tears came like a waterfall, and sometimes they stayed stuck as a cramp deep in my stomach. Either way, this vulnerability was the beginning of fearlessness and the first real sign of warriorship.

Trusting myself to cut a hole in the house using a power tool was the first step in developing the kind of courage I needed to be happy and radically alive. Fearlessness and power tools were the path to bravery and freedom.

I stood on the inside looking out and feeling the light. I felt strong. Confident. Alive. Was it not my birthright to have clear panes of glass to the outside world?

What if I let in even more light? Was a simple transactional change all I was after? Could I exchange one window for another without changing the structure of my house? What if I installed a door? Did I have the confidence to cut a hole that large in my house? Could I face the fear of something terrible happening? I had spent my life reacting to fear. Could I move forward despite it and have faith that nothing terrible would happen?

Chapter 38

nstalling a door would require a significant structural change to my house. This would also be a transformational change, allowing even more light to enter the kitchen through the expanded rectangle, making the inside of my house more visible to the outside world.

The lives we build look different following loss. It is a mistake to believe that we can rebuild life in the same way without our beloved. Allowing for a new structure of life to form allows grief to transform us.

Could I trust myself enough for a change this transformational? I had been dedicated to invisibility and accommodation for so long, always working to fulfill the needs and dreams of others. I was willing to use an umbrella while brushing my teeth and accommodate Klaus's treasure trove while pushing down my need for tidiness and order. But could I now attend to my needs instead of worrying about and accommodating the needs of others?

I considered whether I wanted clear glass to allow people to see in. There was translucent or textured glass that would make the inside less transparent. Smoked glass was out because I didn't want anything to further darken the space. Cutting a hole in my house required faith in myself and faith I wouldn't cut through anything imperative to keeping the house from falling down. Having faith in myself required opening myself to the outside world.

Life was bigger than its changing circumstances. I no longer wanted to be dying inside, driven by fear and doubt. Grief requires faith. Faith had gotten me out of bed in the mornings and kept me vertical when all I wanted was the safety of being under the covers.

At the lumber counter, I said, "I'd like a sliding glass door for my house." I was impersonating Someone Who Knows What They Are Doing.

"Tell me about your project." My answers always began with the same phrase: "I have a quirky old farmhouse I'm learning to take care of." After a detailed explanation of the project, the salesperson said "I think you need a swinging patio door."

After asking about the difference between a sliding door and a swinging door, I learned that a traditional sliding door is made up of two panels. One is fixed to the framework while the other is mobile, allowing it to swing open and closed.

I thought about my life thus far and being fixed to the framework of Klaus, always adjusting to the opening and closing of his ever-mobile panel.

A swinging patio door can open all of the way, allowing for easier flow in and out. But it also takes up more space than a sliding door. You have to allow for the door to open as it swings.

Crossing the new threshold to the outside world, I wanted a door that would open all the way and easily swing to the outside. I was ready to take up more space. I had been dedicated to making myself small long enough. I wanted out of the Candy Pink closet.

"Would you like an inswing or an outswing door? Your interior will have more room if your door swings to the outside."

"Your interior will have more room if your door swings to the outside."

Holy shit. I was already planning to cut a hole that was large enough to gain a new perspective on my view of the outside and allow my inside to be more visible. Now I was being asked to open the door to the outside too. Could I do this? It was as if my soul was asking me to open doors before me and within me.

My response was nearly immediate: "Out-swing please." I was ready for the door to swing open to the outside world on its hinges. I wanted to be mobile and swinging, not permanently fixed to the framework of another.

Door ordered and with dimensions in hand, I ignored the queasiness in my gut and the old messages and tapes warning me that something terrible was sure to happen, I put a new sharp saw blade into my reciprocating saw.

Eventually, faith led me to an understanding that my life could be different, that I could cut a hole in my house allowing in new light and it wouldn't fall down. On reflection, those first steps were taken in the dark when I was utterly vulnerable and stripped of what had previously provided me with confidence. Things were coming together in a new way and it was time to embrace the transformation grief taught me was possible.

Fierce and steady faith kept me moving forward and now supported me as I cut through old beams. I was cutting outside the lines of my old boundaries and into the existing framework of the house, expanding the rectangle filled with cloudy panes. Faith would support adding new doors with large and sparkly panes. Faith would help me to trust that everything would turn out okay.

The door was delivered, and my neighbor helped to hang it. Set in the rough opening, it was evident the door needed a lot of fussing, shimmying, and leveling to fit into the framework that was anything but plumb. Finally nailed into place, the door swung wide to the outside.

The kitchen filled with light as I admired the new view from my house. I thought of Klaus. He would have loved cutting this hole in the house but would have filled it with a jerry-rigged door found on the side of the road. What would this new life I was creating for myself look like? First, I wanted a new door hung right.

"I think we should build a deck here," I announced. Building a firm platform on the other side of the new threshold seemed like the next obvious step.

With the help of our neighbor/mentor/Project Manager, a plan was made, and dimensions were agreed upon. Shopping list in hand, I stood at the contractor's counter at the local lumber yard and announced, "I am here to order material to build a deck."

"Sure, I can help you with that." His response startled me because I'd been listening to the voice in my head that was screaming, "Who do you think you are, thinking you can build a deck?"

"I would like pressure-treated lumber," were the words I actually said, drowning out the tape.

"Excellent choice—your deck will withstand Minnesota weather." Materials ordered and delivery date scheduled, I moved forward, outlining the outside perimeter of the deck just like I had seen Klaus do decades before. Orange construction twine wound on wooden stakes marked the new space. I was ready for the next step with a sharp new saw blade loaded into the circular saw.

As I laid the decking lumber onto the sawhorse, I thought about the confidence I had gained while learning to fix the house. A few years ago, I would have never had the confidence to be standing in this place, scary power tool in hand, cutting on the line I had measured and marked in pencil. I had fought against the seduction of bitterness and now was building a deck onto my home.

Together with Sonja, Peter, and Alex, I measured and cut the decking according to the directions from our neighbor. Decking pieces were laid on the new framework, ensuring the bubble of air inside the vial of encased liquid was exactly horizontal to the earth's surface.

Emotions and feelings since losing Klaus had been anything but level to the earth's surface. With Nancy's help, I was learning to navigate widening emotions and manage feelings with tools more effective than pink closets and cookies.

Each swing of the hammer had its own resonance, its moment of power or failure. Would I hit the nail head or miss? I didn't know, but I kept swinging. This swing, and the next, and the next, and the next, brought resonance to move forward. As I screwed each piece tightly to the underlying framework, I reflected on how I, too, felt more firmly grounded in a new foundation. Just as in grief, if we do not deal with the structural issues, other problems will begin to seep out of the cracks of our existence.

Then came the time to lay the threshold, a small piece of wood that fits snugly into the space between the old and the new. This new crossing to the outside needs to fit tightly to keep cold air out and mud from washing in. What would this new threshold represent for me? Did I have the skills to navigate it, and would I be brave enough to cross it?

I remembered a writing group I was in, early in grief, when we were asked to write about the life we wanted that was taken from us. I wrote about growing old with Klaus, chasing grandchildren through the garden, planting sunflowers with them, and helping them carefully lift chicken eggs out of the nesting box. Then we were instructed to tear the page in two, vertically, pasting the two halves of our writing on either side of a larger sheet of paper with a gap in between them. The space between the torn vision of growing old with Klaus was blank. The assignment was to fill the page with a new vision for my life moving forward.

At that time, raw grief had prevented me from filling that blank space with a life that I didn't want. Clutching the table, I pronounced emphatically to my fellow group members, "I don't want to cross this threshold."

And now, years later, a literal threshold lay before me, representing a separation of what was from what is not yet to be. This can be a site of danger and risk; crossing may be perilous and a threat to safety or a departure from one way of being into a way of being not yet known.

Standing on the threshold required a new definition of home and of my life as I saw it. I had done the inner work. Could I now apply that work to the outside?

I had come to a threshold in my understanding of myself, who I thought I was, and who I thought myself to be. In spaces of not knowing, I had always lived on high alert, full of tension and constriction. I wanted to move forward with awareness and curiosity, into a space that invited movement and growth. I wanted to move forward with the understanding that I deserved to love myself.

I reflected on the skills I had gained since those days. Now I was asking myself to leave the familiarity of my house and do something I had not yet done.

Rosie, my chocolate lab puppy, stood buckling her knees. Fear was evident in her shaking. She paused and sniffed. And, finally, taking a deep breath, she jumped, her ears flapping behind her. I followed close behind.

Crossing onto my new deck felt like a bridge. I might finally be able to cross from one space into the other. I was seeking the kind of wholeness that comes from accepting myself so that I could grow into the person I aspired to be. Transformation had allowed this to happen. I stepped on the threshold for a moment to allow my eyes to adjust to the new bright light.

CHAPTER 39

"Klaus - wo bist Du?" There was a deep unraveling inside me and a profound longing as I searched through one empty room after another of a large, unfamiliar house. I knew I was in Germany. Outside, I saw the Bodensee where we often sailed together. With the clear understanding that comes only in dreams, I knew Klaus was somewhere in the house, but I didn't know where.

I followed the deep familiar voice that was calling, "Susanne!"

"Where are you, Klaus?" I cried, moving from room to room. I had waited years for Klaus to come to me in a dream, so long that I no longer expected it. The week after he died, he appeared in a friend's dream, buying leeks in the grocery store. "He was with two older German women that were dressed in clothes that looked like they were from the 1940s or 1950s. He said to tell you that he is fine."

Creamed leeks had always been one of my favorite dinners. Thinly sliced leeks were sautéed down in a little bit of butter until they were soft. Cream was added to bind the leeks together and complement their savory sweetness. Sliced ham provided a punch of saltiness. All was served over boiled Yukon Golds. I hoped the women at his side in the grocery store were enjoying the leeks as much as I did.

Now, I called after him again and again, stumbling forward, tripping through the large house.

His voice suddenly became much louder, and I knew he was in the next room. From behind the closed door, I heard his voice say gently, "Susanne, es muss weiter. Es geht immer weiter." It was the calm and resonant voice he used when my thoughts were swirling quickly and about to disappear down the toilet drain. "Susanne, you have to move on. It is time to move on." Waking up prevented me from entering that room and embracing him or from telling him I loved him, that I now had a neatly mowed lawn without tufts of violets, and that I cut a hole in my house.

A new season had crept into me, a softer season of acceptance. I could feel the sky, the earth, and the water, and I could revel in being a part of the world around me without a chasm of pain opening at the thought of living the rest of my life without Klaus. I could stand firmly rooted against the wind. The core of me wasn't lost; rather, I was discovering who I was with each screw I drove into the decking.

Yet memories still could abruptly take me over and drag me down, as could speculation: what you would be doing now, or what would you look like? Would your salt and pepper beard be all white? It has been over thirty years since I arrived to live with you on your birthday and you greeted me with twenty-one red roses. Jobless and full of hopeful anticipation, I moved in with you based on a relationship that had been built on thin airmail paper, expensive phone calls, and less than 14 days together.

Nostalgia is a bitter sentiment filled with "if only" and wistful affection for the past. Memories that can pierce our hearts with suffering and hold the sadness of life in balance with the beauty of the world. I looked at the gladiolas blooming along the picket fence and thought of the beauty you've left behind. None of us go through life untouched.

Instead of letting memories drag me down and leave me powerless, I looked at the gladiolas blooming along the picket fence and thought of how memories open us to possibilities inherent in every moment.

When do you accept that someone you love is gone? Is it when the doctor tells you they are gone? When you see it with your own eyes? And what then? Do you move on as if they never were?

Except Klaus wasn't gone. He was still snuggled safely in my closet. Was I different or was the world different? Although I had crossed the threshold to my new outdoor space, I hadn't yet fully embraced it with flying ears like Rosie. With new sparkly glass, an out-swinging door, and a wider opening to the outside world, I was still looking for a sense of home and place in the world that did not include Klaus. What was missing from my definition of home, and where would I find it? It was going to take more than a sniff and simple trust. It was going to require embracing new truths and the relinquishment of old beliefs I had held as truth.

Carrying my belongings on my back and questions in my head, I hoped to find answers walking the Camino. I packed my bags for a journey of understanding, traveling for spiritual reasons, and searching for meaning, purpose, or truth. Typically, a pilgrimage is a journey to a location of importance to someone's faith. I was taking a metaphorical journey searching for a sense of home and belonging to myself. Many countries have lifted prison sentences in place of walking the Camino. Perhaps I could release myself from the self-imposed prison of self-doubt. I considered how I could reduce the baggage I was carrying in my life.

With each step, I realized that I was looking in the wrong places for home. Until now I asked myself questions about where I belonged. Germany? Minnesota? Klaus? I had felt as if I could not live my life without a permission slip.

While walking, I began to feel a remarkable sensation: hope. I did not need to walk to the Compostela to find my spiritual home. It was in my heart and on my small plot of land with a quirky farmhouse that had cocooned me for over two decades. I now had the instruction manual for my farmhouse, and I could learn to give myself permission slips for living. Leaving my boots on a makeshift altar of stones, I returned home committed to living a life uncovering strength previously unknown. I was going home in a new and different way, belonging to myself.

Grief had slapped me in the face like a tidal wave and would have washed me away had I not found myself on this ancient path. Grief had drained me of every emotion and sapped my strength and will. It had stripped me bare, down to the dirt floor of my soul, and left me with a blank page at the end of a partly written book. It had also given me a choice, either to leave that page blank or to keep writing the story with hope and light.

Klaus had to have a final resting place that freed him as well as me. In nearly six years, he had made it from my trunk to my closet. I still did not know where to put him to rest. My plumbing and septic were still not conducive to his remains, nor did his requested option leave me feeling fulfilled in a resting place. Did I want to place him in a cemetery? I could not bear to confine him behind a chain-link fence surrounded by scrappy trees. He would have hated that. He wanted nothing more than to be free. Finally, the answer was clear.

"On Sunday at ten, I'm leaving to put your dad's ashes in the Mississippi. It's up to you if you'd like to come."

He loved the water, and he loved America and Germany. He would finally have the freedom he longed for. Sonja and I carefully unwrapped the black velvet bag and opened the plastic jar of ashes.

We stared down into the dark water where his ashes had stopped swirling at the surface. Water bubbled up from the bottom. "Klaus, are you having the last word? Are you saying what I desperately wanted to say to you: Klaus, I loved you so much and I never doubted you loved me."

I have no idea what the future will bring. The only certainty I have about my future is that it will contain an orderly garage.

Acknowledgments

I never set out to write a book, but at some point, somewhere between being through enough raw grief that I could look at pictures of Klaus and me, and having had enough therapy to apply some humor to my life, I felt like I had a story inside myself that needed to be told. During this time so many remarkable people supported me and believed in me. Without all of you, this book would not have been possible.

Deep gratitude to those who held Klaus as he lived and celebrated his life when he died: the Unitarian Fellowship of Northfield and minister Kristin Maier. For most of his life, Klaus felt like a misfit toy. You loved him into being real and he loved you back with all his heart. Particular thanks to the choir members, and Lee and Bev Topp whom Klaus called his "big friends." You remain my "big friends" and have been there to support me every step of the way.

To Mark Ekeren and his team at Integrity House Services, who insulated the walls of my house protecting me and my family from the elements, and built my house back up when we hit the dirt bottom.

Serendipity and good fortune landed my writing in the hands of Gillian Steinberg. I am indebted to her for having faith in my early work and encouraging me to continue and for her keen eye when editing the final draft.

My book would never have reached the final stages without my writing cohort from the Loft Literary Center in Minneapolis, led by mentor and author Nicole Helget. Weekly you listened to me struggling with words on a page and emotions in my heart and provided loving and thoughtful feedback. Nicole, you teased the story out of me in spite of myself.

To my neighbors...Carolyn, who washed towels, made coffee and French toast, and always made sure my water glass was full to replace the fluid deficit from persistent crying, and Karl who answered endless questions about my house. Gary who was my "consultant" during the deck addition and encouraged me to embrace skills I didn't know I had, like cutting a hole in my house.

Wayne, you came hours after Klaus died and promised "you never have to worry about plowing your driveway again." You have kept your word and I am beyond grateful. I have the best-plowed driveway in Greenvale Township.

To my labor and delivery friends from United Hospital. You came in droves beginning with the day Klaus died. Sheila who climbed into bed with me, took me to the funeral home, made meatballs, and made my children laugh the day after their father died. Joannie who took my children funeral clothes shopping, made chili, and did laundry, and the countless others who bought me slippers when I couldn't stay warm and always had my back.

I am particularly grateful for my spiritual haven at Unity Church-Unitarian. Thanks to the Reverend Janne Eller-Isaacs whose simple invitation, "we have a grief group on Tuesday, would you like to come?" welcomed me into a community that has walked with me and held me in my grief. And to the Reverend Karen Hering (*Trusting Change: Finding our Way through Personal and Global Transformation*), whose work on living through change helped me cross the threshold into life beyond raw grief. Particular gratitude to my widow buddy Linda. We have walked the journey of widowhood together and I will never take your friendship for granted.

I am beyond grateful to my colleagues and friends at St. Olaf who have listened, cajoled, and encouraged me: Diane, Mary, Rosalyn, Anna, Katie, Trish, Sian, and Judy.

Rita, you believed in me and helped me realize having PhD behind my signature.

My appreciation to Steve at Ice Cube Press, who had the faith to keep reading even when he wasn't accepting anything new.

Nancy, my therapist. Your impact on my life has been so huge that Alex and Megan have said they would name their first baby "Nancy" regardless of gender. I have no words to express the level of gratitude for the profound impact you have had on my life.

And finally, the most immense gratitude goes to my family. To my brother Peter and cousin Vera who haven't left my side and have provided a protective layer of bubble wrap to insulate me during the most painful times. And to Megan: you came into our family and made it better.

And last, deep, deep gratitude to my children. You gave me a reason to be vertical and have hope.

Peter: Thank you for compelling me into the garden again, for cooking countless dinners and spreading gravel on the sidewalk so I don't fall.

Sonja: Thank you for being my buddy, giving me koala bear hugs, and for gently teasing me out of my misery at just the right times.

Alex: Thank you for putting your arms around me when I need it most and saying "It'll be OK mom."

It is an honor to be your mother.

Susan Huehn was born in a sleepy German town in south central Minnesota at the confluence of the Minnesota and Cottonwood rivers. The town was home to her immigrant parents and where she was raised speaking German. A love of German culture was embedded in to her at a cellular level. At a music festival in her home town, she met a German singer and after a transatlantic relationship (before email, Facebook, and WhatsApp!) she moved to Germany, where she lived for three years. She got married during those three years and returned with her husband to live in Northfield, Minnesota, on a small hobby farm.

She studied nursing at St. Olaf College and is currently chair of the nursing department. After completing her PhD in Education she ventured from academic writing to creative writing, knowing she had a story that needed to be told.

In her spare time she loves to cook good food for those she loves, garden and sew aprons.

The Ice Cube Press began publishing in 1991 to focus on how to live with the natural world and to better understand how people can best live together in the communities they share and inhabit. Using the literary arts to explore life and experiences in the heartland of the United States we have been recognized by a number of well-known writers including: Bill Bradley, Gary Snyder, Gene Logsdon, Wes Jackson, Patricia Hampl, Greg Brown, Jim Harrison, Annie Dillard, Ken Burns, Roz Chast, Jane Hamilton, Daniel Menaker, Kathleen Norris, Janisse Ray, Craig Lesley, Alison Deming, Harriet Lerner, Richard Lynn Stegner, Richard Rhodes, Michael Pollan, David Abram, David Orr, Scott Russell Sanders, and Barry Lopez... We've published a number of well-known authors including: Mary Swander, Jim Heynen, Mary Pipher, Bill Holm, Connie Mutel, John T. Price, Carol Bly, Marvin Bell, Debra Marquart, Ted Kooser, Stephanie Mills, Bill McKibben, Craig Lesley, Elizabeth McCracken, Derrick Jensen, Dean Bakopoulos, Rick Bass, Linda Hogan, Pam Houston, Paul Gruchow, and Bill Moyers... Check out Ice Cube Press books on our web site, join our email list, Facebook group, or follow us on Twitter. Visit booksellers, museum shops, or any place you can find good books and support our truly honest-to-goodness independent publishing projects and discover why we continue striving to hear the other side.

Ice Cube Press, LLC (Est. 1991)
North Liberty, Iowa, Midwest, USA
Resting above the Silurian and Jordan aquifers
steve@icecubepress.com
Check us out on Twitter and Facebook.
order on-line: www.icecubepress.com

Celebrating Thirty-Two Years of Independent Publishing.
2023 Iowa Governor's Art Award | MIPA Gold Award 2023

To Fenna Marie, MSW
grief, and happiness,
good tidings and joy
you know it all and more
live long love well